CHILDREN'S GUIDE
TO KNOWLEDGE

WONDERS OF NATURE

MARVELS
OF SCIENCE AND MAN

Published By
PARENTS' MAGAZINE PRESS

A division of
Parents' Magazine Enterprises, Inc.
New York, N.Y.

Subjects

PETS *by George Geygan and Ellis Anderson*

DOMESTIC ANIMALS *by Nicholas Amorosi and Kerwin Bowles*

WILD ANIMALS *by Oscar Liebman and Sheldon Corday*

BIRDS *by Russell F. Peterson and A. Washington Pezet*

BUTTERFLIES, BEES, BUGS AND OTHER INSECTS *by Eve Chambers*

FISHES, SHELLFISH AND REPTILES *by Marvin Fireman*

FLOWERS AND PLANTS *by Claudine Nankivel and Celia Green*

TREES AND SHRUBS *by Marjorie Hartwell and Charles Bradford*

LANGUAGES *by Anne Harris, John Lencicki and Howard Liss*

UNITED NATIONS *by Anne Harris, Howard Liss and Dale Stein*
       Foreword by Mrs. Eleanor Roosevelt

WONDERS OF THE WORLD *by William Hyer, Alec Stone and Kerwin Bowles*

CITIES OF THE WORLD *by Eve Chambers*

SCIENCE *by Oscar Liebman and A. Washington Pezet*

PEOPLES *by Celia Green and Don Cornelius*

INVENTIONS *by Oscar Liebman and Joseph R. Greene*

SPACE EXPLORATION *by Bradford Chambers and George Schelling*

1974 Edition
Copyright MCMLXIII

©

Parents' Magazine Enterprises, Inc.

Library of Congress Catalog Card No. 63-11929
LITHOGRAPHED IN THE UNITED STATES OF AMERICA

INTRODUCTION

This large volume is made up of sixteen children's books or subjects and introduces youngsters to the world about them. The material has been prepared to give children a basic understanding of man's more important achievements of the past and what he is accomplishing right now and of his hopes for the future. It also introduces children to the world not made by man — to the world of animals — wild and domestic, as well as insects, birds, fishes, flowers and trees.

In the area of science, the book includes material calculated to arouse a child's curiosity in things scientific. The whole scope of man's scientific progress is surveyed — from the early attempt to make fire to atomic energy and the conquest of outer space.

The Children's Guide to Knowledge recounts for the young reader the history of man's past, both ancient and modern. It describes the world's cities, the customs of its people, its inventions and its wonders. It acquaints children with the languages of the world and tells them how man is attempting to establish, through the United Nations, a way that will enable all people to live at peace in this world.

To induce a greater interest in reading, every page has been beautifully illustrated with original drawings, many in full color. These paintings have been designed to stimulate an interest in the text that accompanies the pictures and finally to so arouse the curiosity of the young child that he will go on to other books and sources of information and thus broaden his knowledge of the world around him and finally make him a more interesting and successful person.

CONTENTS

II

BUTTERFLIES, BEES, BUGS AND OTHER INSECTS

FISH, SHELLFISH, AND REPTILES

FLOWERS AND PLANTS

TREES AND SHRUBS

LANGUAGES

THE UNITED NATIONS

ANCIENT AND MODERN WONDERS

CITIES OF THE WORLD

SCIENCE

PEOPLES

INVENTIONS

SPACE EXPLORATION

FACT QUESTIONS TO CHECK

Pets

Terriers
Long-Legged Terriers
Short-Legged Terriers
Beagles
Greyhounds
Spaniels
Boxers
St. Bernards
Collies
German Shepherds
Police Dogs
Setters
Dachshunds
Chihuahuas
Bulldogs and Mastiffs
Boston Terriers
Pekingese
Poodles
Great Danes
Doberman Pinschers
Dalmatians
Eskimo Dogs
Pomeranians
Tabby Cats
Persians
Maine
Siamese
Burmese
Maltese
Abyssinians
Manx
Bird Pets
Talking Birds
Singing Birds
Fishes
Caged Pets
Hamsters
Guinea Pigs
White Mice
Rabbits

THE first animals men knew were the wild ones they caught to eat. But while they were hunting for their food, another wild animal that hunted along with them became their closest friend. This was the wild dog.

The wild dogs were faster than men, and could see farther and smell farther, so their help was welcome. But men had learned to make arrows and spears and stone knives to kill the food animals, and when it came time to eat men built a fire. The dogs curled up by the fire, and shared the food they had helped to catch. By these

forest fireplaces dogs and men became friends.

Dogs were the first pets. Pets are special kinds of tame animals that are kept not because they are useful, for food or their wool or skins, or because they help in farm work, but because they are fun to have around. Of course many pets are helpful to their owners. Dogs herd sheep and cattle, help the police, and guide the blind. Cats catch mice. But dogs and cats are also wonderful companions. Later, people found that even mice and birds and fish and rabbits were fun. So all these became pets.

TERRIERS

AIREDALE

THERE are several different breeds of Terrier. They were originally called "earth dogs" (that is what Terrier means), and were used to catch small animals.

Now Terriers are mostly housedogs, and they make fine guardians, because they bark fiercely if an unwelcome stranger comes near. There are long-legged and short-legged kinds.

LONG-LEGGED TERRIERS

THE Airedale is a long-legged Terrier about two feet high and usually colored tan. Bull Terriers, usually white, are the strongest dogs for their weight, and yet they are noted for their gentleness. One dog of this kind, finding it had to fight a tiny Pekingese which teased it, picked the little fellow up and placed it gently in a waste basket.

Fox Terriers, both smooth and wire-haired, are gay, brave, loyal, and lovely to look at. Other long-legged Terriers are the Irish, the Welsh, and the Bedlington.

SCOTTIE

WIREHAIRED
TERRIER

SHORT-LEGGED TERRIERS

THE best known short-legged Terriers are the Scotties. They are shaggy. often black or sand-colored, with small pointed ears and erect tails. Sealyham and Dandie Dinmonts are other short-legged Terriers.

Many Terriers have lived in the White House, among them Theodore Roosevelt's Scamp, Woodrow Wilson's Davie, Calvin Coolidge's Peter Pan, and Franklin D. Roosevelt's Fala.

FOX TERRIER

BEAGLES

THE Beagle is a merry dog, about a foot high, with a short coat of no special color—it can be black-and-white, tan, or a combination. The Beagle is really a kind of hound, and its notion of a good time is to chase rabbits across a rough field.

No dog is more gentle and affectionate than the Beagle, especially if it is treated with kindness. But the kindest thing you can do is to be sure it gets out for a good run ever so often!

GREYHOUNDS

GREYHOUNDS are swift dogs with long, narrow heads. They are not always grey, in spite of their name. They were used for hunting as long as 6,000 years ago. Now they are used as pets and in dog racing.

SPANIELS

SPANIELS get their name from Spain, where they were bred 700 years ago. Spaniels enjoy retrieving because they are really hunting dogs, long trained to find and bring back birds that hunters have shot. Some Spaniels like water so much that they are called Water Spaniels. Cocker Spaniels have their name because they were used to help hunt woodcocks.

BOXERS

BOXERS are big dogs, up to two feet high, with faces somewhat like bulldogs. They are very gentle and intelligent, and are even used as Seeing-Eye Dogs.

Boxers have smooth coats of lovely yellow-brown, called fawn, or a sort of gray color with dark spots, called brindle. Their eyes are somewhat thoughtful, but never worried. No one knows why they are called Boxers, but it is not because they fight.

ST. BERNARDS

THIS powerful dog, with an uncanny sense of direction, was originally bred by monks in the St. Bernard region of Switzerland. St. Bernards rescue people lost in the snow drifts of the Swiss Alps. During the past 300 years, they have saved the lives of more than 2,500 persons.

COLLIES

COLLIES are big, shaggy dogs with long silky coats and long lean heads. Their eyes are very gentle, and they often seem to be smiling. They are often named "Laddie" or "Lassie," and everyone knows the famous film star by that name!

Collies came originally from Scotland, where they were used to tend the sheep, and they are still used more than most dogs for farm work. Yet Collies are favorite house and pet dogs. They are kind, loyal, and able to learn very difficult tricks.

GERMAN SHEPHERDS

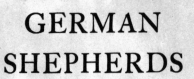

LIKE the Collie, the German Shepherd was originally trained as a sheep dog. It is about two feet high, noble and fearless in appearance, with a rough coat any color from black to gray. German Shepherds are very loyal to their masters.

POLICE DOGS

GERMAN Shepherds are also called Police Dogs, because they can be trained to help the police track down criminals.

German Shepherds are the most loved of all dogs by the blind. As Seeing-Eye Dogs, they lead their sightless masters through crowded streets and into buses and subway trains, where no other dog is allowed.

SETTERS

THE Setter is a dog that loves the outdoors, and needs plenty of exercise. There are several kinds, and they are all known for their beauty and gentleness. The English Setter looks something like a Spaniel, and is one of the foremost of hunting dogs. The Irish Setter is always a golden red and hunts when it can, but because of its beauty it is often bred for dog shows.

DACHSHUNDS

SOMEONE described the Dachshund as half-a-dog high and a dog-and-a-half long. It is very smart and, in spite of its rather funny appearance, very brave.

Dachshunds were originally used in hunting, and one of their "faults," the slowness with which they moved, made them useful in hunting deer, because they did not frighten the animal they were tracking down. There are smooth, long-haired, and stiff-haired dogs of this breed, and they can be tan or black with tan points. Nothing is cuter than a Dachshund puppy.

CHIHUAHUAS

THESE tiny dogs weigh only between two and four pounds. Their name, pronounced "tchee-wah-wah," is that of a state in Mexico, from which they did not come; the name is just a mistake.

Chihuahuas are graceful, gay, and clever. They are also delicate, and must be protected from extremes of weather. Their small size makes them ideal house pets. Some have short hair, others are long-haired, and they come in all colors.

BULLDOGS AND MASTIFFS

PEOPLE who do not know any better take one look at a Bulldog's face, and run. This chunky dog with the wrinkled face is one of the kindest breeds, although it is hard to beat in a fight.

Bulldogs are related to another fierce-looking but gentle dog, the Mastiff, shown at the top of the next page. One of the two dogs that came to America on the Mayflower was a Mastiff (the other was a Spaniel). But while the Mastiff may be almost as big as a Great Dane, a standard Bulldog is not much taller than a Terrier.

MASTIFF

BOSTON TERRIERS

THE only important breed started in America is descended from the Bulldog and the Terrier. This is the neat, gay, and loving Boston Terrier. It has a slight facial resemblance to the Bulldog, but no wrinkles, and its ears are like those of a Terrier.

The Boston Terrier is most often gray or tawny with white markings on its face, legs, and chest.

17

PEKINGESE

THIS small reddish dog with the soft, thick coat has no idea of its size. It is called the "lion-dog" because its face looks somewhat like that of a lion. But it also has the courage and the pride of a lion, in spite of its size. It has a right to be proud. For more than 1,000 years, only the Emperor of China could be the master of a Pekingese.

Less than 100 years ago, the first Pekingese dogs reached England. They were taken from Peking, the capital of China, by British soldiers. Now they are favorite lapdogs, especially liked by ladies. And there is no longer any emperor in China.

POODLES

Poodles are the smartest dogs known. Most circus and show dogs are Poodles. They come in any solid color, and all (except brown ones) have black lips and noses. Their coats are curly, and they are usually clipped in what appears to be a fancy design. This custom began when Poodles were hunting dogs and their coats got in their way in the underbrush.

GREAT DANES

GREAT Danes are three feet tall and have short, thick coats. No other dog stands as proudly. It is one of the oldest known breeds, for its picture was painted by Egyptian artists 4,000 years ago.

DOBERMAN PINSCHERS

DOBERMANN, a German dog lover, made up his mind to breed a terrier (Pinscher in German) so that it would be the size of a shepherd dog. The dog that resulted is brave, intelligent, and obedient. It is a fine police dog and is used as a Seeing-Eye Dog.

DALMATIANS

MANY fire-houses have Dalmatians as mascots. These big white dogs, with black or brown spots, love horses and are also fine watch dogs. They are loyal, brave, and friendly, and they make wonderful pets.

ESKIMO DOGS

In the cold northern regions of America live the Eskimos and their dogs, which are named after them. These dogs are not really pets. They are seldom even allowed to enter an Eskimo house, or igloo. But they are certainly helpful to everyone in the northland, because they pull the sleds hundreds of miles over the snow and ice, and can always find their way home, even when their masters are lost.

POMERANIANS

A COUSIN of the Eskimo Dog is the small, fluffy, gentle Pomeranian. This breed owes its popularity to one woman, Queen Victoria of England, who bought one in Florence and brought it back home.

Queen Victoria's pet weighed about 30 pounds. But the Pomeranian that is carried from home to home today weighs no more than seven pounds. This is the result of breeding, that is, of always picking the smallest puppies to be the parents of the next family.

TABBY Cats

ALL cats are soft, cuddly, and willing to purr when they are happy. They come in many colors and shapes, with long or short hair. Cats are called independent because, unlike dogs, they only love their owners when they are treated with love and understanding. But they really depend on their owners just as dogs do.

Most cats belong to no breed at all, but are mixtures of several breeds. Such cats are often striped, and are called Tabby cats. Their name comes from a kind of striped or wavy cloth called "attabi" by the Arabs.

PERSIANS
AND MAINE CATS

ALL cats probably came from the East, and those with long hair are called Persians. The kittens are fluffy and will grow up with the same color—snow white, creamy white, coppery red, dusky blue, tortoise-shell (a kind of brown

shading to yellow in spots), charcoal gray, or jet black.

The first Persians were known as Angoras, and were a little longer than Persians are now. There are very few pure Angoras left. Some were brought to Maine a long time ago, and a new type, which some call a breed, is the Maine or Coon cat *(shown on page 28)*. It is bigger than the Persian and has a pointed tail, while other long-haired cats have bushy or kinky tails.

SIAMESE

THE best known short-haired cat is the Siamese. This breed comes from Siam (which is now called Thailand), where it is the common housecat. They are not as fluffy as the long-haired cats, and their color often changes. A white kitten may become a light-brown (fawn) or shadow-blue cat, and it will usually have darker shades of the same color on its face, legs, and tail.

The eyes of Siamese cats are almost always blue, and often they are crossed, but this does not mean that they have poor sight. All cats have very keen sight, even when the light is dim. You can see how much bigger their eyes are at dusk or by firelight. But cats cannot see in total darkness, as many people believe.

BURMESE

BURMA is a country near Thailand where the Siamese cats came from. Burmese cats also have short hair and long bodies, but their colors and eyes are different. Most Burmese kittens are light brown which becomes deeper as they grow. They have round eyes, colored greenish or yellowish.

MAINE

(See page 24.)

ABYSSINIAN

MALTESE

MANX, MALTESE, ABYSSINIANS

THE Abyssinian cat has fur that is more like that of a rabbit than that of other breeds of cat. It is usually brown in color, with the tips a darker shade of brown, giving the cat an interesting speckly look. It has big ears, big eyes, and is very rare.

Manx cats are different from all others, because they have no tails at all. Their hind legs are higher than their front legs, so they look like rabbits when they run. They are usually striped, either blue or brown, or solid black or white, and their heads are rather large. Real Manx cats are so rare that sometimes dishonest cat dealers cut the tails from other breeds of cat and sell them as Manx cats.

Maltese cats are beautiful blue cats of no special breed, just like Tabbies.

MANX

29

BIRD PETS

MANY kinds of birds can be tamed and kept in cages. There you can take good care of them. They would not be happy if they were free, like other birds, because they would not know how to take care of themselves.

TALKING BIRDS

SOME birds have voices that are almost human. By listening to human speech they can learn to talk, too. Of course, they do not know what they are saying, and they will never say anything they have not heard someone else say many times over.

Parrakeets are the most popular of talking birds. They have beautiful feathers of many bright colors, green and blue and yellow.

SINGING BIRDS

THE tame bird with the finest singing voice is the beautiful Canary, which is usually yellow. A Canary sings best when it is happy. Whistle or sing to it, and see if it does not answer.

FISHES

A PET fish is no tamer than any other fish, but it is more beautiful. Goldfish are kept in bowls where you can watch them as they dart about. At feeding time, you tap the bowl and they understand. Another pet fish is the Guppy.

CAGED PETS

SOME pet animals are so small that they would get lost or hurt if they were allowed to be free, so they are kept in cages. These cages are their homes. After they know you well enough to go out for a short time, they will come back to their cages and sleep or play there.

HAMSTERS

THE first Hamsters were brought here from Europe in the 1930's. These furry animals are only about six inches long. They have pointed noses and round ears and pouches in their cheeks where they store food to eat later. They love to be petted.

GUINEA PIGS

Guinea Pigs are not pigs at all, and they do not come from the country of Guinea, but from South America where they were tamed by the Indians. They are about six inches long, with chunky bodies of various colors, pointed faces, and no tails at all. They are very gentle and talk by squeaking.

WHITE MICE

White Mice are often kept as pets because they are so pretty and lively. If their cage has a tiny trapeze, such as acrobats use, they will learn to swing on it. They must always be kept in their cages.

RABBITS

SOME Rabbits are white and silky, with broad floppy ears. Others have small, perky ears and short hair. Rabbits love to be cuddled, and to play games. If they are annoyed, they show it by knocking their hind legs against the floor.

Cats may learn to play with Rabbits, but some dogs never learn this because they are trained to hunt hares, which look like Rabbits. Every Rabbit likes to have its own comfortable home which should be built like a wild Rabbit's burrow.

Domestic Animals

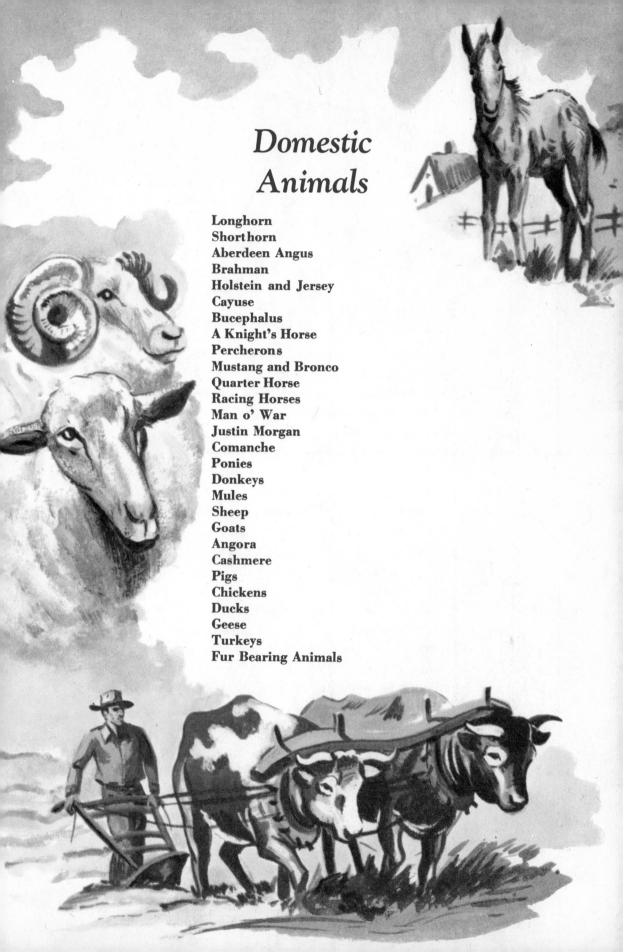

Longhorn
Shorthorn
Aberdeen Angus
Brahman
Holstein and Jersey
Cayuse
Bucephalus
A Knight's Horse
Percherons
Mustang and Bronco
Quarter Horse
Racing Horses
Man o' War
Justin Morgan
Comanche
Ponies
Donkeys
Mules
Sheep
Goats
Angora
Cashmere
Pigs
Chickens
Ducks
Geese
Turkeys
Fur Bearing Animals

Long before men could read or write they
learned to make friends with animals. In
those days all their food came from hunting
or fishing. Some years there were plenty of wild
animals and plenty of food. Other years animals
were hard to find, and men were often hungry.

One time somebody—we do not know who—
caught a pair of wild oxen, a male and a female,
and instead of eating them right away, kept them
until they had baby oxen. The little ones were
not wild. They were saved alive until a bad year
came. Meanwhile they had more baby oxen.
This was the beginning of cattle raising.

Now men could live wherever they could
find food for their cattle. Soon they learned to
raise food for their cattle and for themselves.
They became farmers.

Other wild animals
were taught to live on
farms. Wild sheep and
goats were tamed and
kept, not only to eat, but
for their wool and milk.

36

Wild horses were taught to draw carts and both horses and oxen learned to carry heavy loads. The fierce boars of the forests became farm pigs. Large birds that lived mainly on the ground and were delicious when roasted were kept on farms and became chickens, while their swimming cousins became geese and ducks.

Those animals that could not be tamed continued to be hunted, some of them until there were no more left. Often a few were kept and put in zoos. But all over the world farm animals are kept alive to give men food or hides or wool. These animals which men have tamed are called *domestic* animals.

Longhorn

In 1493, on Christopher Columbus' second trip to the New World, he brought with him horses, sheep, goats, pigs and cattle. None of these animals had ever before been seen in this country. Other Spanish conquerors brought more of these animals.

Massive herds of wild cattle, descended from the stock introduced by the early Spaniards, made their way to the Southwest of what is now the United States, especially to the open prairies of Texas. Anglo-Saxon settlers in this region domesticated these cattle and called them Longhorns.

Shorthorn

NEW breeds were brought to America from the farms of northern Europe. Their meat was better because they did not roam over wide prairies but were carefully fed and watched by the farmers.

The earliest and still one of the best of these breeds came from Scotland and was called the Shorthorn or Durham. The bulls provide fine beef and the cows give plenty of milk.

Aberdeen Angus and Brahman

THE very best cattle are bred to provide either beef or milk, not both.

A fine beef-producing breed is the Aberdeen-Angus, a coal-black animal that comes from the highlands of Scotland. These cattle are much smaller than the silver-gray Brahmans, which are brought all the way from India. Brahmans are usually mated to cattle of other breeds, and in this way a new breed is formed.

Holstein and Jersey

THE black-and-white Holstein and the brown Jersey are two of the best dairy cows. They are raised mainly for the milk they produce. The Holstein provides more milk each day, but the Jersey provides milk that is creamier.

Of course, dairy cows also produce calves. Male calves are not usually allowed to grow up. They are turned into meat, which is very tender and is called veal. Female calves are called heifers until they grow up and become cows. On farms, children often choose a pretty heifer to become a pet.

Cayuse

THE Cayuse is still seen in the West and, of course, in the movies. It is a strong, yet active animal, able to cover difficult ground at a rapid rate without getting too tired. The famous Pony Express was carried by these small horses, bringing the mail across mountains and deserts before the railroads were built. They are also called Mustangs, but the name Cayuse is most often used. Their ancestors were the wild horses of the plains. And there is no horse that brings back the memory of the Old West in the way the Cayuse does, especially when an Indian is in the saddle.

Bucephalus

LONG ago there was a tiny kingdom called Macedonia. The King was buying horses one day. One horse seemed so wild that the King refused to buy him. But the King's son, Prince Alexander, made friends with the black beauty, whose name was Bucephalus, and tamed him.

When Alexander became king, he conquered the world, and wherever he went he rode on Bucephalus. After Bucephalus died, Alexander built a new city and named it Bucephala.

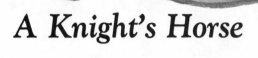

A Knight's Horse

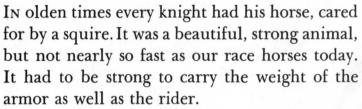

In olden times every knight had his horse, cared for by a squire. It was a beautiful, strong animal, but not nearly so fast as our race horses today. It had to be strong to carry the weight of the armor as well as the rider.

When the knights from Europe fought battles against the horsemen from Asia, the knights were sometimes beaten because their horses were too slow. The horsemen from Asia used fast Arabian animals, more like our race horses.

Percherons

THE Percheron is one of the most famous of work horses. It was brought here from France, and its ancestors were the sturdy horses of the knights and the lighter Arabian horses. For hundreds of years Percherons and other strong horses did heavy farm work and pulled coaches or carts. Now the Percherons are vanishing, because machines have taken their places.

Mustang and Bronco

HORSES first came to America with Columbus. These were called Barbs because they had originally come from the Barbary coast of Africa.

Soon there were Barbs on every ranch in Spanish Mexico. When the Indians captured many of these ranches, the horses escaped. The Barbs wandered wild all over the West for hundreds of years. When the cowboys reached the Far West they caught and tamed these horses.

The cowboys called them Mustangs. Before a Mustang is "broken" or tamed, it is often called a Bronco.

Quarter Horse

A FAVORITE breed on Western ranches is the Quarter Horse. It is usually dark in color and about five feet high. The name comes from its speed in running short distances, such as a quarter of a mile. The Quarter Horse can get in motion so fast that it can head off a steer before the creature can even begin to run off.

Racing Horses

FAST, light horses of all kinds may be called Arabian, because they come from a breed originally raised in far-off Arabia. When they first reached Africa they were known as Barbs. So many Barbs were brought to Spain that the breed was often called Spanish. These were the horses brought to America, from which the Mustang came.

One type of Arabian horse finally reached England, and is now known as the Thoroughbred. All Thoroughbreds today trace their descent from three famous animals—an Arabian named Darley, Godolphin, a Barb, and Byerly, a Turkish horse, who was used in the army before he became famous.

Thoroughbreds are fine saddle horses and racers, but for harness racing the best pacers and trotters are Standardbreds. Just as the Thoroughbreds trace back to particular Arabians, so the Standardbreds trace back to two Thoroughbreds named Messenger and Justin Morgan.

Man o' War

THE most popular racehorse of all time was the chestnut Thoroughbred, Man o' War. He was bought, when a year old, for $5,000, but was so spirited that the trainers could hardly control him. Then, in two years, the horse won 20 out of 21 races and earned $250,000 in prizes.

After Man o' War was retired from racing, he became the father of many other great racehorses. Horse lovers from all over traveled to Lexington, Kentucky, just to get a glimpse of him.

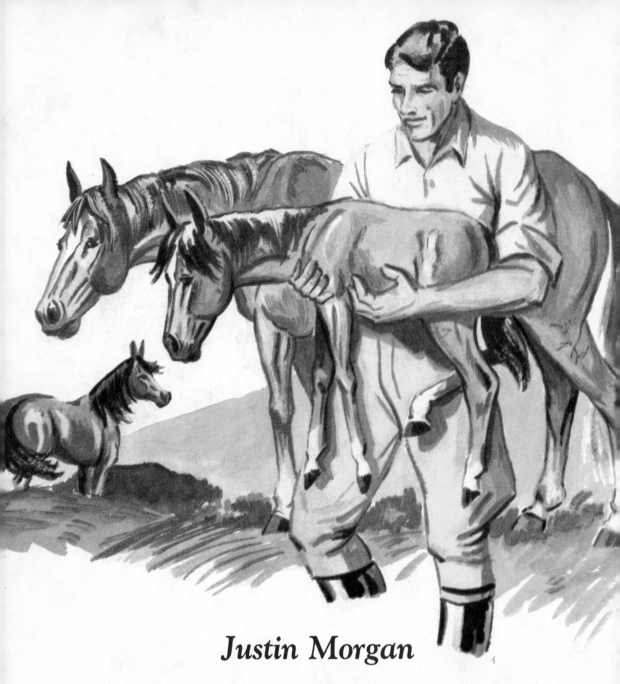

Justin Morgan

SOME of the most famous horses were of no special breed. One horse of this kind, who was mostly Thoroughbred, became the founder of a new breed known as Justin Morgan.

This horse, owned by a Vermont schoolteacher named Justin Morgan, soon gained the reputation of being the best horse in sprinting, pulling, trotting, or any kind of farm work. Justin Morgan, named for his master, was so popular that thousands of fine Morgan horses were descended from him.

Comanche

COMANCHE was another famous horse of no special breed. He won his fame in battle.

Comanche was one of the United States cavalry horses present at the famous Battle of Little Bighorn, which took place in 1876 and in which General Custer lost his life and the lives of his men. The victorious Indians took away the cavalry horses, as prizes of war.

But the six-year-old horse, Comanche, had hidden behind some bushes. He was badly hurt when found the next day by a party of soldiers. When he recovered the horse was received with honor. And in every parade, as long as he lived, Comanche walked behind the flags.

Ponies

PONIES are really small horses of special breeds. Shetland ponies, the most popular, are about 40 inches high. They may be black, brown, or spotted, and they have two coats, a summer coat that is short and glossy, and a shaggy winter coat that comes off in the spring.

Shetland ponies are fine pets, just big enough for a child to ride or drive. They are usually gentle, but some of them can become stubborn at times.

Donkeys

A COUSIN of the horse is the donkey, also called an ass. (If it is male, it is called a jackass.) In spite of its reputation, the donkey is not stupid. It is about the size of a pony, has short hair, and long ears.

In Mexico and South America, donkeys called burros are used to carry heavy loads.

Mules

IF a jackass is mated to a female horse (a mare), the young ones will be mules. They are hard workers, but sometimes they just refuse to work. Then they become "as stubborn as a mule."

Sheep

IN ancient Greece, they told how a hero named Jason sailed to the end of the world to find a treasure called the Golden Fleece. This is just a story, but all over the world farmers keep shy, gentle animals, with woolly coats which can be turned into money or gold. Only tame sheep have these coats. Wild sheep, such as the Rocky Mountain Bighorns, have no wool.

The best wool sheep, Merinos, came from Spain, where the king tried to keep them. But many of them were brought out — Cortes brought some to America—and now Merinos are found all over the world. They produce very fine wool, especially a French type of Merino called the Rambouillet.

In England, they learned to breed sheep like the Lincoln which have very long wool, others like the Hampshire and Dorset which have poor wool but good meat, and still others like the Corriedale which produce wool and meat. The meat of sheep is delicious, as you know, for surely you enjoy lamb chops.

Sheep like to roam over grassland. When they have finished eating, the grass looks as though it had been freshly cut. Often more than 1,000 sheep are guarded in one flock by a herder and his dogs.

Goats

GOATS are like sheep in many ways. All goats have horns, as do many sheep, but the horns of sheep are shaped like a corkscrew, while those of goats fork up and out.

Male goats, called billy-goats, have beards. Female goats, called nanny-goats, are fine milk producers. Their milk is saved for children and sick people who cannot drink cow's milk.

Angora

GOATS have fleece, which is not called wool, but mohair. It is long and silky, and cannot mat. or felt, as wool can. The best fleece-producing goat in this country is the Angora which was first bred in Turkey.

The Angora is smaller than a sheep or a milk goat. It has long ears, horns often more than two feet long, and a noble expression.

Cashmere

FLEECE finer than that of any sheep comes from a goat found only in the valley of Kashmir, in India. Both the goat and the fleece, which is often called wool, have the name of this valley, but spelled differently—Cashmere.

Pigs

Pigs are heavy, thick-skinned animals with short legs, almost no neck at all, and a long snout. They are neither lazy nor dirty, but they do love to roll in mud, just as a dog loves to roll in grass.

Before a pig is a year old it will weigh 200 pounds. Then it is ready to be turned into tasty ham and bacon.

Some pigs are fed corn until they cannot eat any more.

They grow into hogs, weighing as much as 1,000 pounds, and they are very fat. This pleases the farmer, because all the fat on these hogs is valuable. It is turned into lard, which is used for cooking. Other parts of the animal are also useful. Strong leather is made of pigskin, and the tough hairs, called bristles, are made into brushes.

Chickens

IN the jungles of Asia, there is a large bird with brilliant colors—red feathers on the wings, yellow on the neck and head, black on the tail. It is hard to believe that our common chicken is related to this jungle bird, but it is the same animal, except that the chicken is tame.

Almost all farmers raise some chickens, and some raise nothing else. Imagine the noise they must make, all cackling at once! Chickens provide delicious meat and billions of eggs every year.

Chickens cannot fly very high or very far. They eat by picking at their feed with their strong beaks. The little chicks are very lively.

Most American chickens are kept for both meat and eggs. The best egg chicken is the Leghorn, from Italy. If its ear lobes are white, the eggs it lays will be white too, but if the ear lobes are red, it will lay brown eggs. Both are good to eat.

A chicken farm is very noisy, because chickens make all kinds of sounds. The happiest sound comes after an egg has been laid, and the loudest comes early in the morning, when the roosters (male chickens) wake everyone with their crowing.

Ducks

DUCKS are tame water-birds that sleep on land, but their short legs and webbed feet are not much good for walking. In the water, however, they get along fine, and as soon as they come out their feathers are dry. A mother duck gliding through the water, followed by all the little ducklings, is a pretty sight.

Farmers breed ducks for their fine meat. Long Island, in New York, is famous for its tasty ducklings. The most popular breeds are white.

Geese

A COUSIN of the duck is the goose. Its neck and legs are longer than those of a duck, but its feet are webbed and it is at home in the water.

Geese are good to eat, but the best part of all is the liver which is chopped up to make a spread. Goose feathers, which are very soft, are used for stuffing pillows.

Tame geese are gray or white. When a goose wants to talk, it makes a single loud noise, a honk, that sounds like a rusty automobile horn.

Turkeys

TURKEYS are as American as Thanksgiving, when they are almost always served for dinner. The Indians had learned to tame these big, bright-feathered birds. The Spaniards who came over after Columbus discovered America took turkeys back home, and some of them reached England. Then the Pilgrims brought a few of them back to America on the Mayflower. They must have been surprised to find wild turkeys all through the New England woods.

Turkeys, wild or tame, are beautiful birds because of their brilliant colors — green, golden, coppery in some types, although there are plain white ones too. One famous type is called the Bronze, another the Bourbon Red. They are much larger than chickens, and their meat is very solid.

You cannot be hungry after a turkey dinner. Many years ago, when families were larger, with a dozen children and sometimes more, one turkey would be just enough for a good meal. But now, few families could finish eating such a big bird, so the turkey farmers have learned to breed new types that weigh little more than a large chicken.

Fur-Bearing Animals

THE last animals to be raised on farms were those which are valued for their fur. Although they live in man-made homes, they never become tame, and are not pets.

The silver fox was the first animal to be kept on fur farms. Its fur is really black with hairs tipped gray or white, giving the coat a frosty look.

The mink is small, with soft brown fur. Hundreds of minks are needed to make one garment.

The chinchilla is like a squirrel, so small you can hold it in your hand. Its fur is soft and gray and thick. Chinchillas originally came from South America, but so many were killed that they became rare. Now some are raised on farms.

Wild
Animals

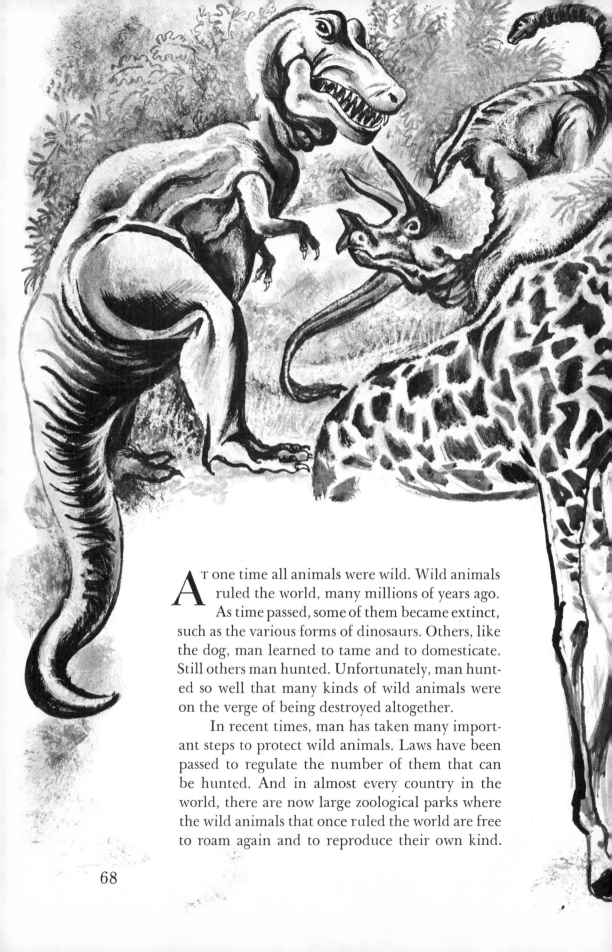

A T one time all animals were wild. Wild animals ruled the world, many millions of years ago.

As time passed, some of them became extinct, such as the various forms of dinosaurs. Others, like the dog, man learned to tame and to domesticate. Still others man hunted. Unfortunately, man hunted so well that many kinds of wild animals were on the verge of being destroyed altogether.

In recent times, man has taken many important steps to protect wild animals. Laws have been passed to regulate the number of them that can be hunted. And in almost every country in the world, there are now large zoological parks where the wild animals that once ruled the world are free to roam again and to reproduce their own kind.

Giraffe

THE African Giraffe is the tallest animal on land. It reaches a height of 19 feet, and its legs are so long that a man can actually stand under them.

People often wonder how this tall, unwieldy animal can protect itself from other wild animals. The Giraffe's protection comes from its hind legs. These are amazingly strong and they can give powerful, deadly kicks.

Zebra

THE Zebra is the wild horse of Africa. It is colored white with black stripes, so that it cannot be seen when it stands in the shadows of branches.

The Zebra has a large head and large ears. The short hair on its neck stands straight up. This animal can see very far, has excellent hearing, and can smell amazingly well.

Gorilla

THE Gorilla is the largest of the apes, growing to over five feet tall and weighing as much as 600 pounds. Even the lion is afraid to fight with this animal. The Gorilla will not harm people unless they attack it. It lives on fruits and vegetables.

The African mountain Gorilla is black. The jungle Gorilla is gray. A captured Gorilla becomes friendly very easily. It is smart but not as smart as the chimpanzee.

Baboon

THE Baboon, shown in the above picture on the right, is called "dog-faced," because it has a snout like a dog. The Baboon really belongs to the monkey family.

Some Baboons live in colonies or tribes, and they are ruled by the elder members. Between the various tribes of Baboons there is constant warfare.

Chimpanzee

THE African Chimpanzee is the smartest animal—next to man. It is about five feet tall and its arms hang down to its knees. It can be taught many tricks, even to roller skate.

Mongoose

THE Mongoose is a famous snake killer. Although only two feet long, it will attack a poisonous snake seven feet long. It is found in Africa and Asia, where there are many snakes. Sometimes the Mongoose gets bitten by a snake, but this does not happen often.

Aardvark

AARDVARK is a South African Dutch name which means earth pig. The Aardvark does look a little like a pig but it is not really a pig.

The Aardvark sleeps in a hole during the day. At night it comes out to look for termites. With its sharp claws, it easily tears open the termite mounds. And with its long, sticky tongue, it licks along the opened mound, gobbling up the termites.

Anteater

THE Anteater lives in swampy forests in Central and South America. The animal's long head comes to a point at the end of its mouth.

The Anteater has no teeth. Its tongue is almost two feet long, and sticky, so it can lick up ants. It uses the long powerful claws on its front feet to dig up large ant hills.

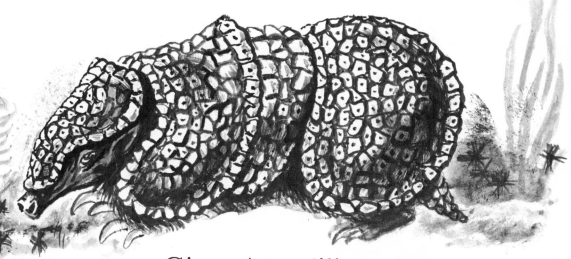

Giant Armadillo

THE Giant Armadillo lives in the jungles of South America. It has a hard protective covering over its head and body, which looks a lot like the armor that knights of the Middle Ages used to wear in battle.

Cougar

THE animal shown leaping through the air on the left side of the picture is a Cougar, or Puma. It is sometimes called a Panther. A member of the cat family, the Cougar is native to America. The Cougar can leap as many as 20 feet with ease, and 60-foot leaps have been recorded.

Jaguar

THE spotted Jaguar, shown in the lower part of the picture, is the most powerful of all the wild cats in America.

Many Jaguars live in the jungles of South America. There the owners of cattle ranches hire professional hunters to hunt the Jaguars, because these animals prey on defenseless cattle.

Cheetah

THE Cheetah of Africa and India is one of the swiftest four-legged animals in the world. Its speed has been officially timed at 48 miles an hour, but some people claim to have seen it travel at 70 miles an hour.

Hippopotamus

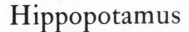

HIPPOPOTAMUS is a Greek word that means river horse, but the Hippopotamus is really related to the pig. It has a very large round body and short legs. It lives in Africa, in the same waters as the crocodile, but the two animals do not bother each other. When the Hippopotamus swims, only its eyes and nose stick up out of the water.

The Hippopotamus can close its nose like a bottle cap and stay under water for as long as 30 minutes. When it comes up and opens its nose with a loud snort, a foot-high spray of water shoots out. The Hippopotamus lives on vegetables.

Rhinoceros

A very large, clumsy animal is the Rhinoceros. It has one and sometimes two horns on its head between the nose and eyes. This animal is very short-sighted and bad tempered. Perhaps this is why it often charges without any reason.

In India there is a belief that a Rhinoceros horn has magical powers. Some natives think that drinking from the horn will keep a person from becoming poisoned. If he is already poisoned, they think it will cure him.

Buffalo

THE Buffalo once roamed all over the North American plains. There were millions of Buffaloes in a single herd. The American Buffalo is also known as the Bison. India is the home of the Water Buffalo. The Cape Buffalo comes from Africa. The Bison is a big powerful animal. There is thick hair around its head and neck and shoulders and a black beard on its chin.

The Bison was a very important animal in the history of America. It was killed for food and clothing by the Indians and the early white settlers. Buffalo Bill was a famous hunter of Buffaloes or Bison. He was hired by the Kansas Pacific Railroad, in 1876, to kill the Buffaloes to keep them away from the railroad tracks. So many were killed that today, there are only a few thousand Buffaloes left.

Deer

DEER inhabit almost every region of the world. We speak of the adult male of most species of deer as a buck. The adult female is called a doe. The fawn is a young deer.

The antlers of male deer are those hard bones that grow from the head and look like tree branches. At the end of every mating season, these antlers fall off, but new ones grow the next year. The Moose is the largest of the deer. Caribou is the common name for our North American Reindeer. Do you remember the names of the eight Reindeer in the lovely poem, "Visit from St. Nicholas"?

Tapir

THE timid Tapir is a strange animal. It has a massive body, short legs, and a long snout. It has five front toes but only three hind toes. The Tapir lives in Central and South America. It is a harmless animal, and is very, very shy.

Sloth

THE Sloth is the laziest of animals. It has long, curved claws which it hooks onto the branches of trees. It hangs upside down, moving slowly along a branch, while eating leaves.

Wart Hog

THE Wart Hog is probably the ugliest of all animals. Its head is very big and its body is small and round with pudgy legs.

The eyes of the Wart Hog squint. On each side of its face are four warts, like huge, ugly pimples. Near the end of its snout are two tusks almost a foot long. It has some whiskers on its face.

The Wart Hog is often found with zebras and antelopes on the plains of Africa.

Bear

THE Bear is a large and powerful animal, with a thick coat of hair and sharp claws. It lives in North America and Northern Asia. The Bear is a good swimmer. It sleeps all winter long. This is called hibernating.

The Polar Bear, shown above, lives in the Arctic. Its coat is white and sometimes a little yellow. It eats seals, walrus cubs, foxes and birds. It is friendly, but only when there is plenty of food around. When it is hungry it will even go after a man. The Grizzly Bear shown on the next page is even more ferocious.

The Eskimos hunt the Polar Bear for food and for clothing.

The Brown Bear and the American Black Bear become very timid in captivity. The Black Bear eats mostly vegetables. Honey is something every Bear likes.

Elephant

THE largest animal that lives on land is the Elephant. The African Elephant grows as tall as 12 feet and may weigh as much as 12 tons. The Elephant uses the long snout, called a trunk, to eat leaves from trees, to drink water, and to bathe itself. It also uses the trunk to scent enemies because its eyesight is very poor. The trunk is strong enough to pull up large trees.

We all know how big the Elephant's ears are. The strange thing is that the Elephant cannot hear too well. The Elephant is astonishingly smart. Once, a herd of Elephants came to a stream which was too shallow to bathe in. All the Elephants started building a dam across the stream. The dam blocked up the water and made a fine deep pool for bathing.

84

Waterbuck

THE Waterbuck on the right of this picture belongs to the antelope family. Its home is in Africa. It is really a land animal. But whenever it is frightened it hides in the water. The Waterbuck is a good swimmer.

Gazelle

THE animal in the lower part of the picture above is the Gazelle. Only the cheetah can outrun it. The deserts of Africa and Asia are the Gazelle's home.

In 1946, newspapers printed a story about a boy who was brought up by Gazelles. Natives saw the boy running with Gazelles and caught him. A doctor said the boy acted just like a Gazelle. Some people thought the boy was left by his mother and the Gazelles found him.

Gibbon

THE Gibbon ape of Asia stands only about three feet high, but its arms are so long that its fingers touch the ground. The Gibbon walks with its hands over its head and looks as if it will fall forward on its face.

In the trees this ape swings easily from branch to branch. It has a loud voice and likes to scream while eating.

Orangutan

THE Orangutan's home is in Borneo and Sumatra. It leans on its knuckles when walking because of its very long arms. A captured Orangutan ape can be taught to ride a tricycle or to put on a suit.

Camel

No animal is better adapted to life in the desert than the Camel. When sandstorms blow, the Camel's eyes are shielded by its very long eyelashes. We all know that the Camel can go without water for days.

Do you think that water is stored in the humps of the Camel? Actually these humps store food, not water, as most people suppose. Inside the Camel's stomach are many pouches or sacks; that is where the water is stored. Sometimes, when desert travelers have no other water supply, they will cut open these sacks and drink the water as a last resort.

Rocky Mountain Goat

THE Rocky Mountain Goat is a little like a goat and a little like an antelope. It is not really either one. It has a thick white coat with horns that curve back. It lives on high mountain peaks. It is very sure-footed and very brave.

Wild Sheep

MANY years ago, all Sheep were wild, like the Angali of Asia. These are thought to be the ancestors of all tame Sheep. They have long, curled horns. Very much like them are the wild Bighorns of our Rocky Mountains. The wild Barbary Sheep of North Africa have shorter horns that do not curl.

Lion

We can certainly understand why the Lion has been named the King of the Beasts. The long flowing hair on its neck, called the mane, is wonderfully majestic looking. But the female Lion, or Lioness, does not have this long mane, and she does not look nearly so majestic.

Lions are the biggest members of the cat family. They sometimes weigh as much as 500 pounds. They are enormously powerful, always dangerous when they are hungry. Lions live in Africa and parts of India. They prefer the open country to the jungle.

Tiger

THE Tiger lives in regions of Asia that extend from cold Siberia all the way to hot India. There are no Tigers in Africa. The Tiger has a yellow-tan color with black stripes which hide it in the jungle. Tigers stalk their prey at night. Of all the cats, the Tiger is man's most dangerous enemy.

Leopard

THE Leopard's home is Africa. It is smaller than a lion or a tiger, but it is more ferocious. The Leopard has black spots in groups of five or six on its body. Sometimes it has so many black spots that it looks all black. The Leopard likes to stay around trees where it can hunt monkeys and birds.

Monkey

THE Monkey that lives in the jungles of Central and South America has a long tail which it uses as an extra hand when swinging through the trees. The Spider Monkey is the best acrobat. It can leap 30 feet through the air.

The Monkey of Asia and Africa does not have a tail that can grasp. This is the kind used by organ grinders and is called the Rhesus Monkey. The funniest looking Monkey lives in Borneo. It is called the Proboscis Monkey because it has a very long snout or nose, and proboscis means a long snout.

Flying Lemur

THE Flying Lemur is the size of a large squirrel. It is found from Malaya to Thailand and in Java, Burma, and the Philippine Islands. A thin, furry skin spreads from its front feet to the back feet, like sails.

The Lemur does not really fly like a bird. It spreads its feet so that the sails catch the wind, then glides through the air from the tops of trees. It only glides at night. During the day it sleeps, hanging from a branch, upside down.

Gnu

THE Gnu, or Wildebeest, of Africa, is the strangest looking member of the antelope family. It has a body like a horse and a head like a buffalo. Its horns curve down and then up, like the handlebars on a racing bicycle. There are very few of these animals left.

Antelope

THERE are many kinds of Antelopes. The Sable Antelope from the southern and eastern plains of Africa is one of the most beautiful. Its long horns curve back gracefully. The Sable Antelope's hair is short and colored black-brown and is very shiny. There are long white spots under its eyes.

The Royal Antelope is the smallest of these animals. It grows to no more than ten inches high. It lives in western Africa.

Gaur

THE Gaur is a wild ox. It is the largest of the wild cattle. Attempts to domesticate it have never been successful. The body is dark brown and the legs are white up to the knees.

In India and Burma, the home of the Gaur, the natives say it can pick up stones in its nose and blow them out at hunters as fast and as straight as bullets. This is only a story. The Gaur is really a very shy animal.

Wolf

THE Wolf is a form of wild dog. Some people think it is the original ancestor of all our domestic dogs. Others think it is an altogether different breed. But we do know that Wolves can be tamed, and then they become as affectionate as the most affectionate domestic dog. Since they are very powerful, they are sometimes mated with sled-dogs, to make a stronger stock.

In the wild state, Wolves can be terribly vicious and destructive. They hunt in packs and will attack sheep and cattle. They make their homes in caves and in hollow tree trunks.

Jackal

THE Jackal is a wild dog that lives in Africa and Asia. Many people call the Jackal cowardly, because it usually attacks smaller animals or animals that have been wounded by others.

Fox

Do you know the sly, clever Fox in the Aesop and "Uncle Remus" stories? The Fox is famous for its cleverness, because of the amazing tricks it will play to escape from pursuers, like running through water or along the tops of fences so as not to leave behind tell-tale tracks.

The female Fox is called a vixen. When baby Foxes or cubs are born, they stay blind for ten days, like baby kittens. And, also like kittens, cubs love to chase each other.

Coyote

COYOTE is an Indian name for the Prairie Wolf. Coyotes hunt in packs at night, uttering the most blood-curdling howls. When they hunt jack-rabbits, Coyotes work in pairs. One gives chase, while the other waits and rests, knowing full well that jack-rabbits run in circles.

Kaola

THE Kaola of Australia looks just like a toy bear. It has no tail. A Kaola is a marsupial. A marsupial is an animal that holds its babies in a pouch on the outside of its stomach.

Kangaroo

ANOTHER native of Australia is the Kangaroo. It stands seven feet high. With its long back legs and long powerful tail, it can jump as far as 20 feet and hop along at 25 miles an hour.

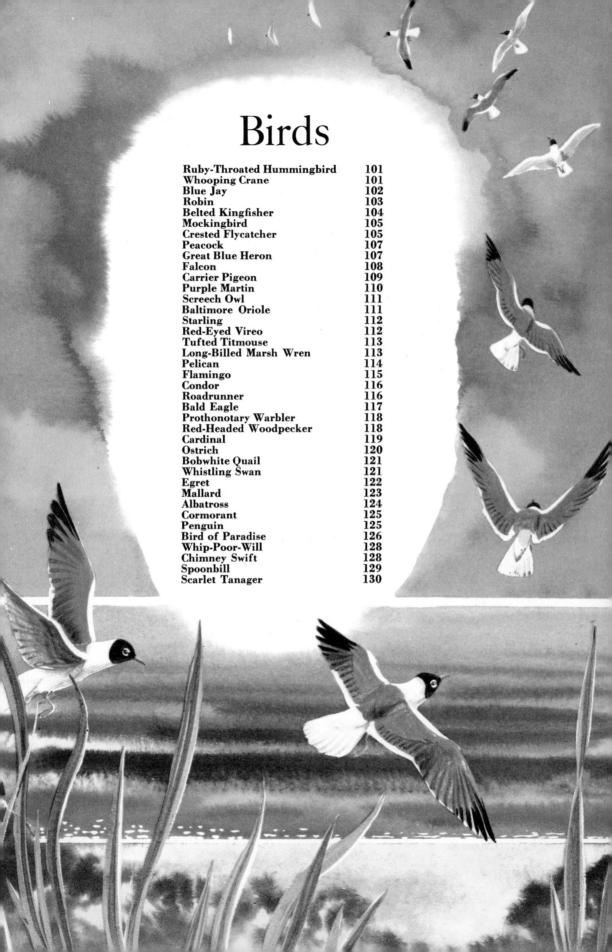

Birds

Birds, like people, have two legs, backbones, and warm blood. But instead of arms and hands, they have wings. They wear feathers in place of clothes. They lay eggs. The mother bird and sometimes the father bird, too, sit on the eggs to keep them warm, until the growing baby bird inside is big and strong enough to break the shell. Baby birds are almost as helpless as human babies. Their parents have to feed them and teach them how to fly.

Birds come in many sizes and in all the colors of the rainbow. The hummingbird's body is not much larger than the bowl of a tablespoon and it weighs less than the letter you drop in the mail box. But the ostrich grows eight and nine feet tall and weighs as much as two men.

The bird on this page is prehistoric. It lived many millions of years ago.

100

Ruby-Throated Hummingbird

THE smallest of all birds gets its name from the humming, motor-like sound of its beating wings. Like a helicopter, it can hover in one place and fly backwards. It can fly 70 miles an hour.

Whooping Crane

THE Whooping Crane is the tallest and loudest bird in North America. It is nearly five feet tall. When it whoops it can be heard all of three miles away. Usually, it lives for 50 years.

There used to be thousands upon thousands of Whooping Cranes in this country. Now there are nearly none left.

Blue Jay

FROM the tip of its beak to the tip of its tail, the Blue Jay is just a bit shorter than your 12-inch ruler. Blue Jays are very blue, very noisy, and great jokers.

On a hot summer afternoon, when owls like to sleep, several Blue Jays will gang up on a sleeping owl and awaken it with their brassy cries. Stealing acorns from squirrels is fun, too. Blue Jays gather and hide many more acorns and beechnuts than they can ever eat. But from these buried nuts forests of new trees have grown.

Strange as it seems, the beautiful Blue Jay is a cousin of the common crow. It is smaller and much more richly colored than the crow. Another Jay bird is the Robber Jay, so called because it steals food from hunters' camps.

Robin

THE Robin is the best known and best liked of all American birds. When the English settled in America they found large numbers of this member of the thrush family. They called it "Robin," because its red breast reminded them of the little English warbler called Robin they had left behind.

No American bird has adapted itself to modern civilization as well as the Robin. Today, it lives not only in villages and suburbs, but even in city parks and on the lawns of city houses. Unlike other migratory birds, it does not go all the way to South America in winter. It stops in Georgia and Florida. So the Robin is the first bird up north to hail the spring with its familiar call, "Cheer up, cheer up!"

Belted Kingfisher

Belted Kingfisher

THE Belted Kingfisher has wide stripes around the body that make it look like a barber shop pole. The males of most birds are richer or more gaudy looking than the females. The male of the Belted Kingfisher is an exception. But he makes up for it with a black crest that makes him look fierce.

The call of the Kingfisher is a harsh, rattling shriek.

Crested Flycatcher

Mockingbird

THE Mockingbird is the best singer and actor of all our birds. It will sing sweetly for hours on end, and then suddenly break off the song to imitate the song, whistle, or harsh calls of other birds.

It will imitate its cousin, the catbird, imitating a cat; and it will meow better than either of them. It will bark like a dog and has even been heard imitating the squeak of a garden gate's rusty hinge.

Mockingbird

Crested Flycatcher

THE Crested Flycatcher likes to fly after large insects and catch them in the air. It prefers to live in woodland country, but an old orchard will do. It will perch on a branch or railing for hours on end, waiting for some insect to fly by. Then it will dart quickly after the insect, snap it up, and return to its perch to wait for another insect.

The Crested Flycatcher's favorite nesting place is an empty woodpecker's hole. It will watch for a snake to shed its skin and will take the old skin to line its nest. If it cannot find any snakeskin, it will use onion skin and even man-made wax paper and cellophane. Its call is a long, loud wheeep!

Peacock

THIS most gorgeous of all birds is a native of India and Ceylon. It still lives in large numbers in the jungles of Ceylon. It has been domesticated for centuries in Europe, and struts about the lawns and gardens of the rich, and in this democratic age, in public parks, too.

The male Peacock has a train of feathers from the lower part of his back and the upper part of his tail, which he can raise and open up like a huge fan of green and blue and gold. The Peacock does this to attract the female bird who has no such fan.

Great Blue Heron

THIS long-legged water bird is a beautiful steel blue, with white markings. Its feet are not webbed like the feet of a duck and many other water birds. Its separated toes are long enough for it to curve its feet around the branch of a tree and hold on.

It builds its nests in the trees that border the swamps of Florida, Louisiana, and Texas. Sometimes as many as 100,000 of these great Herons will nest in the same place. They will return to it each year. They live on fish, frogs, snakes, shrimps, crabs, and mice. In the summer they fly north but return to the south in the fall.

Falcon

THE Peregrine Falcon, a member of the Hawk family, is also called the Duck Hawk. It is a very strong, swift flying, bluish bird with crossbars of brownish black and white spots. It has a cruel, curved beak and powerful talons. It will fly above a wild duck, pigeon, or some other smaller bird and swoop down on it, grasping it with its talons, and then will tear it to pieces with its beak.

During the Middle Ages in Europe, Falconry was a great sport of the nobles. Falcons were trained to capture certain game birds for their masters. In those days, your rank was marked by the quality of Falcon you carried about on your wrist. The sport of Falconry originated in China about 4,000 years ago.

Carrier Pigeon

PIGEONS have been serving men by carrying messages for nearly 3,000 years. Carrier Pigeons have been used mainly to carry secret messages across battlefields. Even in these days of radar, radio, and rockets, the trained Carrier Pigeons of the Army's Flying Telegraph still play an important role.

During World War II, an American Air unit had been ordered to bomb a certain Italian village believed to be held by the Germans. Minutes before the attack was to start, a U. S. Army Signal Corps Pigeon, named G.I. Joe, reached the Americans with a message saying that the town had just been taken by a British Infantry Brigade. G. I. Joe had flown the 20 miles in exactly 20 minutes! Thus he had saved 1,000 British soldiers from certain death.

Purple Martin

THE Purple Martin is the largest member of the swallow family. The male is a glossy purplish black, while the color of the female is a dull purplish black. Like all swallows, the Purple Martin has a very sweet, joyful song.

It is very friendly to people and is probably the most domesticated of all wild birds. Though it spends its winters in the jungles of the Amazon Valley, when it comes north to the United States and Canada in summer, it prefers to nest in a box-house built for it by man. Usually it will have to fight for its house with the ever-present English sparrow. Most often the Purple Martin wins. The English sparrow, by the way, is not a sparrow at all. It is a finch.

Screech Owl

YOU have heard the saying, "the wise old Owl." As a matter of fact, Owls are not as smart as many other birds. What makes them look like scholarly judges or school teachers is the fixed stare of their round eyes. But the Owl cannot look any other way. It cannot roll its eyes the way you can and all other birds do. It can only look straight ahead.

Baltimore Oriole

NAMED for Lord Baltimore, the founder of Maryland, this is the most beautiful member of the blackbird family. It has a glossy black head, neck and back. Its wings are black with a white trim, and all the rest of it is a flaming orange yellow.

It weaves its nest of grass and string, the female using her bill like a needle. The nest hangs from the tip of a high branch, swaying in the wind like a hammock, which makes a rocking cradle for the baby Orioles.

Starling

THE Starling is an immigrant.
It used to live only in Europe,
Asia and North Africa. It was
first brought to New York City's Central
Park, in 1890, to kill off insects that were
destroying the trees. Today, there are
many, many thousands of Starlings in
this country.

The Starling loves company. It
gathers in huge flocks that fly, without
any apparent leader, in perfect and
beautiful formations. It is very intelligent. It has been taught to whistle a
tune and to speak a few words.

Red-Eyed Vireo

THE Red-Eyed Vireo's nest is so well built that it will last for
several years. The Vireo is the victim of the lazy cowbird which
sneaks its egg into the Vireo's nest. And the Vireo will sit on it,
hatch, and bring up the young cowbird as if it were its own!

112

Tufted Titmouse

THE Tufted Titmouse is a perky, six-inch bird. The feathers on the top of its head stand up like the peak of an old fashioned nightcap. It does not go south in winter, but stays in swampy bottomlands.

It hunts for hidden insect eggs in the company of chickadees which belong to the Tit family, too. In summer its favorite food is caterpillars. This makes the Tufted Titmouse very popular with farmers. In winter as well as in spring and summer, the Tufted Titmouse is a loud and regular singer.

Long-Billed Marsh Wren

THIS little bird is not much larger than a hummingbird. The male usually has two or more wives. But these Wrens always build more nests than they have wives. Then, when attacked by big hawks or crows, the cagey male stands over the empty nest and chatters angrily at the attacker, while the wives sit quietly on their eggs or young ones.

Pelican

HERE is a well-known saying about this peculiar bird:
> "There is an old bird called the Pelican
> Whose bill can hold more than his belly can.
> He can put in his beak
> Enough food for a week
> And I just don't see how well he can."

This is how the Pelican does it. Its bill is from nine to 13 inches long, and underneath the bill is a bag which is like a balloon with no air in it. This bag can be filled with food and stretched until it holds three and a half gallons! That is equal to 14 quarts of milk! The huge bill and the bag are used to scoop up water with fish in it. After making its dive, the Pelican raises its head high into the air. As the water flows out, the bag gets limp and small again and the fish slide down the Pelican's throat.

114

Flamingo

THIS vivid pink water bird is four feet tall from the tip of its bill to its toes. It breeds in the swamps of Louisiana and Florida.

The Flamingo does not build a nest in the trees or shrubs, as other birds do. But on the mud flats it builds a wide-bottomed, cup-shaped nest of clay and sticks, and lays its single egg in the center of this nest.

Sometimes, so many Flamingos build nests in the same place that they are called Flamingo cities. The birds stick their stubby, curved beaks into the mud and shallow water, and root out the shrimps and crabs they love to eat.

You might not think it, but ducks and geese are cousins of the Flamingo. The Flamingo makes a call that sounds like the deep honk-honk of many kinds of geese.

Condor

THIS is a South American vulture. It is the greatest and most powerful bird of prey in the world. It lives high in the Andes mountains of Peru and Chile. It flies higher than any mountain peaks in the United States.

The Condor never builds a nest but lays its eggs in saucer-shaped rocks. If very hungry, Condors will hunt in pairs, swooping down into the valley and carrying off a sheep, a deer, or some member of the llama family. Once plentiful, Condors today are very rare. Soon they will probably become extinct.

Roadrunner

ON dirt roads, from Kansas to California and south to Texas, you may see a funny-looking track with two toes pointing forward and two backward. They were made by the Roadrunner, a bird that can run as fast as a man.

It has a foot-long upright tail, long power-packed legs, and short rounded wings.

116

Bald Eagle

THE Bald Eagle is not really bald. It has white head feathers to match its white tail feathers. But its large body, its great wings, and strong legs are covered with dark brown feathers, so that from a distance it actually looks bald.

This great American bird, with its big eight-foot wing spread, lives high up on rocky cliffs. With its keen eyesight, it can watch the surface of rivers and lakes far below. From its high perch, it can swoop down upon fish, waterfowl, or upon rabbits racing for cover. With its huge, sharp talons it can scoop up these animals and carry them up to its nest.

Prothonotary Warbler

In England, many years ago, there was a kind of Chief Clerk of the courts. This man was called a Prothonotary. He wore a bright yellow hood. It seems like a big name to have given a sweet, little Warbler, just because it, too, has a golden yellow head.

Red-Headed Woodpecker

The Red-Headed Woodpecker has been called the Carpenter Bird because it spends a lot of time drilling into trees with its strong, sharp-edged bill. When you see a Woodpecker drilling into a tree, it is either making a nest or looking for insect eggs that make up its food.

Cardinal

THIS rich red, crested, black-faced bird gets its name from the color of the robes worn by a cardinal of the Roman Catholic Church. It makes its home in any area that has thickets and tangles near open spaces.

It will eat insects and fruits but its favorite foods are the seeds of sunflowers, melons, and squash. When people place such seeds where wandering Cardinals can get at them, these birds become regular residents of the locality. They repay these human favors with their rich, loud and happy singing.

Ostrich

THE Ostrich is the largest bird in the world. It cannot fly. But with its small wings it can run along the ground, making giant strides, at speeds of more than 50 miles an hour.

An Ostrich egg weighs three pounds and would make an omelet large enough for 14 people. The feathers on the body of the Ostrich are black but those on its tail are white. These Ostrich plumes have been prized for centuries. They used to be worn by kings and knights.

Bobwhite Quail

THE Bobwhite is the American Quail. It differs from European Quail because it does not go south in winter.

Most of the year, it is not afraid of man. It will come out on the road or visit your garden. But it *always* seems to know when the hunting season starts. Then it hides deep in woods or in tall grass. A whole flock will sleep together in a circle, with their tails pointing in and their heads out, so that they can see in all directions. People in the South call this bird a Partridge.

Whistling Swan

HAVE you ever wondered why a Swan's neck is so long and so beautifully curved? That makes it possible for the Swan to reach plants and fish at the bottom of streams and shallow ponds, without having to dive down after them.

Our native American Swan is called the Whistling Swan. But it is not the one we usually see in our parks and lakes. That is a large white Swan which is imported from Europe. All Swans make a hissing noise when they are excited. With their powerful wings, they ward off enemies.

Egret

THE Egret is a beautiful white, long-necked bird of the heron family. It eats fish, frogs, snakes, and some water insects.

It was once commonplace up and down our coast. It was bad luck for the bird that during the breeding season, as many as 50 beautiful, long white plumes would grow out of their backs. For these *aigrettes,* as they were called, were worth 25 dollars each to adorn women's hats and heads. The birds were killed off by the thousands until hardly any were left. For many years the Audubon Society and others fought to save them. Finally, laws were passed to stop the killing. Women became ashamed to wear *aigrettes.* And so the lovely Egret lives happily again.

Mallard

THE Mallard is the common American wild duck. Wild geese are related to it. Both domestic ducks and geese were tamed from the wild varieties.

The Mallard has a broad head, a flat bill, very short legs and webbed toes. The bird is about two feet long. The upper part of the male is grayish brown and it has a chestnut-colored vest. The neck and throat are very dark green, while a thin white collar goes around its neck. The female is mostly brown, with streaks of black and buff.

Most ducks, however, are colored white, with rusty colored vests and a blue band on the wings. They all nest in the reeds along the shores of rivers and bays and other inlets of the sea. In summer they go far north and in winter as far south as Panama. There is one sort of wild duck that builds a nest which floats on the surface of the water.

Albatross

THE great white Albatross is not only the largest water bird, but in some ways the largest flying bird in the world. Though not as large of body as the mighty condor, its wing spread is 14 feet, which is as large as a small two-seated airplane.

The Albatross nests on high land overlooking the sea, but spends most of its time flying far out over the ocean. It can fly thousands of miles and fast enough to keep up with an ocean liner. For days it will follow a steamer. Each day when the garbage is thrown out at the stern, the Albatross will scoop up and eat whatever floats on the water. It can be tamed quite easily. For this reason, lonely sailors have grown very fond of the Albatross. They will tell you it is very bad luck to kill one.

Cormorant

THE Cormorant is a big, black bird with a white or yellow face. Cormorants live along the world's seashores.

In Chinese and Japanese waters, they have been trained to catch fish for man. A ring of hemp (of which we make rope) is tied around the bird's neck so that it is unable to swallow. Thus prevented from eating the fish, the Cormorant carries it in its bill to the boat of its owner and drops it in the boat. When the boat is full, the ring is taken off and the Cormorant is rewarded with fish for itself.

Penguin

THE Penguin lives in the far south of the world around the South Pole. It

looks and acts as if it were human.

When a Penguin stands and walks erect on its stubby legs, its paddle-like wings at its sides, and with its stout body, white in front and black at the back and sides, it looks just like a short, fat man in full dress evening clothes.

Bird of Paradise

IT is truly, the Birds of Paradise, for in and around the big island of New Guinea, in the South Seas, there are more than 40 different kinds of these unbelievably beautiful birds. Not only do these birds have beautiful, rich colors on their feathery bodies, but they have extra feathers of still other colors bursting out all over them. They look like living fountains of color.

They have tails like corkscrews, movable shields of feathery color, and extra sets of wings. Their calls range from the clang of temple gongs to a harsh scream. They live on fruits and berries.

Whip-Poor-Will

THE Whip-Poor-Will is colored brownish with a few white markings. The odd thing about the Whip-Poor-Will is that nearly everyone has heard it but hardly anyone has ever seen it. That is because it sleeps all day and lives and travels by night.

It does not build a nest, like other birds, but lays its eggs on a pile of dead leaves on the ground. At night and especially before a storm, it can be heard calling on the world to "whip-poor-will," in tones so sad, that once heard you will never forget them.

Chimney Swift

THIS little bird with narrow, slightly curved wings, and not much tail, really lives up to its name. It is the fastest living thing that flies. It can go 100 miles an hour. It has been known to cover 1,000 miles in a single day.

Then, too, it likes to roost in unused chimneys. It feeds on the many small flying insects that fill the air in summertime.

128

Spoonbill

THE Spoonbill is one of the funniest looking birds. But it is also one of the most beautiful. It has a white breast, but the rest of it is a wonderful shade of rose.

It gets its name from its silly bill which looks just like a very large spoon held in its mouth, with the bowl end out. This silly looking thing is one of the most practical eating machines in Nature. With it the Spoonbill is able to scoop up shrimps and crabs and other shell fish that it cannot even see in muddy waters.

Scarlet Tanager

MOST of the Tanager birds live in South America and the
West Indies. A few kinds, the Scarlet Tanager among them,
make the long trip up from Peru, Bolivia and Ecuador to spend
their summers in the United States.

The Scarlet Tanager is the most widely known of the
Tanagers. It is colored a gorgeous vivid red, and is the most
brilliant of all our northern birds. You may have heard it
called the "Firebird."

In our country this beautiful bird was almost killed off
by men who sold its feathers to make women's hats. Laws were
passed to stop this killing and one of our loveliest song birds
was saved.

Butterflies, Bees, Bugs and Other Insects

W<small>E</small> all know that butterflies, bees and bugs are insects. But have you ever wondered just what an insect *is*? Many people wonder whether or not an insect is an animal. An insect is very definitely an animal. As a matter of fact, insects are the most numerous of all the animals in the world. There are also more different kinds of insects than there are of all the other kinds of animals in the world put together.

An insect can be identified by the fact that it has six legs. It never has two legs, like a human being, or four legs, like a dog or a horse. Nor does it ever have more than six legs, like a spider or a centipede. Spiders and centipedes belong to a closely related order of animals but they are not true insects.

Another way you can tell insects from other animals is by the peculiar shape of their bodies. The bodies of all insects are joined into three parts: the head, the chest or *thorax,* and the abdomen. Almost all insects have *antennae* or feelers. These may be long or short, pointed or club-shaped, but they stick out of an insect's head like the antennae on a television set.

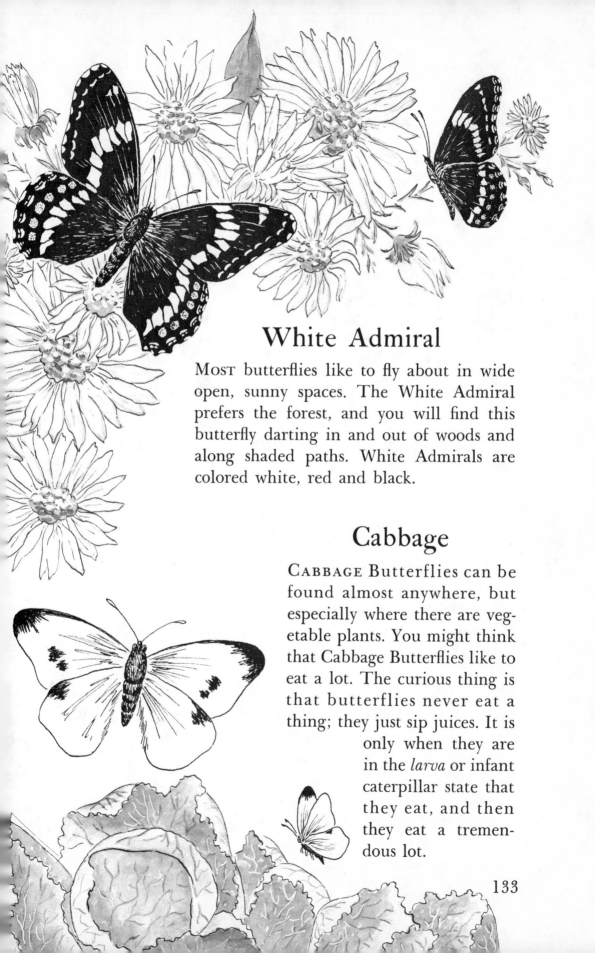

White Admiral

MOST butterflies like to fly about in wide open, sunny spaces. The White Admiral prefers the forest, and you will find this butterfly darting in and out of woods and along shaded paths. White Admirals are colored white, red and black.

Cabbage

CABBAGE Butterflies can be found almost anywhere, but especially where there are vegetable plants. You might think that Cabbage Butterflies like to eat a lot. The curious thing is that butterflies never eat a thing; they just sip juices. It is only when they are in the *larva* or infant caterpillar state that they eat, and then they eat a tremendous lot.

133

Tiger Swallowtail

SWALLOWTAILS are probably the handsomest of our butterflies. There is no doubt that they are the largest. You can easily spot a Swallowtail by its great size and by the tail-like parts of its hindwings. The Tiger Swallowtail has yellow wings with black stripes, like a tiger's coat.

All butterflies face the danger of being eaten alive by birds, especially when they are in the caterpillar state. Nature has a wonderful way of protecting the Swallowtail caterpillar. The front of its tiny green body has two big round yellow spots which look like the eyes of a snake. And hidden in its head are two orange horns which resemble a snake's forked tongue. These horns suddenly shoot out when the caterpillar is frightened. Birds think they have come upon a snake and are frightened away.

Monarch

BY far the favorite American butterfly is the orange and black Monarch. Of all butterflies, this one is certainly the most accomplished traveller.

In the fall Monarchs gather in great swarms to start their famous migration to the south.

Buckeye

THE Buckeye is a born fighter. This butterfly of medium size will pick a fight with larger butterflies, and it will even pit its strength against big grasshoppers or birds.

The upper spots on the hindwings of the Buckeye are so large and staring that they look like the eyes of a buck deer, which is how this little scrapper got its name.

Silverspot

A GRANDER name for the Silverspot Butterfly is the "Great Spangled Fritillary." Its wings are a rich yellowish brown, the edges splashed with black, and the underwings have gorgeous spots of shining silver.

Viceroy

THE Viceroy looks just like a small Monarch Butterfly, yet it belongs to an entirely different family. This helps the Viceroy because birds have learned from experience that Monarchs have the most terrible taste. Viceroys do not have a terrible taste but because they look just like Monarchs, the birds keep away from them too.

Mourning Cloak

THE Mourning Cloak, with wings that seem to be torn at the edges, is the first butterfly to make a spring appearance.

When winter has gone, you can find Mourning Cloaks perched on bushes and tree stumps. Their chocolate brown color, with edgings of creamy yellow, make it difficult to distinguish them from the clumps of brush.

136

Hummingbird Moth

UNLIKE butterflies, moths generally prefer the darkness of night to the light of day. The Hummingbird Moth is an exception to this rule.

Though this moth often seems to stand still in midair, you would have difficulty catching one with a net. Humming-bird Moths are fast little fellows. When you start to chase after them they will dart away at speeds of up to 35 miles an hour.

Bombyx Moth

SILKWORMS are not really worms but the infant caterpillars of the Bombyx Moth. Like most moths, Bombyx lives only a few short days.

The eggs which Bombyx lays hatch into the important silk-making caterpillars. These caterpillars, spinning protective threads of silk round their cocoons, eat up a ton of leaves to make one pound of silk.

137

Polyphemus Moth

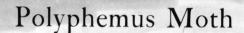

THE great Polyphemus is one of the largest of our North American moths. It is best known for the giant round "eyespots" on its hindwings. Of course, these are not real eyes but natural markings, often used by scientists to tell the moths apart. You can see why this moth is named after Polyphemus, the legendary one-eyed giant who was blinded by Ulysses.

Io Moth

THE Io Moth has "eyespots" only on its hindwings. Scientists think that Nature put these spots on the wings of some moths and butterflies to frighten away their enemies.

Cecropia Moth

HERE is the king of the moths. He is the largest moth you will find anywhere in our country. As a matter of fact, Cecropias are so large that people often mistake them for bats.

138

Luna Moth

IF you were asked to pick the queen of the entire insect world, could you make a better choice than this majestic moth, the beautiful Luna? The wings are gracefully curved, like the crescent of a new born moon, and when the Luna flies the tails stream behind like luxurious flowing robes.

Luna Moths lay their eggs on the twigs of walnut and hickory trees. The eggs take about two weeks to hatch into caterpillars. As fall approaches, each caterpillar curls itself up inside a leaf; there it waits to become what is known as a *pupa*. It sleeps in this peculiar state throughout the long winter. But during that time astonishing changes are taking place. By late spring or early summer, what was a caterpillar has been completely transformed into a full-grown adult moth. Then the Luna wriggles out of its pupal state and flies away to mate and to lay eggs and to start the marvelous process all over again.

Field Cricket

CRICKETS are the musicians of the insect world. Their cheerful chirps are really mating calls. Only the male crickets make music. The females find their mates by listening for the serenades of the males.

Have you ever wondered how crickets make their music? The veins on their front wings are very thick and along their hind legs are tiny ridges. The sounds come when the ridges of the hind legs are scraped against the wings, somewhat the way a violinist draws the bow along the strings of a fiddle. This insect's ears are situated, of all places, on the shins of its forelegs!

Camel Cricket

WE do not need anyone to tell us why this hump-backed insect is called the Camel Cricket. It is especially fond of damp places, and you can usually find it under the stones and logs in cellars and caves.

140

Katydid

WHEN you hear the familiar "Katy did, Katy she did, she did," you can be sure it is a male Katydid singing. But he is no tattle tale, for that is all he ever says about her.

Katydids do not really sing, of course. Like all insects, they do not possess such a thing as a voice. To sing out "Katydid," the male rubs his wings together three times; to say "she did," he rubs them twice.

Walking Stick

THIS insect could not be better named. It looks exactly like a stick that walks and when it is not moving you would be certain to mistake it for a stick or twig. This is one more example of Nature's marvelous way of protecting her own.

The color of the Walking Stick changes with the seasons. It is green when the leaves are green, during the spring, and when the leaves turn brown in the fall so does the color of the Walking Stick.

Grasshopper

GRASSHOPPERS belong to the same chirping family
as crickets and katydids. They are the acrobats of
the family. A blade of grass makes a fine trapeze
for the Grasshopper. With its long hind legs and
strong muscles it can leap far into the air. It uses its wings
to glide gracefully back to the ground.

It is not easy to catch Grasshoppers. If you have ever
tried you probably found that they shot "tobacco juice" at you.
This "tobacco juice," which Grasshoppers spit out of their
mouths, is dark brown and it has a bad smell, thus keeping
the Grasshopper's enemies away.

Grasshoppers make their chirping sounds by rubbing their
hind legs together. Only male Grasshoppers chirp though;
and the silence of the females has led to this saying:

"Happy are the Grasshoppers' lives
They all have noiseless wives."

Praying Mantis

THIS interesting fellow usually looks as if he were kneeling to say his prayers before going to bed. That is the typical way he stands, and that of course is how he got his name of Praying Mantis. But do not let his peaceful looks fool you. He is a ferocious fighter, feared even by insects many times his size. You might call him the hobgoblin of the insect world. With his powerful front legs he can crush an enemy to death in an instant. But because he kills so many different kinds of destructive agricultural pests, he is known as the farmer's best insect friend.

You can make a wonderful pet of the Praying Mantis. You can train him to drink water out of a teaspoon and to eat chopped meat from a saucer. After every meal he will wash his face, just like a cat does with its front paws. From his corner he will follow your every move, his head cocked perkily to one side, like a playful puppy.

Longhorn Beetle

BEETLES have much harder shells than other insects. The shell on a beetle's back is divided into two parts which act as shields. These shields protect the beetle's delicate wings. It is only when the beetle is in flight that you can see the shields unfold.

This particular beetle is known as a Longhorn. Its antennae or feelers are amazingly long, many times the full length of its body.

Whirligigs

SOME families of beetles make their homes in pools and lakes—like these Whirligigs. They love to swim in groups.

Whirligigs get their name from the way they go whirligigging about in circles, twirling around and around, like we do when we dance the jig or polka.

Water Scavenger

THE savage Water Scavenger preys upon all forms of life that inhabit the world of pools and lakes. Unlike Whirligigs, it enjoys the land as much as the water. It is especially attracted to electric lights.

144

Scarab Beetles

THERE are many families of Scarab Beetles. One is the well-known "tumblebug." Its name comes from the clumsy way it rolls the dung of cows and horses into round balls.

Another type of Scarab is the Unicorn. On the top of this page is a picture of a male Unicorn in flight. You can see from this picture how the protective covering of a beetle unfolds into two shields when it is flying. Still another member of the Scarab family is the Stag Beetle, so called because its jaws look something like the antlers of a male deer or stag.

Ladybird Beetle

You probably know these small, spotted beetles by their nick-name of "ladybugs." Did you know that they are perhaps our most valuable insects? The reason is that Ladybird Beetles love to eat mealy bugs and mealy bugs are terrible pests.

Japanese Beetle

In contrast to the helpful Ladybird, this beetle is one of our worst insect enemies.

Adult Japanese Beetles eat the foliage and fruit of a large variety of plants, while their young damage the roots by sucking the juice out of them.

Firefly

FIREFLIES are the fairy lamplighters of the insect world. They can turn their lights on and off whenever they want to, just as we would use a battery flashlight. But Fireflies do not use their lights for the same purpose we do, to see their way at night. Their lights are mating signals.

The female of this strange member of the beetle family does not have wings and she cannot fly in the air. When it is dark the female Firefly crawls up on a high blade of grass where she waits for the flashing signals of male Fireflies passing overhead. Then she blinks her own lights on and off, so that one of the males will see her signals and fly down to mate with her.

Dragonfly and Damselfly

THESE insects have the wings of airplanes and they speed through the air and swoop down upon their prey like mighty bombardiers on the attack. The Dragonfly is larger than its near relative the Damselfly. It is also a stronger flier. Dragonflies can zoom through the air at a mile a minute, making them the fastest insects known.

You may have heard the Dragonfly spoken of as "the devil's darning needle." It is also supposed to sew up the mouths of naughty children. These are superstitions, of course.

The best way to tell a Dragonfly from a Damselfly is when they are standing still. The Dragonfly always rests with its wings outstretched, whereas the Damselfly keeps its wings close together when not in flight.

Bumble Bee

THE furry bee up at the right of this page is a queen Bumble Bee. You can be sure that all the Bumble Bees you see flying about in the fall will be queens just like her. For each one you see will be the lone survivor of a large colony of Bumble Bees, and each one will be looking for some spot to spend a lonely winter.

All winter long the queen Bumble Bee will stay by herself. She will not come out of her retreat until spring, when she will start to search for a snug hole in the ground, preferably an abandoned mouse nest, which she will make into a home of her own. She will carefully line the sides of the nest with dried bits of leaves and grass. Then she will gather pollen and nectar from flowers. When at last she has stored up a sufficient quantity of food she will lay her eggs.

When these eggs have hatched and grown into a great colony of Bumble Bees, they will include a number of females or queen bees like herself. Except for these queens, the entire colony will perish when cold weather comes.

Honeybee

Is there anything more fascinating in the whole insect world than a Honeybee hive? It is a manufacturing center, a nursery, and a queen's palace.

Every hive is a community made up of thousands upon thousands of individual bees. Like people, different bees do different kinds of work, which is why Honeybees are called *social* insects. The most important member of this bee community is the great queen bee. In size she is bigger and longer than the others. She also lives longer than all the rest. Her task is to lay eggs and she performs her task amazingly well. During a queen bee's life — she lives about three years — she may lay as many as a million eggs!

Wherever the queen bee goes she is always followed by a special group of bees who feed and take care of her. These bees who form the queen's royal court are called worker bees. They even clean and comb the queen's beautiful shining coat.

In addition to the queen and the worker bees, there is a third kind called drones. They are idle, clumsy fellows who never do anything at all except mate with the queen.

Worker bees are the most numerous group of bees in any hive and it is they who do practically all the work. While some take care of the queen, others are kept busy at housework, and still others are nursemaids who tend to the hive's nursery. Each of the queen's many eggs is hatched in a separate room or *cell*. The nursemaid bees keep these cells immaculately clean, and they bathe and feed the baby bees. It is also the worker bees you see flying from flower to flower in the summer months as they gather pollen and nectar which they change into honey. A great deal of this honey is made inside the hive itself. The honey we eat is what is left over after the bees have finished feeding themselves. Fortunately for us, Honeybees make much more honey than they need.

Mud Wasps

THESE wasps make their homes of mud and clay. They have been using these building materials for millions of years, long before man got the idea of using clay bricks to make houses. The Potter Wasp builds beautifully proportioned nests of clay that look like small jugs or vases.

Mason Wasps prefer underground holes but sometimes they hang their nests from the branches of trees. And you will usually find the nests of the thin-waisted Mud Dauber Wasps in attics or barns.

Paper Wasps

NOT all wasps build their homes of clay. Some use paper, and those that do may be truly called the world's oldest papermakers. They make the paper for their nests by chomping on bits of wood until it becomes a pasty pulp.

We have learned to make paper in much the same way, except that we use machines. Among the many families of Paper Wasps are the Yellowjackets.

Ichneumon Wasp

A CURIOUS relative of the wasp family is the Ichneumon. The female lays eggs in the strangest places. What seems to be her long curled up tail is not a tail at all but a sharply pointed hollow tube. She uses it to pierce through several inches of tree trunk to drop her eggs in places where there will be food when the eggs hatch.

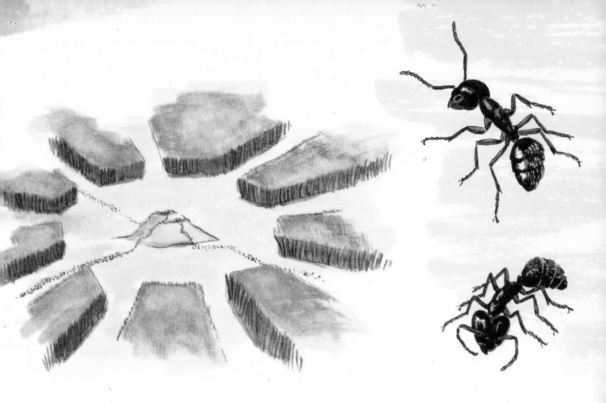

Ants

IF you have ever disturbed an ant colony, perhaps by turning over a stone under which ants were living, you may have seen them rushing about in every which way. You may have wondered about the reason for all this frantic hurrying, what it was they were carrying between their jaws, and where they were going when they suddenly disappeared into the ground.

Ants are the most highly developed of the social insects. By *social,* of course, we mean that they have developed the habit of living together, as in families or communities. Every ant community has its queen, a number of kings or males, and a great many workers. Some even have a special class of warriors or soldiers. The important thing is that each member of an ant colony has some special task to perform.

Individual ants do not work for themselves alone but for the good of their fellows. Thus, the ants you saw when you overturned the stone were probably worker ants. They were scurrying about with little *pupae* in their jaws, infant ants, which they were carrying away to safety in their underground communities.

Ant Lion

We have all heard of the word "doodlebug." It has several meanings, but it is also used as the nickname for the larva of the delicate four-winged Ant Lion. Like so many insects, the young Ant Lion does not look a bit like the adult. It looks more like an ugly monster, and in a way it is.

The funnel-shaped pit on this page is the young Ant Lion's trap for some unsuspecting insect like an ant. When an ant steps over the edge of the pit it starts a miniature landslide which carries it down into the Ant Lion's waiting jaws. If the ant tries to crawl back out of the trap, the Ant Lion will shoot grains of sand at it to knock it back down again. You will find these pits near almost any ant colony. If you drop a little twig down the sides, you will see the Ant Lion hurling up grains of sand. The sand will come up like machine-gun fire.

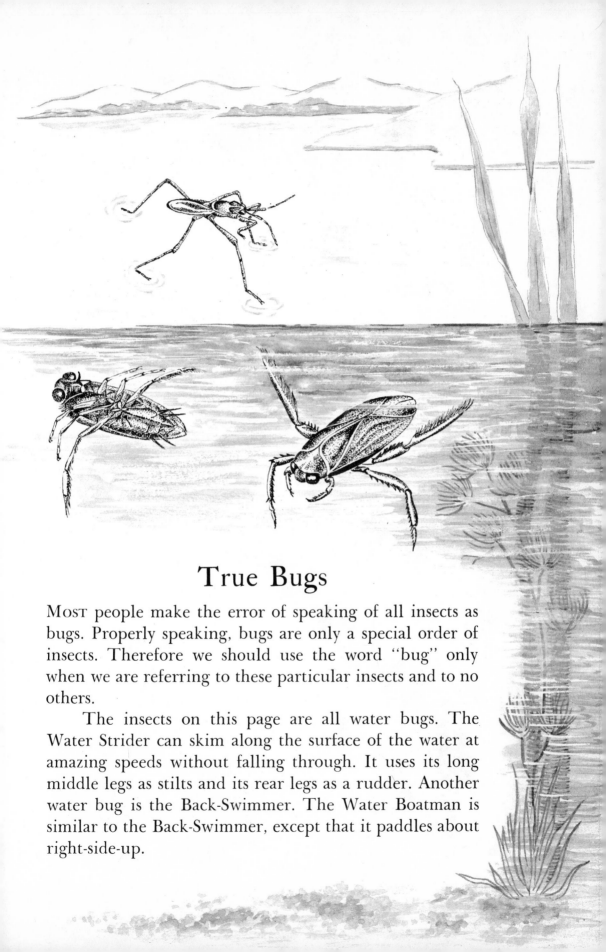

True Bugs

MOST people make the error of speaking of all insects as bugs. Properly speaking, bugs are only a special order of insects. Therefore we should use the word "bug" only when we are referring to these particular insects and to no others.

The insects on this page are all water bugs. The Water Strider can skim along the surface of the water at amazing speeds without falling through. It uses its long middle legs as stilts and its rear legs as a rudder. Another water bug is the Back-Swimmer. The Water Boatman is similar to the Back-Swimmer, except that it paddles about right-side-up.

Cicada

THE Cicada is another true bug. It is the biggest of all the bugs. You have probably heard of the "seventeen-year locust." This is a family of Cicadas whose baby nymphs live underground for all of 17 years while they are maturing into adults.

Treehopper

THIS odd-looking fellow is a Treehopper, sometimes called the "Brownie" of the insect world. There are many different kinds of Treehoppers. But they are usually colored yellowish brown and green. And they all have the oddest shapes.

Chinch Bug

THE Chinch Bug is one of the farmer's worst insect enemies. Chinch Bugs are not large. They are quite tiny actually. But they reproduce rapidly and unless controlled they can destroy grain fields very quickly.

Harlequin Bug

THE gaily colored, clown-like insect on the right is the Harlequin Bug, another insect enemy of farmers. It is one of those insects popularly called "stink bugs." The odor these bugs give forth *is* horrid but it is quite harmless. Harlequins use the odor for the same reason skunks do—as a protection against enemies.

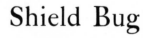

Shield Bug

THIS true bug, shaped in the form of a shield, is also a member of the "stink bug" family. The eggs of Shield Bugs are most interesting. They are beautifully ornamented, and they are always laid in clusters that look something like barrels piled in rows, one on top of the other.

Crane Fly

THE insects on this page and the next are all true flies. They have a single pair of wings, which is what distinguishes them from other types of flying insects. The long-legged fly on the left is the Crane Fly, often mistaken for the "daddy long-legs."

Housefly

You know that Houseflies are dangerous because they can carry the germs of diseases. But do you know how they carry germs?

This is how. The Housefly feeds by sucking, and so solid bits of food must always be softened before they can be digested. To do that the Housefly lets out a drop of liquid from its mouth onto the food and then sucks some of it back in. If we leave food uncovered, especially during the hot summer months when Houseflies are numerous, the food can be contaminated by these drops of liquid.

Robber Fly

THE big, hairy Robber Fly, with eyes that bulge, will pounce upon an insect flying in midair. Its legs form a basket which it uses to capture its prey while still in flight. Another name for this fly is the Assassin Fly.

Mosquito

You will never be bitten by a male Mosquito. Only female Mosquitos bite. And the only reason they ever bite is that at least once in their lifetime they must suck the blood of some warm-blooded animal before their eggs will develop properly. The larvae of Mosquitos are called "wrigglers," and they breed in ponds and pools.

Prehistoric Insect

THIS strange creature is believed to be the biggest insect
that ever lived. Its wing measurements are two feet from
tip to tip and the body alone is 15 inches long.

Archaeologists discovered the insect imbedded in
stone where it had been preserved for millions and millions of years.

162

Fish, Shellfish and Reptiles

Plankton
Jellyfish
Crabs
Lobsters
Shrimp
Shellfish
Coral Reefs
Spawning and Migration
Mackerel
Herring
Salmon
Tuna
Black Sea Bass
Porgies
Cod
Flounder
Grass Pickerel
Catfish
Sunfish
Trout
Spotted Whip Ray
Swordfish
Sharks
Whales
Flying Fish
Porpoise
Octopus
Eels
Crocodiles
Turtles
Seals
Betta
Marlin
Four-Eyed Butterfly Fish
Clownfish
Angel Fish
Sea Horse
Sailfish

HAVE you ever stood by the edge of the sea and looked out over the endless waters that stretch way off into the horizon, and beyond? "How pretty," you must have thought as you watched the sun's rays dance merrily on this great blanket of water.

If only you were able to see through this blanket, down deep into the water, you would see sights such as you never thought existed. For just below this blanket of blue, there lives in the sea a silent world, a world of beauty, mystery, and sometimes danger.

With our new and better underwater breathing equipment, more and more of us have been able to go into this strange, silent world.

As the brave men who explore our ocean world return, they bring with them the pictures and stories of the things they have seen. As you turn the pages of this section, you will be able to share in some of the secrets and beauty of the fish, shellfish, and amphibians that live in our undersea world.

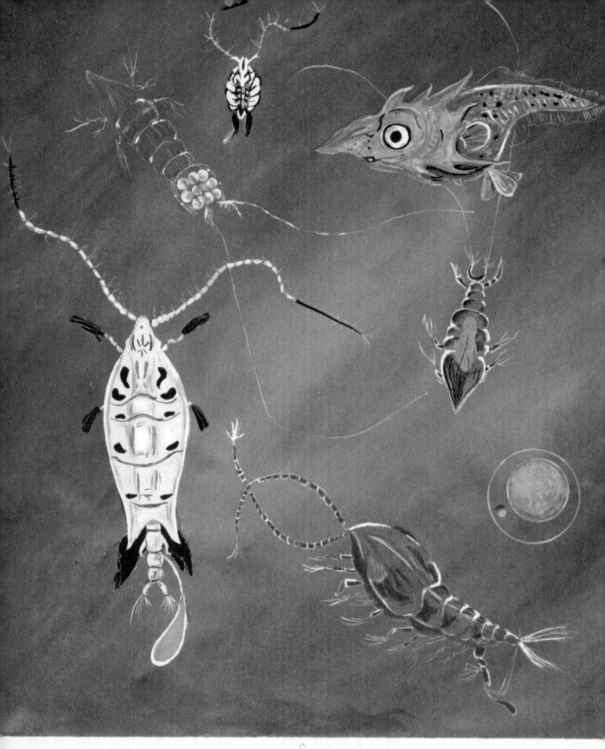

Plankton

OUR oceans are full of tiny animals called Plankton. Even though Plankton are no larger than specks of dust they are an important food for many of the fish that live in the sea.

Jellyfish

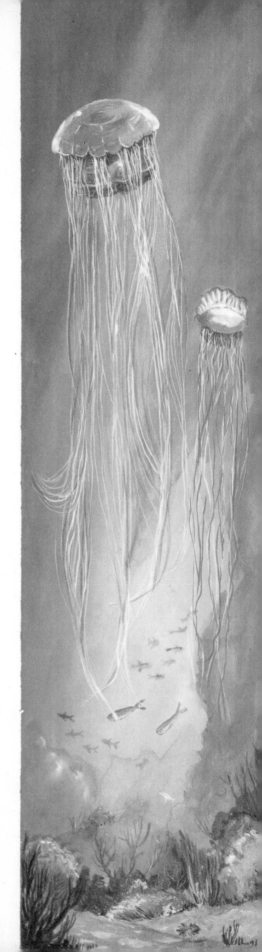

JELLYFISH are among the simplest creatures that live in the sea. There are many kinds of Jellyfish. Some of them have clear bodies that look like glass. Others have a pink or orange color. Some Jellyfish shine in the dark.

Along our shores we may find Jellyfish that are no bigger than a half dollar. In the ocean there are pink Jellyfish that grow as big as the top of a barrel. The larger Jellyfish, in the picture on this page, is a pink Jellyfish.

The smaller Jellyfish, in the picture on this page, is a Portuguese Man-of-War. The Man-of-War has tentacles that contain a deadly poison. When a fish is stung by this poison it becomes paralyzed. The Man-of-War's poison is also dangerous to man, and the slightest sting can cause great pain.

Crabs

MOST Crabs make their homes in rocks and seaweed under the sea. All Crabs walk sideways, and when they grow too big for their shell, they grow a new one.

Crab-meat is good to eat. The Crab shown on the top of the page is a Market Crab. Market Crabs have much meat and are an important food for man.

Lobsters

A LOBSTER is more like a spider than a fish. Like a spider, the Lobster walks on its many long thin legs. In the front of its body are two large claws that are used to catch and crush food.

Most of the Lobsters that we eat come from the ocean waters near Maine and lower Canada.

Shrimp

SHRIMP look like small lobsters without claws. They live near sandy beaches all over the world. Shrimp hide from their enemies by covering themselves with loose wet sand. Shrimp make tasty food.

Shellfish

ON the side of this page are popular shellfish animals. From top to bottom they are: the Snail, the Hermit Crab, the Scallop, and the Oyster. All these animals grow their own shells except the Hermit Crab.

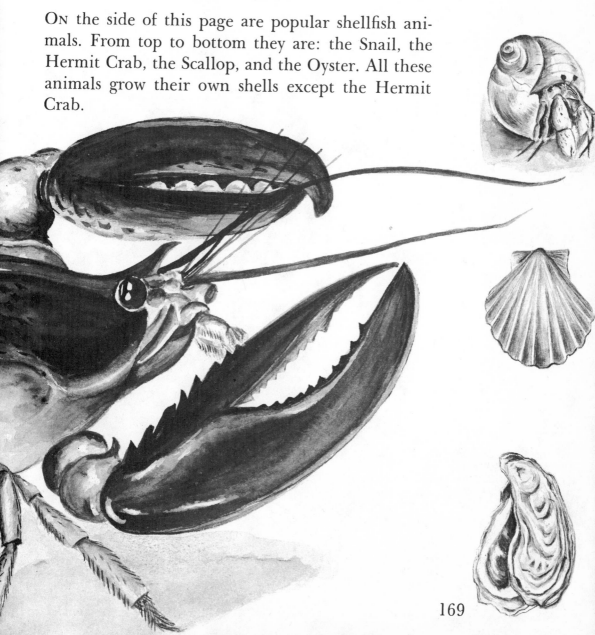

Coral Reefs

IN our southern seas there are many mountains that are miles long and hundreds of feet high. These mountains are made of Coral. The Coral is a small animal that lives in the warm waters of the tropics. There are many kinds of Coral, and they all have beautiful colors.

When Coral die they leave a hard skeleton for other Coral to live on. The Coral stick together and pile on top of each other until great mountains of Coral are made. These mountains of Coral are called Coral Reefs. Some of these Coral Reefs are millions of years old.

Sometimes these Coral Reefs grow so high that their tops stick out of the water and become small islands. Coral Reefs can be dangerous to man. If a ship crashes into a hidden reef it may be wrecked.

Under the sea many fish make their homes in the small caves that are found in Coral Reefs. Wherever there is Coral many fish and plenty of food can always be found.

Spawning and Migration

THE seasons change, and summer turns into winter. In the sea, fish can no longer find food and shelter. The sea becomes cold and empty. The fish must move. Unless they find food and shelter they will die.

Millions of fish gather together with their families. They are ready to begin their long yearly journey. This journey is called *Migration*.

Somewhere along the way, or sometimes at the end of their travels, the fish find a safe place for the females to place their eggs. When fish lay and hatch eggs, we say they are *Spawning*.

After the eggs are hatched the fish continue their trip. Soon millions of fish appear in our bays and along our beaches. Fishermen have been waiting for them with lines and nets. Thousands of fish are taken from the sea. Some fish are put into cans for food, and other fish are sent fresh from the sea to the markets.

Fish are good to eat. They are full of vitamins and minerals, which help make us big and strong.

Mackerel

ONE of the strongest food fish found in the sea is the Mackerel. Even though it is not much bigger than the herring, it has great strength and speed. It swims in groups that stretch as long as 20 miles. The Mackerel never seems to stop to rest but is always moving.

The Mackerel is always hungry and it will eat plankton, other small fish, or herring.

Every spring many Mackerel come to the waters of the North Atlantic Ocean to find food, and a place to drop their eggs. They have no one favorite spawning ground, and they will put their eggs wherever it is safe for the eggs to hatch.

At the top of this page there is a picture of an Atlantic Mackerel. Another kind of Mackerel is the Spanish Mackerel. This fish makes its home in our southern seas.

The Atlantic Mackerel is found in the North Atlantic Ocean along the American and European coasts. The Atlantic Mackerel usually grows to about 12 to 16 inches long, and weighs from one to three pounds.

The Mackerel is a very important food fish and is sold in stores in both North and South America, and Europe.

174

Herring

OF all the fish that live in the sea, the one that is most important to man is the Herring.

The Herring is a small fish that never grows much more than 12 inches long. Herring swim together in large groups called schools and each school may have a million or more fish in it. There are so many Herring in our oceans that we cannot even guess at their number.

Every year many Herring die. Thousands are caught by fishermen, and many more of these fish are attacked and eaten by bigger fish.

Strange as it seems, in spite of all these dangers the number of Herring in the sea never gets smaller. One reason for this is that each female Herring may have up to 30,000 babies a year, and for every male Herring there are three females. Another reason may be that Herring always have plenty of food. They eat plankton and only have to open their mouths to strain in plankton from the sea water whenever they are hungry.

Fished for by man and eaten by the other fish in the sea, the little Herring feeds the world and somehow is still the most plentiful fish found in the sea.

Salmon

PACIFIC Salmon are born in fresh water lakes and streams. The young fish swim to the Pacific Ocean where they stay until they have grown into strong adults. Then they return to the inland lakes and streams. To get there, they must fight upstream against strong rapids and jump over large rocks and waterfalls.

Tuna

TUNA are big, strong fish. They grow as long as ten feet and may weigh up to 1,000 pounds. They swim through the water at very high speeds and always fight very hard whenever they are attacked.

One of the favorite members of the Tuna family is the Bluefin Tuna. These fish swim in large schools and are found in the warm waters of the Atlantic and Pacific Oceans.

Fishermen catch Tuna with nets, harpoons, or strong fishing poles. Most of the Tuna's meat is put into cans and sent all over the world for us to eat.

177

Black Sea Bass

THE Black Sea Bass makes its home on rocky or rough bottoms and near old shipwrecks. Most large Bass are found near the shores of New York and New Jersey. Sea Bass usually weigh about two to five pounds and are very good to eat.

Porgies

THE Porgy is a popular food fish found in the Atlantic Ocean along our northeastern shores. They grow to about nine inches long, and live on the bottom of the ocean where they feed on small fish and worms.

Cod

THE Codfish is one of the most important food fish in the world. These fish are found in the cold waters of the North Atlantic Ocean. The Codfish weighs from ten to 35 pounds. There are always many Cod in the sea. One Codfish can lay as many as four million eggs!

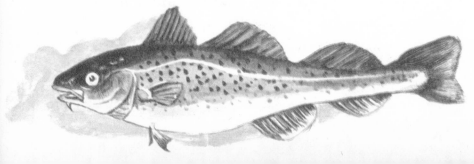

Flounder

To most people the Flounder may seem to be a very ordinary fish, but this is far from the truth. When the young Flounder begins life it swims upright, like all other fish. As this strange flat fish becomes an adult it turns and swims on its side. The young Flounder has eyes on each side of its body. As the Flounder grows, one eye begins to move upward, so that it can see properly as it swims on its side.

Flounder rest on the bottom of the ocean. Their undersides are almost colorless, but their top sides can change color to blend with the ocean bottom. Their color may be anything from a sandy tone to shades of dark brown.

There are winter and summer Flounder. Winter Flounder live in shallow cold water in the North Atlantic Ocean. Summer Flounder prefer warmer waters and many of them are found during the summer months along the New York shores.

Grass Pickerel

GRASS Pickerel live in lakes and quiet streams. They like to make their homes in shallow water where there are weeds and a muddy bottom.

The Grass Pickerel is a small fish and often people mistake it for a baby northern pike.

As a sport or game fish, the Grass Pickerel is not very important because of its small size.

Catfish

CATFISH are among the most popular fish in America. There are many different kinds of Catfish living in our fresh water lakes and streams.

Most Catfish like warm muddy waters. They will eat almost anything that they find on the muddy bottom.

All Catfish have small eyes and long feelers that look like a cat's whiskers. Unlike most other fish, Catfish have no scales.

Catfish are very hardy and can live out of water longer than most fish. Many people like to eat Catfish.

Sunfish

THE little Sunfish is one of the most popular fresh water fish in the United States. There are many different kinds of Sunfish living in our streams and lakes. Most of these fish are only three to eight inches long. Sunfish have bright blue, yellow, and orange colored skins.

These fish are always plentiful and are easy to catch on a small hook baited with a worm. Even though they are small they make a tasty meal.

Trout

SPORTSMEN have fished for Trout since the days when America was first settled.

Most Trout live in cool, rushing streams. They eat insects, worms, and other small fish.

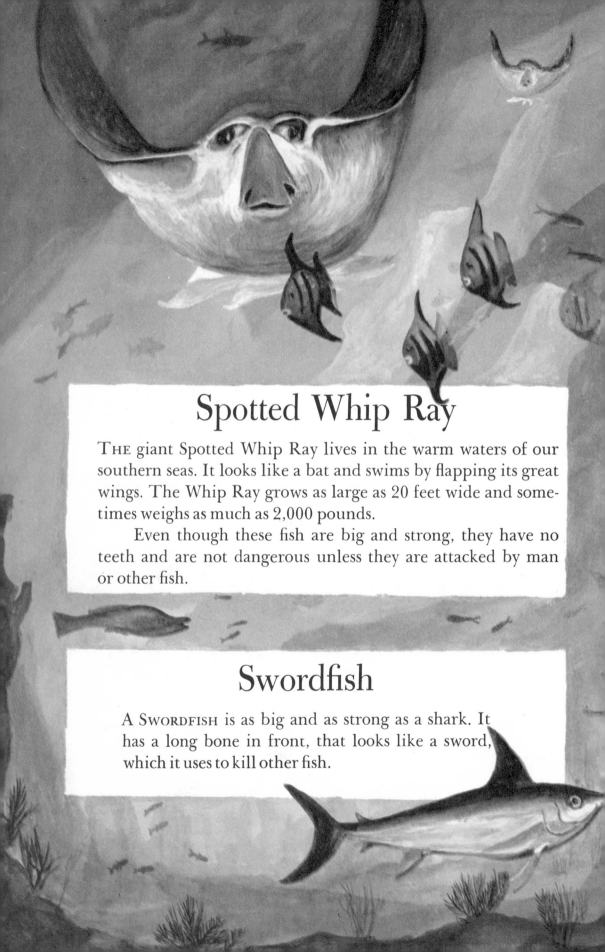

Spotted Whip Ray

THE giant Spotted Whip Ray lives in the warm waters of our southern seas. It looks like a bat and swims by flapping its great wings. The Whip Ray grows as large as 20 feet wide and sometimes weighs as much as 2,000 pounds.

Even though these fish are big and strong, they have no teeth and are not dangerous unless they are attacked by man or other fish.

Swordfish

A SWORDFISH is as big and as strong as a shark. It has a long bone in front, that looks like a sword, which it uses to kill other fish.

Sharks

SHARKS are feared by men and fish. But most Sharks will not attack fish or man unless they are sure they will win.

The most dangerous Sharks are the big man-eating White Sharks. These Sharks attack anything, and fear nothing.

Whales

WHALES, the largest animals in the world, spend all their lives in the water, like fish, but they really are not fish. Whales are mammals. A mammal is an animal that has hair and warm blood. All mammals take care of their children. Dogs, cats and cows are mammals that live on land. Can you think of others?

Unlike fish, Whales must breathe air, and cannot stay under the water for more than 20 or 30 minutes.

Sperm Whales, like the one you see in the picture above, are valuable for the oil they carry in the top of their heads. Man uses this oil to make soap and perfume.

184

Flying Fish

THE Flying Fish does not really fly, but it can glide hundreds of feet through the air. This small fish, although never more than 12 inches long, has very large fins that look like wings. When the fish jumps out of the water it spreads its fins and glides over the waves like a bird.

Porpoise

PORPOISE are mammals like the whales. Porpoise always swim in large schools. They can swim very fast and they often jump out of the water high into the air. Porpoise have sharp teeth which they use to fight sharks.

Porpoise are very smart and can be taught to do many tricks. They are friendly animals who love to have fun and to show off.

Octopus

THE Octopus is an ugly monster that lives among the rocks on the bottom of the sea. It has eight strong arms and a mouth that looks like a parrot's beak. When an Octopus is attacked, it will wrap its arms around its enemy and pull it to the bottom of the sea.

Eels

EVEN though the Eel looks like a snake it is a true fish. All Eels are born far out at sea. They swim thousands of miles until they reach inland streams. When the Eel is ready to spawn it returns to the sea where it was born.

Crocodiles

CROCODILES are amphibious reptiles that can live on land and in water. Crocodiles are found in tropical countries all over the world. They like to make their homes near sluggish rivers or open swamps.

Crocodiles have webbed feet which help them walk easily on soft wet ground. Crocodiles feed on small animals and fish, which they swallow whole. Sometimes a Crocodile will attack a large animal or even a man.

Crocodiles lay eggs. They bury their eggs under sand or in nests of weeds and plants. The female Crocodile guards the nest until she can hear her babies grunt. Then she digs the babies out of the nest.

Crocodiles are important to man. They have a tough skin which is made into leather for shoes, handbags, and traveling bags. We make perfume from the oil in their glands.

Turtles

THE Sea Turtle is born on land but its life is spent in the sea. When the mother Sea Turtle is ready to lay her eggs she leaves the sea and climbs onto some sandy beach. On the beach she finds a safe place away from the water, and digs a hole in the sand. After burying her eggs in the sand the mother Turtle, who is now very tired, slowly crawls back into the sea. She will never see her children. Soon the eggs hatch and the baby Turtles go down to the sea where they will spend the rest of their lives.

On the top of this page is a picture of a Hawksbill Turtle. The shell of this Turtle is used to make beautiful tortoise-shell combs and jewelry.

The picture just above is that of the Green Turtle. This Turtle can grow to be over four feet long and weigh more than 500 pounds. This big Turtle is used to make Turtle soup.

Seals

THE Seal is an air-breathing mammal. Even though the Seal spends part of its time on land, its real home is the sea. There the Seal is a graceful animal, but on land it is clumsy and awkward. Whenever there is danger the Seal rushes to the safety of the sea.

In the picture below, on the left, is a Sea Lion. Sea Lions are the smartest members of the Seal family. Most of the performing circus Seals are Sea Lions.

The Sea Elephant on the right is the largest member of the Seal family.

Betta

THE Betta is a small, tropical, fresh-water fish that is never longer than three inches.

Whenever two male Bettas meet there is a great battle, and they fight to kill. When fighting with a male, or breeding with a female, the male Betta spreads his fins like an ostrich and shows off his beautiful colors. Because of their great beauty, these small fighting fish are bred and kept in aquariums by people all over the world.

Marlin

STRIPED Marlin are found only in the Pacific Ocean. They are huge fish that weigh 600 pounds or more.

It is thrilling to see this fish streak through the water at top speed and then leap high into the air. The Marlin is famous as a game fish because of the great fight it puts up when it is caught on a fisherman's hook.

Four-Eyed Butterfly Fish

THIS little fish lives in the waters of the West Indies. It is a very colorful fish and very popular among tropical fish lovers all over the world. This fish got its name because of the large black spot that it has on each side of its back fin. The spot looks like another eye.

Clownfish

ONE of the greatest enemies of small fish is the sea anemone. The sea anemone looks like a flower, but it has long, waving tentacles that are full of poison.

For some strange reason, the sea anemone does not harm the Clownfish. Whenever this funny looking fish is threatened by danger, it swims in among the anemone's tentacles where other fish are afraid to follow.

Angel Fish

THE Angel Fish is one of the most colorful fish found near coral reefs.

It has a flat, brightly striped body that shines in the water as it swims lazily along.

This fish is called an Angel Fish not only for its beauty, but because its fins look like wings.

192

Sea Horse

THE Sea Horse is a strange looking creature. It is a true fish, but it swims in an upright position and has no tail fin.

Like all other fish, it breathes through gills which are on both sides of its head. Its body is covered by tiny scales that join together to make a hard suit of armor.

One of the strangest things about the Sea Horse is that the father has the babies instead of the mother. The father has a pouch like a kangaroo. The mother puts her eggs in this pouch and then goes on her way, leaving the father to hatch the eggs. When the eggs are hatched, about 200 baby Sea Horses swim out of the father's body.

Most Sea Horses are only three or four inches long. They are found along the shores of most tropical seas.

Sailfish

SAILFISHING is an exciting sport enjoyed by many people. The Sailfish lives in the Atlantic and Pacific Oceans. When it is caught on a fisherman's hook, it will leap high out of the water and fight ferociously to get the hook loose.

The Sailfish is not very good to eat because its meat is very oily. Fishermen like to stuff and display this beautiful fish in their homes.

Flowers and Plants

Garden Flowers
Iris
Rose
Lady-Slipper
Crocus
Lily-of-the-Valley
Lily
Pansy
Bleeding-Heart
Dahlia
Sweet Pea
Camellia
Carnation
Bachelor's Button
Peony
Gardenia
Hibiscus
Amaryllis
Zinnia
Daffodil
   Tulip
   Hyacinth
   Gladiolus
   Poppy
   Aster

Chrysanthemum
Rhododendron
Clematis
Violet
Wild Flowers
Bluebell
Goldenrod
Buttercup
Dutchman's Breeches
Honeysuckle
Venus's-Flytrap
Ferns
Carnivorous Flowers
Foxglove
Pitcher Plant
Desert Flowers
Hedgehog Cactus
Saguaro or Giant
   Cactus
Useful Plants

Cotton
Peanut
Peppermint
Parasitic Plants
Orchid

Every living thing is either animal or plant. Plants can grow up into the air or down into the ground. They cannot go from place to place as animals do. Animals have to move to hunt for food. Plants make the food they need out of sunshine, air, and minerals from the soil.

With a wonderful chemical called chlorophyll, which makes their leaves green, plants manufacture sugar. This sugar is the source of

all the food in the world. For animals eat plants or other animals which have eaten plants. So it all goes back to the sugar in the plants.

Trees, shrubs, grasses, vines, and weeds are all plants. Like all living things, plants can reproduce their kind. The flowers make this possible. Just as animals are male or female, so flowers are *staminate* and *pistulate*. The stamens hold the pollen. Deep within the pistils are the ovules or seeds of life.

Nature makes flowers beautiful, gives them a lovely smell, and fills them with honey-sweet nectar so that they will lure the insects. When butterflies, bees, and hummingbirds go from flower to flower gathering nectar, they carry pollen to the seeds. These unite in the miracle of creation.

Garden Flowers

GARDEN flowers are those that we plant, water, weed, fertilize and otherwise take care of ourselves. This is called cultivation. All of our cultivated flowers were once wild flowers.

Flowers we replant each year are called annuals. Perennials are those that will bloom year after year.

Iris

IRIS is so hardy that it will survive the cold of Siberia and also the heat of India. Iris is the Greek word for rainbow, and it comes in all the colors of the rainbow. Blue Flag, a wild Iris, grows in meadows in this country. Iris is the state flower of Tennessee.

Rose

THE most beautiful and best known of our garden flowers is the Rose. There are wild Roses in many of the cooler parts of the world. They have been cultivated for many hundreds of years in China, Persia, and Europe. Cultivated Roses are like domestic cats and dogs. People have cross-bred different kinds of Roses to make new and more beautiful kinds.

The most beautiful of all Roses, the American Beauty Rose, was really an accident. One day some years ago, it appeared in the corner of a garden in Washington, D. C. The bees had mixed up the pollen and seeds of Roses that would have been kept strictly apart if the garden had not been neglected.

Lady-Slipper

THE Lady-Slipper, a cousin of the orchid, gets its name because one part of it is shaped like a lady's slipper.

There is a smaller kind that hides away in deeply shaded bogs. It is called the Fairy Slipper. Another, which the Indians called Moccasin Flower, can be replanted and grown in your garden.

Crocus

LIKE the robin, the Crocus tells us that spring is on the way. This tough, little flower pushes up through late snow.

Sometimes it is so white it cannot be seen. But it grows in your favorite colors too. From the orange-streaked flowers of one kind of Crocus comes the coloring used on candy and cakes.

200

Lily-of-the-Valley

THE Lily-of-the-Valley is a dainty, little member of the lily family. Its blossoms look like nodding, small, white bells. It has a lovely, sweet scent. It grows wild in the woods of Europe and northern Asia. In the United States, it grows in the woods of our eastern mountains.

Lily

THE Lily is a very large family of flowering plants. It includes not only Lilies and lilies-of-the-valley, but also such flowers shown on other pages as iris, hyacinth, tulip, and daffodil. And believe it or not, asparagus, leek, onion and garlic are in the same family as Lilies.

Pansy

Pansy is from the French *pen-sée* which means thought or re-membrance. Pansies have funny little clown faces made by darker markings on light ones.

Bleeding-Heart

This pretty flower has heart-shaped, deep pink blossoms and fern-like leaves. You will find the Bleeding-Heart in many gardens.

Dahlia

The original Dahlia was a small red flower with a yellow center.

Sweet Pea

The Sweet Pea comes in more different colors than any other flower.

Camellia

THE Camellia Japonica is the beautiful blossom of an evergreen shrub closely related to the tea plant. In the south it is called just Japonica.

Carnation

THE Carnation is probably the most popular flower after the rose. The Red Carnation is the state flower of Ohio. Related pink Carnations grow wild.

Bachelor's Button

IT is said that an unmarried man wears this flower to find out if his girl loves him.

Peony

PEONIES are native to eastern Asia and southern Europe.

Gardenia

THE Gardenia has very shiny, deep green leaves. The flower is a waxy-looking white, a creamy yellow, and it has been produced in a pinkish white.

The Gardenia is native to the hot parts of Asia and Africa.

Hibiscus

THIS is the name of a large, showy, bell-shaped flower. It is sometimes seven inches wide and may grow on a stem seven feet tall. It may be white, rose, or pink.

Hibiscus is also the name of a very large group of related plants. One kind is the tall, graceful Hollyhock and the Althea or Rose of Sharon.

Amaryllis

AMARYLLIS is the name of a whole family of beautiful flowers. It comes from a Greek word meaning to sparkle or twinkle. Amaryllis have bulbous roots and look like lilies.

Zinnia

THE Zinnia was once an ugly, little flower that no one wanted. But cultivation has made it into a beautiful garden flower. It now comes in different shades of scarlet, rose, orange, yellow, purple, and red. There are double-flowering Zinnias and a little pompom that blooms for weeks. The Zinnia is the state flower of Indiana.

205

Daffodil

DAFFODILS and the related
jonquil look alike, but you
can tell them apart because
the jonquil has no leaves on
its stem. Both flowers grow
from bulbs planted in the
fall. They blossom in April.

206

Tulip

HOLLAND cultivates Tulips of every solid color and combination of colors, and sends millions of Tulip bulbs to the rest of the world. Now we grow Tulips too, especially in the state of Michigan.

Hyacinth

THE small blossoms come in blue, purple, lilac, pink, red, or white. They are closely packed in bell-shaped clusters.

When Hyacinths were brought to America in colonial days, a wild Hyacinth grew here. It was so prized by the Indians that when white men trampled a field of them, it started an Indian war.

Gladiolus

THE purple, red, orange, yellow, or white blossoms of the Gladiolus grow on only one side of its long stem facing the sun. The bulbs have to be stored away from frost in warm cellars each fall and replanted in the garden when spring comes.

Poppy

THE Poppy is native to many different lands and climates. The beautiful, golden-yellow Poppy is the state flower of California. The oriental Poppy of Turkey and Armenia is a flaming red with a purple-black center.

Aster

ASTERS are among the commonest of wild flowers. There are also many different garden varieties. Most of the wild Asters are blue, lavender, or pinkish. All these have yellow centers. The cultivated Chinese Asters have no yellow center. There is a giant California Aster which grows three feet tall.

Chrysanthemum

THE Chinese cultivated the Chrysanthemum more than 2,500 years ago. The Japanese made it their national flower.

Today we raise it in red, purple, yellow, and white. It comes in dainty, little button-hole flowers and in huge eight-inch soft balls on stems four feet long.

Rhododendron

THE Rhododendron is an evergreen shrub or tree. Sometimes it is only six feet high, but some kinds are 15 and 20 feet high. It has showy, shiny, deep green leaves.

The big flowers are from three to six inches across. They may be lilac-purple, pink, or white. They grow wild in the mountain woods of Virginia and south to Georgia. They also grow on the Pacific coast. The Rhododendron is the state flower of Washington.

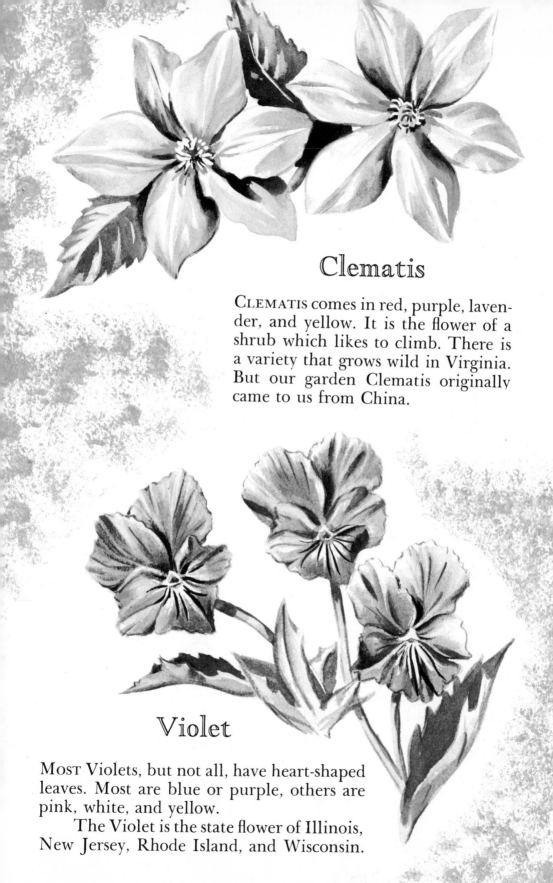

Clematis

CLEMATIS comes in red, purple, lavender, and yellow. It is the flower of a shrub which likes to climb. There is a variety that grows wild in Virginia. But our garden Clematis originally came to us from China.

Violet

MOST Violets, but not all, have heart-shaped leaves. Most are blue or purple, others are pink, white, and yellow.

The Violet is the state flower of Illinois, New Jersey, Rhode Island, and Wisconsin.

Wild Flowers

WILD flowers are those that will grow without any help or care from us. They grow out in the country, in fields, in the woods, on mountains, and in the valleys. Some wild flowers grow in swamps, others in the dry, parched land of deserts.

Wild flowers will grow by the roadside with cars zooming by all day and night. They will grow on the lawns of houses, and even amid the trash of empty city lots.

There are more than 3,000 different kinds of wild flowers in the United States. Some of the commonest, such as asters, cornflowers, goldenrod, milkweeds, orchids, and violets, will grow in all parts of the country. Others will only grow in certain places. Dutchman's breeches, for instance, is to be found only in the northeastern sections of the country. The golden poppy grows only in California and in the nearby parts of Nevada and Arizona.

Bluebell

THE stems of Bluebells are straight from one to two feet high, then bend under the weight of the blossoms which nod downward. This keeps the rain from washing out the pollen. The flower is first pink, then turns lavender and then blue.

Goldenrod

GOLDENROD is the state flower of Alabama, Kentucky, and Nebraska. There are more than 100 kinds of this bright yellow flower in the United States. They grow in all parts of the country.

Buttercup

THIS little flower looks like a cup and is the color of butter. It has large, green leaves forked like crow's feet and is sometimes called Crow's Feet, too.

There are 40 different kinds of Buttercup in the United States. The giant Buttercup grown in gardens is from China and is called Trollius.

Dutchman's Breeches

THESE white blossoms with yellow centers are shaped like a heart and have feathery, fern-like leaves, but they *do* look like little Dutch boy's pants hanging on a line upside down.

These flowers grow wild from Canada to South Carolina and westward to the Great Plains. They are closely related to the bleeding-heart which came to us all the way from China.

Honeysuckle

THE small, trumpet-shaped Honeysuckle flowers are red outside and deep yellow inside. The lovely trumpets give out no sound, but a heavenly, sweet smell.

Honeysuckle may be either a shrub or a woody climber. This kind will twine its way through the woods or over a porch trellis.

217

Venus's-Flytrap

THE Venus's-Flytrap is a carnivorous plant and grows in the south. It has two trap leaves, one on each side of the flower. These leaves are four inches long.

On the inside surfaces of the leaves are tiny trigger hairs. When an insect steps on two of these hairs, the leaf starts to fold. In less than one second it has snapped shut with the insect locked inside. It takes the leaf a day to digest a small insect, but a week for a big one.

218

Carnivorous Flowers

CARNIVOROUS means flesh or meat eating. So a carnivorous plant is a plant that eats flesh or meat. This sounds rather strange when we recall that plants are living things that manufacture their own food. Well, these carnivorous plants are nature's exception.

Carnivorous plants are unable to get enough nitrogen from the soil as other plants do. So they have to get nitrogen in the same way you do, by eating things that contain it. But as these plants cannot move to go hunting, they trap insects in strange ways to get their steaks and chops.

There are two such carnivorous plants shown in this book. One, the Venus's-Flytrap, is on page 218. You will find the other, the Pitcher Plant, on page 221.

Ferns

AMONG plants that have no flowers, the most beautiful are the Ferns. Their bright green leaves grow in a lovely, lacy pattern. Some are so small you can keep them in flower pots at home. But in the tropics they grow as large as trees.

Foxglove

THIS beautiful European garden flower has large, long bell-shaped blossoms. It may be three to five feet high. The blossoms are white or the light shades of pink, lavender, and yellow, with deeper spots of color on the light shades like an orchid.

Pitcher Plant

THE odd plant shown here is another carnivorous plant, just like the Venus's-Flytrap. Here is how this plant gets its nitrogen: Its tall flower is shaped like a tall pitcher. And just like a pitcher it can hold water.

A spider, fly, mosquito, or other insect landing on the slippery lip of the Pitcher flower, slips down into the rain water that has collected. Then the flower digests it.

221

Desert Flowers

AFTER one rain the desert turns into a carpet of flowers. But they bloom for only a day or two. Typical are the belly plant flowers. They are so small and close to the ground that you have to lie on your belly to see them. Just as typical is the 40-foot tall cactus.

Hedgehog Cactus

THE Hedgehog Cactus shown on this page is a native of the higher land in Arizona. It is one of the few cacti whose flowers last more than a day. Its beautiful red-wine colored, shiny flower lasts five days. Its purple fruit is delicious to eat.

Saguaro or Giant Cactus

THE flower of the tree on the right is colored a creamy, waxy white with a large, bright yellow center. It is the state flower of Arizona. The Cactus has roots that are able to absorb huge quantities of water, which are sucked up into its stalk and branches.

Useful Plants

THERE are many flowering plants that are good for more than the beauty of their blossoms. There are herbs that give us peppermint for candy and dill for pickles. There are the plants that give us peanuts, cotton and many other useful things.

Cotton

THE white blossom of the Cotton plant blooms for one day. It leaves a pod called a boll on the end of the stalk, which bursts open a few weeks later. Then the Cotton is ready to pick for the manufacture of thread and cloth.

Peanut

THE Peanut is not a nut at all. It is a tiny vegetable in a pod like a pea. When the pod starts to form, the stem of the Peanut plant turns downward and pushes the pod underground, where it matures so the plant will grow out of the ground again.

224

Peppermint

THIS three-foot high plant is a herb and a member of the mint family. It has a small, pale blue flower. Its oval, shiny leaves are toothed and pointed. They give an oil used to flavor chewing gum, candy and ice cream. In medicine this oil is used to help relieve indigestion, toothache, and, in menthol inhalers, for hay fever and colds. It is also used in ointments to help headache. Michigan produces one half of the world's supply.

Parasitic Plants

Parasites are plants which attach themselves to other plants and draw food from them. Mistletoe is a typical parasite. The tropical orchid also attaches itself to the bark of trees. But it does not take food from them. It sends its roots into the air from which it gets nourishment.

Orchid

There are 10,000 different kinds or species of Orchids. No other plant in the world has so many different species. The most beautiful Orchids are the kinds that are grown in greenhouses and in the tropics.

Trees and Shrubs

Birch	Palm
Maple	Cypress
Ash	Poplar
Chestnut	Sycamore
Elm	Mulberry
Butternut	Eucalyptus
Beech	Fig
Balsam Fir	Rubber
Hemlock	Hickory
Pecan	Basswood
Persimmon	Black Walnut
Magnolia	Teak
Sassafras	Mahogany
Cedar	Cacao
Oak	Huckleberry
Redwood	Cottonwood
Spruce	Willow
Pine	Azalea
Apple	Privet
Cherry	Hydrangea
Dogwood	Forsythia
Lilac	

TREES are really plants. They are the largest of all the plants in the world.

Individual trees grow only in one place. But because their seeds are carried by the breezes and the winds, forests of trees actually move. They move forward slowly, a few feet at a time, but in millions of years forests can move across whole continents. In a few cases, like the coconut tree, they have even moved across whole oceans.

Shrubs are plants, too. They are smaller than trees, as a rule. Yet it is sometimes difficult to tell the difference between large shrubs and small trees. A good way to tell them apart is by the form they take. You will find that most trees have only a single stem or trunk, while shrubs generally have many stems.

Trees and shrubs are very important to all of us. They supply us with food. They give us protective shade from the hot summer sun, and protective shelter from the violence of wind storms. And what is just as important, they help make the world a more beautiful place to live in.

Birch

IF you have seen a Birch tree, you know how slender and graceful it is. A variety of Birch tree is called the Paper Birch because
the bark, when peeled off, can be used to write on. The outside
bark is white and marked with lovely charcoal-colored streaks.
The Indians made canoes from the bark of Birch trees,
because it is waterproof. The bark of the Sweet
Birch is dark brown, with lots of short white lines.
From the Sweet Birch comes wintergreen oil.

229

Maple

THE Sugar Maple has a sweet sap which is used to make maple syrup. But this tree has other uses, too. The wood is used for furniture and also for fuel. In the spring there are yellow-green blossoms on the branches of the Maple. Each seed possesses a wing. There are always two seeds joined together so the two wings can be carried by the wind. And from these winged seeds new Maples grow.

The Sugar Maple is but one of about 115 different varieties of Maple. Other popular members of this tree family are the Norway, Oregon, Silver, Moosewood and Japanese Maple.

Ash

STRANGE as it seems, the Ash is a member of the olive tree family.

In the old myths of the Scandinavian peoples, the Ash held a very important place. They believed that the world was supported by a mighty Ash tree, and that it was from an Ash tree that the first man was formed, while the first woman was formed from an Elm tree.

Chestnut

SOME time ago, the Chestnut trees of our Appalachian woods were nearly all killed by a bark disease. Today, young twigs are growing out of the old trunks. Perhaps they will be able to grow into fine trees again. Most of us know how good the nuts are to eat.

231

Elm

THE American Elm looks like a bursting sky rocket. The trunk
splits into branches which grow up and away from the main
trunk and then curve suddenly down towards the ground.

Many Elm trees are planted in New England towns along
both sides of a street, and the high branches overhang to form
a beautiful archway.

232

Butternut

THE leaves of the Butternut tree are light green early in the summer. During the summer they slowly turn yellow. The Butternut tree is found in northern North America all the way west to the Rocky Mountains.

The Butternut is not a strong tree and does not live long. But it does have a delicious tasting nut about one to two inches long. The nut is very pasty, sticking to the branches after the leaves have fallen off.

Beech

THE Beech is a fine shade tree, because its spreading branches have so many thin leaves. The wood is hard and is used for fuel and for lumber. It belongs to the same tree family which includes the chestnuts and the mighty oaks.

In the winter, the trunk of the tree is smooth and gray. In the autumn, nuts fall to the ground from hard, thorny shells. The meat in the nut is very sweet.

Balsam Fir

MOST of our Christmas trees are Balsam Firs. They are a popular choice, because the needles do not fall off quickly and because they have a pleasant pine scent. Unlike the spruce, whose cones grow down, the cones of the Fir grow up.

It belongs to a large group of trees called evergreens. They are called evergreens because they stay green all year round.

234

Hemlock

THE Hemlock is the best known evergreen in North America. In the forest, it grows as high as 100 feet. The wood makes excellent lumber. The leaves of this tree are delicate, short and flat. The top of the leaf is bright green. The bottom of the leaf is light green and silvery.

The flowers of the Hemlock blossom in the spring. They turn into small cones, colored red-brown. They do not fall off the tree until the next spring.

Pecan

The Pecan tree belongs to and is the largest member of the hickory family. Some Pecan trees grow as high as 150 feet. They have very big trunks. The Pecan nut is shaped like a very tiny football that has a thin shell which can be cracked easily to get to the very tasty nut meat.

Persimmon

The playful possum loves to sleep in the branches of the Persimmon tree. He eats the fruit and then goes to sleep hanging by his tail. The Persimmon is an odd looking tree. The trunk is straight, but the bark is cracked into small pieces, and the branches curve out from the top in the funniest shapes.

The fruit of the Persimmon looks like a small yellow apple. It is wonderful to eat, but only when it is ripe. Persimmon wood is very hard and is used to make the wooden heads of golf clubs. Persimmon trees grow best in the southern part of the United States.

Magnolia

THE southern Magnolia tree has so many
leaves that it is hard to see the trunk. The
flower of this beautiful tree is the state flower
of Louisiana.

The rich green leaves have the texture
of leather. The Magnolia has lovely
sweet-smelling white flowers that
bloom in the spring.

Cedar

The nice-smelling wood used to make cedar closets and cedar chests comes from the Red Cedar tree. The wood is very hard and it has a light red color. The fruit of the Red Cedar is a small blue berry.

There is also a northern White Cedar whose fruit is a cone. When it is ripe, the cone peels open like a banana.

The southern White Cedar has cones which split open from the center.

Sassafras

The Sassafras tree is most unusual. Each branch has three leaves of different shapes but evenly colored a beautiful green. Most Sassafras trees are small and slender. But some grow up to 100 feet tall. In the fall the leaves turn to a gorgeous scarlet.

There is a big caterpillar that makes its home in the Sassafras tree. It turns green when it eats the green leaves. This caterpillar becomes the beautiful swallowtail butterfly. Sassafras tea is made from the roots of the tree. The dried and powdered leaves are also used to flavor Creole gumbo soup.

Oak

YOU may have heard the saying, "From tiny acorns mighty Oak trees grow." These acorns are the nut-like fruit of the Oak trees, and they contain the seeds which grow into new Oak trees. Roasted acorns are good to eat.

There are two main kinds of Oak: the Black Oak and the White Oak. The White Oak is a majestic looking tree. The great strength of its wood makes it excellent for building ships and furniture. The bark of the Black Oak is very dark and its wood is not so strong as the wood of the White Oak.

Redwood

REDWOOD trees are the oldest and the tallest of all living things. A Redwood can grow as tall as 350 feet and as wide as 22 feet. Some of these giant trees have holes cut in them so that cars can drive right through.

A sister to the Redwood is the still wider Big tree. These trees grow to an unbelievably old age, and many are more than 2,500 years old!

Spruce

THE Spruce is another evergreen tree. The leaves of the White Spruce are colored a whitish-green. There are many of these trees along the coast of Maine. The White Spruce is one of the favorite Christmas trees.

There is a Norway Spruce which is wonderfully suited for building tall masts and spars on sailing vessels. Most of the wood used for paper-making comes from Spruce trees.

Pine

THE Pine is still another variety of evergreen tree that keeps its needle-like leaves all year long. There is an easy way to tell Pines from other evergreen trees. The needles of the Pine grow in peculiar small bunches of two to five each. The Sugar Pine of California and Oregon is the tallest of the many kinds of Pine trees.

Apple

THE Apple tree has a short, thick gray trunk that is twisted like a piece of clay. In the spring white, sweet-smelling flowers bloom from the tree. But the apples do not ripen until fall. The twigs on the branches that hold the apples are short and thick. They cannot sway in the wind, so the apples are not damaged by knocking together.

No one knows why, but if you plant a seed from one of our sweet apples, such as the McIntosh, the new tree will grow small apples that have a sour taste. That is why new Apple trees are grown from twigs and not from seeds.

242

Cherry

BLACK Cherry trees have dark red buds, long leaves and bark that turns black with age. The cherries that come from this tree are not colored black, as you would imagine, but purple. The early American settlers prized the Cherry tree very highly. They used its strong wood to make beautiful cabinets and furniture.

Dogwood

ONE of the most beautiful flowering trees is the Dogwood. In New England the flowers are pure white. They bloom early in spring before most of the other trees. The Dogwood is not a tall tree, and the white flowers blooming next to the dark trunks of taller trees make a particularly lovely sight.

Palm

THE Palm is a tropical tree. In the United States it only grows in the southern parts of California and Florida. The trunk of the Palm does not get thinner towards the top, as do most North American trees. It grows straight, like a wide pole with a bulge at the very bottom. There are no branches on the Palm tree, but great leaves grow out of the tree top.

A common Palm tree in California is the Canary Island Date Palm. The orange-colored date fruit hang down in bunches.

The coconut of the Coconut Palm is the biggest seed in the world. The white liquid inside it is called coconut milk and it is very nourishing. On some tropical islands the coconut makes up an important part of the native diet. The coconut looks something like a monkey's face.

244

Cypress

THE Cypress is a sad, gloomy looking tree, which is probably why many ancient civilizations used it at funerals and as a symbol for mourners.

The Bald Cypress, which grows in swamps in the southern part of the United States, is an especially strange tree. The bottom of the trunk has ridges like a half-opened umbrella. Part of the roots stick up out of the water all around the tree and look like bent knees. No one knows exactly why they stick up. But they are ideal for making the curved bottoms of wooden boats. Cypress wood is also used to make railroad ties.

Poplar

THE Poplar is easy to recognize. It grows straight up and is very narrow. The branches grow out from the trunk only a little before they curve almost straight up.

In parts of Europe, the people grow long rows of Poplars along the highways and rivers, because they act as effective windbreakers.

Sycamore

THE Sycamore is sometimes called the Buttonwood or Buttonhole tree. In the winter, the tree's fruit look like little balls hanging from strings on the upper branches. The Sycamore is the oldest hardwood tree on earth. The branches grow at different angles. While the bottom of the trunk is always white, the upper bark is colored beautiful shades of white, gray and purple.

Mulberry

You will often find the White Mulberry in old New England towns. The trunk of this tree is short and it has a wonderful way of leaning to one side. It is a good shade tree. The fruit ripen a few at a time all summer long rather than all at once like the fruit of most trees. People do not like to eat mulberries but birds love them.

The Mulberry is the tree silkworms live on. If you cut a twig when the sun is hot, you will see the white sap which the silkworm uses to make silk.

George Washington had many Mulberry trees brought to the United States. He had hoped to start an American silk industry, but the early settlers found that it was not a profitable venture in this country. Today, most of our silk comes from Japan and India.

Eucalyptus

THE Eucalyptus tree is grown in California as a windbreaker. It grows high above the houses, and the trunk of the tree usually slants to one side. The leaves are long and thin and are colored blue-green. They hang in bunches. When the sun is hot the leaves roll up and turn their edges to the sun so they will not be dried up. Eucalyptus oil is made from crushing these leaves.

Fig

THE Fig tree has been the main source of food in regions around the Mediterranean Sea for thousands of years. The figs it gives are very plentiful. That is because of the astonishing fact that instead of bearing fruit only once a year, like most fruit trees, the Fig tree gives two crops every year.

Today, Fig trees are grown in the United States, too, especially in California and Texas.

Rubber

THE Rubber tree grows only in tropical climates. The tree is tall and thin. The bark is smooth and light colored. The flowers are green with yellow centers.

It is the juice of this tree that is used to make rubber. The juice, which is between the outer bark and the inner wood, is white and looks like thick milk. That is why it is called latex. Latex comes from a Latin word which means milk. Workers tap the Rubber tree for this latex by cutting narrow grooves in the bark. They slant the grooves downward. Then they place a cup at the bottom of the tree, and the latex drips into it.

249

Hickory

HICKORY wood is hard and heavy and is used to make tool handles, like axes. Hickory wood is also burned to smoke meats, like hickory-smoked bacon. The bark looks shaggy. That is why the Hickory is also called the Shagbark tree.

The Hickory grows best along water banks and on hillsides through most of the eastern half of the United States. The meat inside the Hickory nut is very delicious. Another Hickory is called the Bitternut because its nuts have a bitter taste.

250

Basswood

In the summer, groups of yellow flowers shaped like stars cover the Basswood or Linden tree. The flowers have a very strong smell. Bees love them.

The wood from the Basswood is used to make toy airplanes and Venetian blinds.

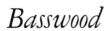

Black Walnut

The Black Walnut has many light green leaves that look very pretty next to the dark bark. These lovely leaves fall off at the end of the summer before the leaves of any other tree. The nut of this tree has a most unusual flavor and is used in ice cream and cakes.

251

Teak

THE Teak tree grows in southern Asia and in great numbers in Burma. The wood is used for ship building, especially for decks. It is also used for fine furniture. Teak wood lasts a long time. Houses built of this wood have lasted for hundreds of years.

During the rainy season, small white flowers appear at the tips of the branches of the Teak tree. These trees may grow as high as 150 feet and as wide as 15 feet, but they take 100 years to reach that size.

Mahogany

MAHOGANY is one of the most popular woods. Today most Mahogany wood comes from Central America. The wood comes in different shades of brown, polishes easily, and is very strong. It is used to make furniture, musical instruments and expensive boats. Some Mahogany trees are grown in southern parts of Florida and California for decoration.

252

Cacao

WHEN Columbus came to the West Indies and Central America, he found the Indians drinking something they called chocolate. It was made by grinding and roasting the seeds of the Cacao, a beautiful evergreen with leaves that are reddish on the back. The seeds, as big as almonds, are in a brown pod. This is the fruit of the Cacao tree. We have changed its name to cocoa and use it not only to drink, but to make candy and cake.

Huckleberry

THE Huckleberry shrub is found throughout North America and Europe. The leaves have yellow scales on the undersides. The berry fruit is blue or sometimes black. It has always been considered good to eat, especially in pies.

Blueberries are better tasting, though, and now that more blueberries are being grown, the Huckleberry may become less popular.

254

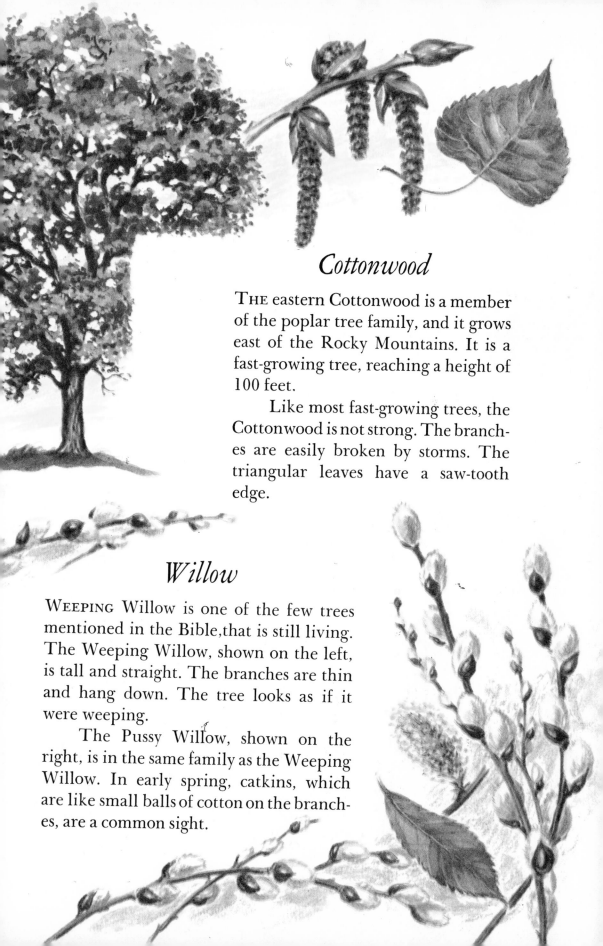

Cottonwood

THE eastern Cottonwood is a member of the poplar tree family, and it grows east of the Rocky Mountains. It is a fast-growing tree, reaching a height of 100 feet.

Like most fast-growing trees, the Cottonwood is not strong. The branches are easily broken by storms. The triangular leaves have a saw-tooth edge.

Willow

WEEPING Willow is one of the few trees mentioned in the Bible, that is still living. The Weeping Willow, shown on the left, is tall and straight. The branches are thin and hang down. The tree looks as if it were weeping.

The Pussy Willow, shown on the right, is in the same family as the Weeping Willow. In early spring, catkins, which are like small balls of cotton on the branches, are a common sight.

Azalea

THE Azalea is one of the most lovely garden shrubs in the world. It comes in many colors, and it would be difficult to imagine a new home in the temperate or northern parts of the United States, where the Azalea grows best, that does not have one of these lovely shrubs in its garden.

Privet

A VERY popular garden hedge is made with the Privet shrub, because it grows straight and is easily trimmed. The Privet will grow rapidly in almost any soil and grows very well in the northern states. The leaf is smooth and green. There are small black berries which do not taste good, but birds like them.

256

Hydrangea

HYDRANGEA shrubs have beautiful clusters of pink, white, or blue flowers. They bloom along sea shores where it is not too cold. The French Hydrangea is a large round bush and has very shiny leaves. The Oak-leaf Hydrangea grows around New York City. There is a Climbing Hydrangea, shown below, which climbs up walls and trees and has large white flowers in June.

Lilac

THERE are at least 500 different kinds of Lilac shrubs. In the spring the flowers are very colorful. The common Lilac is the oldest shrub planted in American gardens. It is also the state flower of New Hampshire.

The most popular Lilacs used to be the purple and white bushes. Today, people like some of the other kinds better, like the Korean Lilac. It has pink flowers and blooms earlier than most of the others.

Forsythia

THE Forsythia shrub is also known as the Golden Bell. The flowers bloom early in spring and the leaves stay green until late fall. One kind of Forsythia, called the Ovata, was brought to the United States from Korea. It has yellowish flowers which bloom before any of the other Forsythias.

There is a new kind of Forsythia called Spring Glory. The many large yellow flowers should make it very popular.

258

LANGUAGES

A LANGUAGE is a set of rules which a group of people uses to communicate with each other. Often, when groups live near each other their "rules" are quite similar; for example, Norway and Sweden are neighbor countries, and their people have little difficulty understanding each other.

A language cannot live without people to speak it, and for this reason some languages have died out when the last speaker was gone. This happened only recently, when the Dalmatian dialect on the island of Veglia, in the Adriatic Sea, disappeared because all the old people who spoke it died out. But when there are many people speaking a language it grows stronger, takes on new words, and even changes with the times.

The ancient wise men had a saying which all of us could well take to heart: "Learn another language; it will help you to understand your own all the better."

INTRODUCTION

WHEN American Indians saw smoke rising from a mountain top in a certain way they knew it was a signal. Today, when a soldier hears certain bugle calls he understands that they are signals which mean "chow," "charge," or "lights out." Sailors understand navy blinkers and flag signals. In just the same way languages are signals.

There are about 3,000 languages around the world, and naturally it would be impossible for this book to tell about all of them. But many of them can be described briefly; we will discuss those which are spoken by most of the peoples of the world.

Languages come in families. For example, the Germanic family, the Romance family, etc. These families are broken up into groups. For example, the Germanic family is broken up into English, German, Dutch, etc. These groups are then broken down into dialects. For example, dialects of Dutch, the language of Holland, are Flemish and Afrikaans.

For the purposes of this book there will be ten families: Germanic, Romance languages, Slavonic languages, languages of India, languages of Asia and the Orient, languages of Africa, Arabic languages, Ural-Altaic languages,

262

Celtic, and then all the others left over.

All languages are important to the people who speak them. Perhaps someday all the peoples of the world may speak the same language.

While many languages will be mentioned in this book it is important to remember that there are only thirteen languages which are spoken by 50 million or more people. These can be considered the chief languages of the world: English, Spanish, Italian, French, German, Chinese, Japanese, Portuguese, Russian, Malay, Hindustani, Bengali and Arabic.

Thanks.
Hello.
Yes.
Today.
Play.
House.

ENGLISH

ENGLISH is a strange language because it came from so many other languages. Basically it is in the Germanic family, but much of it also comes from French and Latin. The German part was brought to England by the Angles and Saxons, the French part mostly by the nobles who came with William the Conqueror; and the Latin by the few educated people who continued to speak that language until about 300 years ago.

More than 250 million people speak English, in such places as the United States, Canada, Great Britain, Australia, New Zealand, Alaska and Hawaii.

When you read about the other languages you will want to know how they compare with English. For that purpose we will use the six common words listed above.

A B C D E F G H I J K L M N O P Q R S T U V W X

GERMAN

NEARLY 100 million people speak the German language, especially in Europe. There it is spoken in Germany and Austria, and in parts of Hungary, Poland, Switzerland, Italy and Yugoslavia. All the latter countries (except Switzerland) were within the Austro-Hungarian empire before the first World War, and the people in that area found it convenient to learn German in addition to their own native languages.

Like most languages German is a mixture of many others. Many hundreds of years ago the Germanic tribes met the invading Roman armies; later on they mixed with the people of Denmark and other exploring Scandinavian countries. It is easy to see why all the languages in the Germanic family are related to each other.

Thanks.
Danke Schon
(Dankeh shoen)

Hello.
en Tag (Gooten tagh)

Yes.
Ja (Ya)

Today.
Heute (Huyteh)

Play.
Spiel (Shpeel)

House.
Haus (House)

SCANDINAVIAN LANGUAGES

MORE than 15 million people speak the Scandinavian tongues. All four of them, Norwegian, Danish, Swedish and Icelandic, are members of the Germanic family. Icelandic has never changed, and sounds much the same as it did in the days of the Vikings. But the other three are geographically close, and each understands a great deal of the other. Swedish people can understand Norwegians and Danes, for there is not a great deal of difference in their languages.

However there is a great difference between German and the Scandinavian languages, even though they both come from the Germanic family.

A B C D E F G H I J K L M N O P Q R S T U V W X Y Z AE Ø

	DUTCH
Thanks.	Dank (Danku)
Hello.	Dag (Dag)
Yes.	Ja (Ya)
Today.	Vandaag (Vandaag)
Play.	Spelen (Spielen)
House.	Huis (H-wees)

OTHER GERMANIC LANGUAGES

ABOUT 10 million people in Holland speak Dutch, which is a member of the German language family. Dutch is also spoken in lands which either once were or still are Dutch possessions, like Indonesia and Surinam.

Flemish, which is very close to the Dutch language, is spoken by about half the people in Belgium (the other half speak French).

There are about 2 million people who speak a form of Dutch called Afrikaans. These people live in South Africa and are the descendants of the Dutch Boers, who colonized the land many years ago.

	NORWEGIAN
Thanks.	Takk (Tak)
Hello.	Hallo (Hallo)
Yes.	Ja (Ya)
Today.	Idag (Eedag)
Play.	Lek (Lek)
House.	Hus (Heus)

C D E F G H I J K L M N O P Q R S T U V W X Y Z

A B C D E F G H I J L M N O P Q R S T U

ITALIAN

ITALIAN is the first of the family of Romance languages, which derive from Latin. It is most like Latin because of geography. Italian was the language of central Italy, around the capital city of Rome. There are many words which are almost the same in Latin as Italian; "tempus" in Latin and "tempo" in Italian both mean "time."

Italian is also the language of music. Directions for playing symphonies and operas are written in Italian. For example, "con brio" means " with fire!" Or, "forte" means " loudly."

About 45 million people, including many in Switzerland and other parts of Europe, in addition to many immigrants in the United States, speak Italian.

| Thanks. | Grazie | (Gratzia) | Yes. | Si | (See) | Play. | Giocare | (Jocara) |
| Hello. | Ciao | (Chayo) | Today. | Oggi | (Odji) | House. | Casa | (Casa) |

268

SPANISH

SPANISH, another Romance language, is one of the easiest languages to learn, and also one of the most beautiful. The language even warns the reader before a question is asked. In such cases you have a question mark at the end, and also an upside down question mark before the sentence! For example "¿como estas?"—how are you?

Nearly 125 million people speak this lovely tongue. Five hundred years ago, when the Spanish fleets were large and powerful, they controlled the oceans around the New World. The Spanish influence spread all over America; today, Spanish is the language of most of the South American countries, as well as the first language of more than ten million citizens of the United States. Spanish is also an important language in the Philippines.

Thanks.	Gracias (Grasias)
Hello.	Buenos dias (Boo-aynos dee-as)
Yes.	Si (See)
Today.	Hoy (Oy)
Play.	Jugar (Hugar)
House.	Casa (Casa)

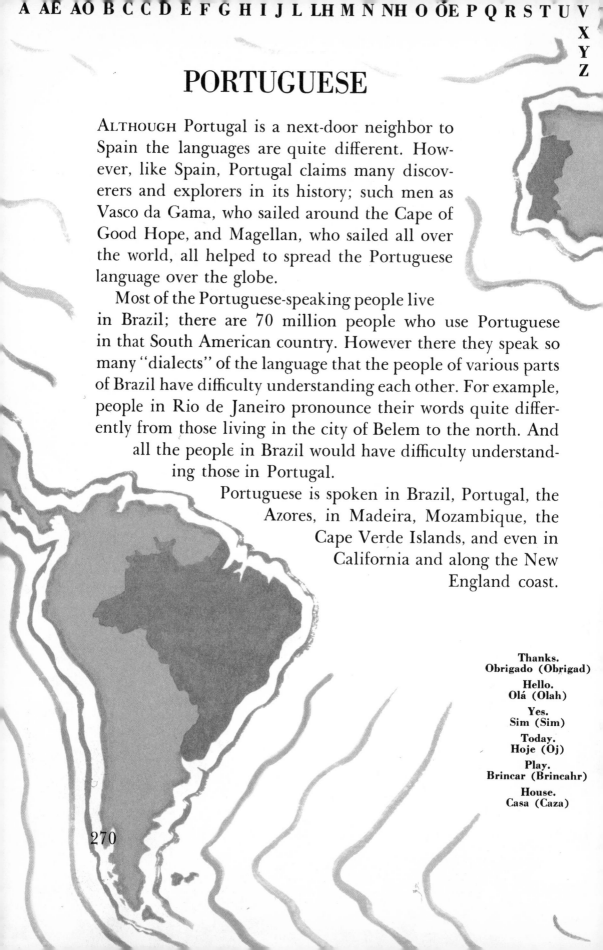

PORTUGUESE

ALTHOUGH Portugal is a next-door neighbor to Spain the languages are quite different. However, like Spain, Portugal claims many discoverers and explorers in its history; such men as Vasco da Gama, who sailed around the Cape of Good Hope, and Magellan, who sailed all over the world, all helped to spread the Portuguese language over the globe.

Most of the Portuguese-speaking people live in Brazil; there are 70 million people who use Portuguese in that South American country. However there they speak so many "dialects" of the language that the people of various parts of Brazil have difficulty understanding each other. For example, people in Rio de Janeiro pronounce their words quite differently from those living in the city of Belem to the north. And all the people in Brazil would have difficulty understanding those in Portugal.

Portuguese is spoken in Brazil, Portugal, the Azores, in Madeira, Mozambique, the Cape Verde Islands, and even in California and along the New England coast.

Thanks.
Obrigado (Obrigad)

Hello.
Olá (Olah)

Yes.
Sim (Sim)

Today.
Hoje (Oj)

Play.
Brincar (Brincahr)

House.
Casa (Caza)

270

FRENCH

FRENCH was once called "the language of diplomacy," because it was spoken by most of the world's diplomats. It still ranks with English as an international language, and millions of people still use it as a second language. It is the official language of more than 80 million people.

French is very close to Latin, and so it is a Romance language. Thousands of years ago the Latin-speaking Romans occupied France and spread their language there.

French is spoken in France, and in parts of Belgium and Switzerland; in Algeria, Belgian Congo and other parts of Africa; in some sections of Asia where the French once had colonies; in French Guiana and Haiti, which once belonged to France; in Canada, where descendants of French colonists still live. French can also be heard in New Orleans and in some New England towns where French-Canadians live.

Thanks.
Merci (Mehr-see)

Hello.
Bonjour (Bon jour)

Yes.
Oui (Wee)

Today.
Aujourd 'hui
(Oujourd wee)

Play.
Jouer (Juay)

House.
Maison (May zon)

RUMANIAN

A Ă Â B C D Ḑ E É Ĕ Ê F G H I Ĭ Î
K L M N O Ó P R S Ș T Ț U Ŭ V X Y

RUMANIAN

Thanks.	Mulțumesc (Mool-tsoo-mesk)
Hello.	Noroc (No-roak)
Yes.	Da (Da)
Today.	Azi (Ahzy)
Play.	Joc (Juk)
House.	Casa (Casa)

А Б В Г

OTHER ROMANCE LANGUAGES

SEVERAL other languages have Latin as their root, and therefore can be called Romance (really "Roman") languages. Rumanian is spoken by nearly 20 million people, in Rumania and in parts of Yugoslavia, Russia and Hungary. A language called Catalan is spoken in the Pyrenees of Southern France, in Catalonia, Spain, and in parts of Spanish Valencia.

Sardinian, which is the language of central and southern Sardinia, is very much different from Italian.

Other Romance languages, all spoken in various parts of Europe, include Romansh, one of the official languages of Switzerland; Provençal, spoken in a few parts of southern France; and a few dialects which are spoken in Italy, such as Piedmontese and Lombard.

272

RUSSIAN

Spreading out in Europe to the northeast and east are the Slavonic languages. By far the largest number of people using these languages, well over 100 million, speak Russian. Russian is the official language of the Soviet Union (the U.S.S.R.).

The Russian alphabet looks strange to us, for it is partly based on the one used by ancient Greece. The Russian alphabet has 33 letters.

Although Russian is an official language of the U.S.S.R. there are more than 100 other languages and dialects spoken in that area. Two major languages, quite close to Russian, are outstanding in this group of Slavonic tongues: Ukrainian, spoken by more than 40 million people in southern Russia, and White Russian, with 10 million speakers near the Polish border.

З И I Й К Л М Н О П Р С Т У Ф Х Ц Ч Ш Щ Ъ Ы Ь Ѣ Э Ю Я Ѳ Ѵ

RUSSIAN

Thanks.
Спасибо
(Spasi bo)

Hello.
Здравствовать
(S dva fst vovat)

Yes.
Да
(Da)

Today.
Сегодня
(Sevo dn ya)

Play.
Играть
(Igral)

House.
Домъ
(Dom)

A Ą B C Ć D E Ę F G H I J K L Ł M N Ń O Ó P R S
U W Y Z Ź Ż CH CZ DZ DŻ DŹ IE RZ RŻ ŚĆ SZ(SZ

POLISH

Thanks.
Dziękuję
(Djen Kuya)

Hello.
Dzień Dobry
(Djen Dobry)

Yes.
Tak
(Tak)

Today.
Dzisiej
(Dishey)

Play.
Bawić Się
(Bavich Shen)

House.
Dom, Budynek
(Dom Budynek)

POLAN

CZECHOSLOVAK

POLISH

THERE are 35 million people in Poland; 25 million of them speak Polish. There are also about 3 million Polish-speaking people in the United States, located mostly in the mining and industrial areas of Pennsylvania, Ohio, Illinois and Michigan. This makes Polish the second largest of the Slavonic family of languages. Although Polish is not spoken much outside the borders of its own country, the language is understood in parts of Russia and other nearby lands.

274 Nearly 10 million inhabitants of Poland speak languages other than Polish. These tongues include White Russian, Ukrainian, Lithuanian, and some Yiddish and Kashube.

OTHER SLAVONIC LANGUAGES

Two closely related languages are spoken in Czechoslovakia, Czech and Slovak; in fact, that is where the nation gets its name. These two tongues are quite different from Russian, and if they are similar to any other language it is Polish. Czech and Slovak use an alphabet like ours, called "Roman," instead of the Russian alphabet which is used by most of the other Slavonic languages.

Serbo-Croatian, the language of Yugoslavia, has some parts of Bulgarian and some parts of Ukrainian in it, and uses the alphabet of Russia in Serbia and Croatia.

Bulgarian is spoken by about 8 million people, and is closer to Russian than to Polish, but is not really like either one. A good way to understand this difference is to remember Spanish and Portuguese. Although both are Romance languages they are different from each other. This same holds true of Bulgarian and Russian.

UKRAINE

BULGARIA

YUGOSLAVIA

CZECH

Thanks.	Díky	(Dyke)
Hello.	Nazdar	(Naz dar)
Yes.	Ano	(Ano)
Today.	Dnes	(D nes)
Play.	Hrát si	(Harat see)
House.	Dům	(Doom)

C Č D Ď E É Ě F G H I Y Í Ý J K L M Ň O Ó P Q R Ř S Š T Ť U Ú Ů V X Z Ž

CHINESE

Thanks.

謝謝

(H sh ieh H sh ieh)

Hello.

您好

(Nin Hao)

Yes.

是

(Shih)

Today.

今天

(Chin Tien)

Play.

遊戲

(Yu Hsi)

House.

房屋

(Fang Wu)

276

ASIA AND THE ORIENT

MORE than one thousand million people live in Asia! This is about half of all the people on earth. Of course this number would include parts of Russia, all of China, Japan, India and many smaller countries. With so many people inhabiting this area it is not surprising that there are so many different languages spoken.

About half of these billion people speak Chinese. However, not all Chinese is the same, at least when it is spoken. There are many dialects of this language: Pekingese, Cantonese and Mandarin, to name but a few. And it is quite difficult for the speakers of each dialect to understand each other. Yet, strangely enough, the writing is the same. Although they cannot understand each other's speech they can well understand each other when they put the words on paper.

It all depends on the tone of voice that each dialect uses. At times, in one sentence, each word has a different tone in the speaker's voice, so that the same word would mean one thing in one dialect and another thing in a different dialect.

Thanks.		(Ari ga tow)
Hello.		(Kon nichi wa Moshi Moshi)
Yes.		(Ha ee)
Today.		(Ke o)
Play.		(Ah so bi)
House.		(I ye)

茶本帝

JAPANESE

THE Japanese language is entirely different from the Chinese. Even the writing, although based on ancient Chinese, is different from modern Chinese. Nearly 100 million people speak Japanese on the Islands, and in Korea many speak Japanese as well as their own tongue. There are Japanese-speaking people in Hawaii, and some in the Philippines and various other Pacific islands.

The problem of dialects is not troublesome to the Japanese speakers. Most of the people can understand each other easily enough. This is because their alphabet is phonetic: that is, they are able to sound out each letter. Chinese writing does not have this system.

Although Japanese is written in "pictographs" like the Chinese (each letter is a sort of small picture), in recent years the system has been standardized and simplified.

278

MALAY

MALAY, in the Republic of Indonesia, is referred to as "Indonesian," and in other places where the language is spoken as Malay. However, not all people of that country speak the same tongue. Actually there are a variety of Malayan languages, none of which are like the Chinese or Japanese. In fact Malay can nearly be considered a family by itself. There are dialects or variations spoken on the Indonesian islands of Java, Sumatra, Borneo and Bali; the island of Madagascar, near Africa, speaks a dialect called Malagasy; and Easter Island in the Pacific Ocean has still another Malay dialect. In addition the islands of Fiji, Tahiti and the Solomons speak another variation, while the Philippines speak a language related to Malay which they call Tagalog (although both Spanish and English are important languages of those islands).

About 100 million people speak some form of the Malay language, spread over islands which are thousands of miles apart.

MALAY

Thanks.
Terima Kasih
(Tree ma Ka seeh)

Hello.
Tabe
(Ta bay)

Yes.
Ia
(Ya)

Today.
Ini Hari
(Ee nee Ha ree)

Play.
Bermain
(Ber main)

House.
Roemah
(Roo mah)

OTHER ORIENTAL LANGUAGES

THERE are many other Far-Eastern tongues, some related to Chinese, some related to Japanese. The most used of these smaller languages is Korean, which is similar to Japanese. Nearly 30 million people speak Korean, and most of them can understand Japanese as well.

In southeastern Asia there are many variations of Chinese; such languages as Siamese, Burmese and Tibetan have many traits in common with Chinese, although they are not the same language by any means. They, like the Chinese, usually use only words of one syllable.

KOREAN

Thanks. 고맙습니다
(Komapsupnida)

Hello. 여보세요
(Yoboseyo)

Yes. 네
(Neh)

Today. 오늘
(Onul)

Play. 논다
(Nonda)

House. 집
(Jip)

PAKISTAN
RUSSIA
IRAN

INDIA
CHI

JAPAN
KOREA
INDONESIA

LANGUAGES OF INDIA

A GOOD part of the thousand million people of Asia live in India. and Pakistan. More than two hundred languages are spoken by the 400 million inhabitants of these two countries, including English, since both countries were once under the control of England. However the two chief languages are Hindustani and Bengali.

The Hindus of India call Hindustani "Hindi," while the Muslims of Pakistan call it "Urdu." Besides the difference in names the Hindus write the language with letters that come from Sanskrit, while the Muslims write with Arabic letters.

The Bengali language is spoken primarily in East Pakistan and in the Indian province of Bengal, especially in the great city of Calcutta.

URDU

Thanks.	شکریه	(Shukriya)	Today.	آج	(Adj)
Hello.	السلام علیکم :	(A salaam aleikum)	Play.	کھیلو	(Kale)
Yes.	ہاں	(Han)	House.	گھر	(Kar)

ا ب ج ح د ر س ش ص ض ط ظ ع غ ت ق ک ل م ن ء ی

PERSIAN

Thanks.	خطر	(Tashakar)
Hello.	سلام	(Salam)
Yes.	الله - له	(Albateh-B-ali)
Today.	امرو	(Amrouz)
Play.	بازی کردن	(Bazikardan)
House.	خانه	(Kane)

OTHER LANGUAGES OF INDIA

IRAN, formerly called Persia, speaks a group of languages which are much like those spoken in northern India. The ancient tongue of Persia was Sanskrit, but many Arabic words have come into the language.

West of Bengal, in northeastern India, a language called Bihari is spoken; other languages on the Indian part of the continent include Marathi, spoken around Bombay; Punjabi, in the Punjab area; Rajasthani, north of Bombay, and also Gujarati, in roughly the same section.

On the Island of Ceylon there are two major languages: Tamil, in northern Ceylon, and Telugu, which is also spoken in southeastern India.

GAELIC

Thanks.

ʒuʀ ᴀ ᴍᴀɪᴢ̇ ᴀʒᴀᴢ

(Gur a maith agat)

Hello.

Ðɪᴀ's ᴍᴜɪʀᴇ 'ʒuᴢ

(Dia's muire 'guit)

Yes.

Ṡᴇᴀᴅ·

(Sha)

Today.

ɪɴᴅɪū

(Inyu)

Play.

ᴀʒ ɪᴍɪʀᴄ

(Egg imert)

House.

ᴄᴇᴀċ

(Tchak)

CELTIC LANGUAGES

THESE languages are spoken almost entirely in and around the British Isles. Of course most of those speaking Celtic understand English as well.

The Irish language sounds strange to our ears, and the writing comes from a form used by the monks of the Middle Ages. Very similar to Irish is Scots Gaelic, which is spoken in the Highlands of Scotland by about one hundred thousand people.

There are other variations of Celtic spoken in nearby areas. Manx is spoken on the Isle of Man; Breton can be heard in French Brittany, just across the channel from England; Welsh is the tongue of about a million people in Wales.

Another Celtic tongue, Cornish, was once spoken in Cornwall, in southwestern Britain, but it has almost died out.

All Celtic languages are fairly similar to each other.

Thanks.	Kiitos	(Kee tos)
Hello.	Hei	(Hi)
Yes.	Kyllä	(Kee la)
Today.	Tänään	(Tan an)
Play.	Leikkiä	(Ley kia)
House.	Talo	(Tah lo)

TURKISH

Thanks.	Tesekür Ederim	(Teshekuer Ederim)
Hello.	Merhaba	(Merhaba)
Yes.	Evet	(Eh veht)
Today.	Bugün	(Bu geen)
Play.	Oynanmak	(Oi nan mak)
House.	Ev	(Ehv)

HUNGARIAN

Thanks.	Kösönöm	(Kus un um)
Hello.	Jö napöt	(Yo naput)
Yes.	Igen	(Eegen)
Today.	Māma	(May ma)
Play.	Jatzany	(Yutz ony)
House.	Haz	(Haz)

URAL-ALTAIC

SOME of the most colorful nations in the world speak some dialect of the Ural-Altaic family of tongues. The Finns, the Lapps of the Arctic Circle and the Estonians speak a language of the Uralic branch, so called because they come from the area of the Ural Mountains. All three of these languages have a good many similarities.

A different language of the Uralic branch is Magyar, or Hungarian, spoken by the people of Hungary, and in some small parts of Rumania, Yugoslavia and Czechoslovkia.

The Turkish language, considered part of the Ural-Altaic family, is the most widespread of this group. In addition to Turkey the language (or a dialect of it) is spoken in parts of Albania, in Bulgaria, in Greece and in sections of central Asia and Mongolia. This is because it was carried from Mongolia by invading armies of Turks, Tatars and Mongols, many years ago. They left parts of their language wherever they went. The name "Altaic," used for Turkish and related languages, comes from the Altai Mountains of central Asia.

FINNISH:

A D E G H I J K L M N O P R S T U V Y Ä Ö

HUNGARIAN:

A Á B C D E É F G H I Í J K L M N O Ó Ö Ő P R S T U Ú Ü Ű V X Y Z CS CZ DS GY

TURKISH:

A B C Ç D E F G Ğ H I I J K L M N O O Ö P R S Ş T U Ü

FINLAND
ESTONIA
CZECHOSLOVAKIA
HUNGARY
YUGOSLAVIA
RUMANIA
BULGARIA
GREECE
TURKEY

'Y ZS DZS

285

ARABIC and HEBREW

ARABIC is one of the most important languages of the Semitic Family. It is spoken by more than 50 million people over a large area that includes north Africa, the Fertile Crescent and the Arabian peninsula. In its written form it is the language of a vast literature that began before 600 A.D. and continues to the present. It is the language of the Koran and of Islam's prayer and therefore is important as the religious language of the Muslim world.

Closely related to Arabic is Hebrew, the language of the Old Testament. Hebrew has been revived as a living language and is now the language of the State of Israel. Although Arabic and Hebrew have many similarities as they are spoken, each has its own alphabet for writing. In Hebrew and Arabic the words are written from right to left, the opposite of the way we write.

وما كان شُوْمى الذى فَرَق يِنى

ARABIC

Thanks.	تَشَكُّرَت	(Ta shak ko rat)
Hello.	سَدامُ	(Sa lam)
Yes.	بَكِى	(Ba li)
Today.	اليَوم	(Al yom)
Play.	لعبِ	(La 'b)
House.	بَيْت	(Bayt)

HEBREW

Thanks.	תּוֹדָה	(To dah)
Hello.	שָׁלוֹם!	(Sha lom)
Yes.	כֵּן	(Kane)
Today.	הַיּוֹם	(Ha yohm)
Play.	נשחק	(Le sac heck)
House.	בַּיִת	(Ba yit)

HEBREW

ך ק ץ צ ף פ ע ס ן נ ם מ ל כ י ט ח ז ו ה ד ג ב א
ר

ARABIC   287

ا ب ت ث ج ح خ د ذ ر ز س ش ص ض ط ظ ع غ ف ق ك ل م ن

AFRICAN

AFRICA is the second largest continent in the world. Can you name the world's largest continent? Africa is populated by very diverse peoples whose languages fall into three principal language-family groups: Bantu, Khoisan and Western Sudanic.

Most of central and southern Africa is populated by people who speak one of the Bantu languages. Swahili is one such language; it is not only the mother-tongue of many Africans but also serves as an international language among many African peoples.

Khoisan is the language spoken in southern Africa by Bushmen and Hottentots. The peoples of West Africa speak one or another of the closely related Western Sudanic languages.

French, English, Dutch, Italian and Arabic are also spoken in parts of Africa.

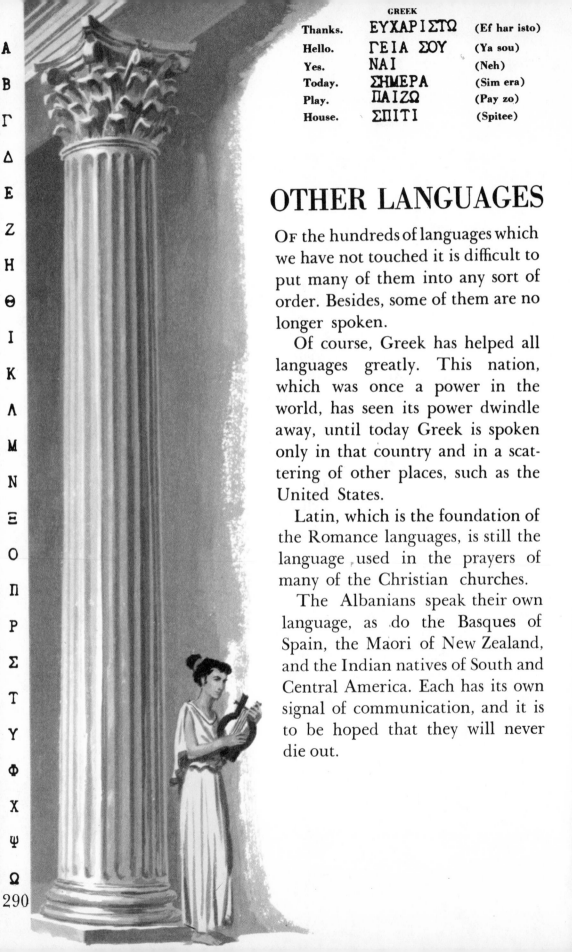

A B Γ Δ E Z H Θ I K Λ M N Ξ O Π P Σ T Y Φ X Ψ Ω

290

GREEK

Thanks.	ΕΥΧΑΡΙΣΤΩ	(Ef har isto)
Hello.	ΓΕΙΑ ΣΟΥ	(Ya sou)
Yes.	ΝΑΙ	(Neh)
Today.	ΣΗΜΕΡΑ	(Sim era)
Play.	ΠΑΙΖΩ	(Pay zo)
House.	ΣΠΙΤΙ	(Spitee)

OTHER LANGUAGES

Of the hundreds of languages which we have not touched it is difficult to put many of them into any sort of order. Besides, some of them are no longer spoken.

Of course, Greek has helped all languages greatly. This nation, which was once a power in the world, has seen its power dwindle away, until today Greek is spoken only in that country and in a scattering of other places, such as the United States.

Latin, which is the foundation of the Romance languages, is still the language used in the prayers of many of the Christian churches.

The Albanians speak their own language, as do the Basques of Spain, the Maori of New Zealand, and the Indian natives of South and Central America. Each has its own signal of communication, and it is to be hoped that they will never die out.

THE
UNITED NATIONS

        This book will tell many children
something about a great world organization,
to which 79* countries belong, which is
trying to establish machinery to help the
people of the world keep peace. The idea
that through talking to each other we can
settle problems instead of using force is
such a new one that we have to grow accustomed to it. Every nation should be learning
as much as they can about it so they will
help their own country to work well as part
of this organization.

        You will find in reading this book
that there are many ways in which you can
help the United Nations, and one of the
first things you can do is go and visit the
headquarters in New York City and see just
how the work is done there.

                              Eleanor Roosevelt

ER:pb

*Since this was written other nations
 have been admitted. The complete list
 is on page 299--Ed.

Why The U.N. Was Formed

THE "United Nations" was a name devised by a president of the United States, Franklin D. Roosevelt. It was first used in the Declaration by United Nations of January 1st, 1942, when representatives of 26 nations pledged their governments to continue fighting together against Germany, Italy and Japan.

During that war many countries were bombed, whole cities lay in ruins, and many thousands of people were killed or injured. The freedom-loving nations of the world decided that as soon as World War II was over they would form an organization which would try to settle disputes between countries in a peaceful way. In the Spring of 1945 representatives of 50 countries met in San Francisco, California, and drew up a Charter for the new organization.

On October 24th, 1945, nearly two months after the war was ended, the Charter was ratified and the United Nations officially came into existence. Fifty-one nations pledged themselves to keep international peace and security; to develop friendly relations with all nations; to co-operate in solving all nations' problems and respect human rights and freedoms. Today October 24th is celebrated as United Nations Day.

At first the United Nations Headquarters were at Lake Success, in Flushing, New York. However, Mr. John D. Rockefeller, Jr. donated some land along the East River, in New York City, to serve as permanent headquarters. The buildings were erected, and in 1950 the United Nations began the task of moving all their records to the new site. In 1952 the U.N. settled down in their permanent home.

All organizations need money to carry out their programs, and the same holds true with the United Nations. Each member nation contributes money to the U.N. in proportion to its population, and its ability to pay.

Membership

MEMBERSHIP in the United Nations is open to all nations, large and small, which agree to live up to the United Nations Charter. When a country applies for membership a committee is usually appointed to study the application. The committee decides whether the new nation is willing and able to live up to the Charter.

Originally there were fifty-one member nations; today there are over a hundred. It is hoped that all nations will join the family of the United Nations.

However, just as new nations can join the U.N. other members can be expelled. Any nation that breaks the rules of the United Nations Charter may be suspended or expelled.

Member Nations

Afghanistan
Albania
Algeria
Argentina
Australia
Austria
Barbados
Belgium
Bhutan
Bohrain
Bolivia
Botswana
Brazil
Bulgaria
Burma
Burundi
Byelorussian S. S. R.
Cambodia
Cameroon
Canada
Central African Republic
Ceylon
Chad
Chile
China
    (People's Republic of)
Colombia
Congo
    (People's Republic of)
Costa Rica
Cuba
Cyprus
Czechoslovakia
Dahomey
Denmark
Dominican Republic
Ecuador
Egypt
Equatorial Guinea
El Salvador
Ethiopia
Fiji
Finland
France

Gabon
Gambia
Ghana
Greece
Guatemala
Guinea
Guyana
Haiti
Honduras
Hungary
Iceland
India
Indonesia
Iran
Iraq
Ireland
Israel
Italy
Ivory Coast
Jamaica
Japan
Jordan
Kenya
Kuwait
Laos
Lebanon
Lesotho
Liberia
Libya
Luxembourg
Malagasy Republic
Malawi
Malaysia
Maldive Islands
Mali
Malta
Mauritania
Mauritius
Mexico
Mongolia
Morocco
Nepal
Netherlands
New Zealand
Nicaragua

Niger
Nigeria
Norway
Oman
Pakistan
Panama
Paraguay
People's Republic of Yemen
Peru
Philippines
Poland
Portugal
Qatar
Romania
Rwanda
Saudi Arabia
Senegal
Sierra Leone
Singapore
Somalia
South Africa
Spain
Sudan
Swaziland
Sweden
Syria Arab Republic
Thailand
Togo
Trinidad and Tobago
Tunisia
Turkey
Uganda
Ukrainian S. S. R.
Union of Soviet Socialist
    Republics
United Arab Emirates
United Kingdom
United Republic of Tanzania
United States of America
Upper Volta
Uruguay
Venezuela
Yemen
Yugoslavia
Zaire
Zambia

Languages

MANY languages are spoken by the member nations of the U.N. Few delegates can understand more than a few-languages, and so it is necessary to have special people called "interpreters" who can speak almost every language that is used today.

There are five official languages used in the United Nations: English, French, Spanish, Russian and Chinese. If a delegate makes a speech in any other language he must furnish his own special interpreter to translate the speech into one of the five official languages. Other delegates listen to these interpreters through headphones. They simply flick a switch for the language they wish to hear. Also, other people who come to watch the United Nations at work can listen to the interpreters. There are headphones for every seat.

The United Nations interpreters come from all parts of the world, and are specially trained for their jobs. which are civil service.

Organization

IN order that the United Nations run smoothly the work has been divided up between various groups called "organs." Each organ has its own tasks, although sometimes they may work together.

There are six organs which make up the United Nations: The General Assembly; The Security Council; The Economic and Social Council; The Trusteeship Council; The International Court of Justice; and The Secretariat.

Working through the Economic and Social Council are groups called "agencies." They include UNESCO, WHO, FAO and others. Both the organs and the family of United Nations agencies will be described in the following chapters.

301

The General Assembly

THE General Assembly is composed of all member nations of the U.N. Each nation, no matter how big or small, has one vote. The General Assembly meets once a year, unless it is called together in an emergency. In such a case either the Security Council or a majority of the U.N. members would call the meeting.

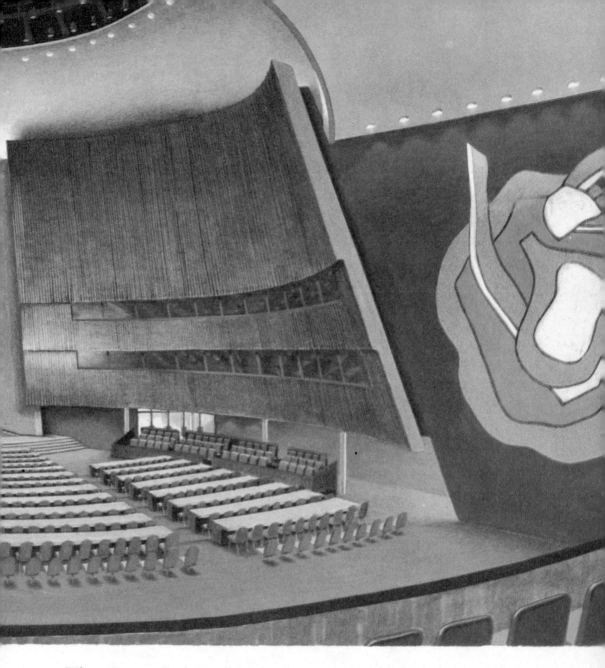

The General Assembly makes recommendations on cooperation between countries, on keeping the peace and security, on disarmament.

If the Security Council is unable to agree on any decision they may turn the matter over to the General Assembly, where it will be discussed and voted upon. On ordinary matters majority rules; if the matter is very important then a two-thirds majority is needed to pass the General Assembly.

The Security Council

THE Security Council is made up of 15 nations. Five nations
—Nationalist China, the Soviet Union, United Kingdom,
United States and France—will always be members of the
Security Council. Ten other nations are elected for two-year
periods by the General Assembly.

A measure accepted by any nine members is accepted by

the Security Council, except that if any one of the "Big Five" nations disagrees with the others it can "veto" the problem under discussion. When this happens the matter may be turned over to the General Assembly for discussion and vote, since there is no veto in the General Assembly.

The Security Council maintains the peace and tries to settle disputes between nations. If any nation disturbs the peace the Security Council tries to decide what action to take.

The Economic and Social Council

THE Economic and Social Council deals with such matters as health, education and culture and arranges studies of economic and social conditions of various nations. It tries to promote respect for human rights and freedoms, and provides assistance for countries which need such help. The Economic and Social Council makes the plans to send trained scientists, doctors, engineers and farming experts to help solve various problems which those nations could not solve by themselves.

The Trusteeship Council

COUNTRIES may come under the supervision of the United Nations Trusteeship Council in three ways: if they were under the supervision of the old League of Nations; if they were colonies of countries which were enemies of the U.N. during World War II; and if they ask to be placed under Trusteeship supervision.

Originally there were eleven trusteeship countries that came under U.N. supervision. Almost all these countries have now gained their own independence except for the Pacific Islands administered by the United States.

The International Court of Justice

THE International Court of Justice is not located in the United Nations building in New York City. It meets at The Hague, the Netherlands. It is made up of 15 judges, elected by the General Assembly and the Security Council; each judge serves a nine-year term. No two judges can be from the same country.

The International Court decides matters according to the laws used by the civilized nations of the world. It judges legal disputes and gives opinions on legal matters.

Every member nation of the U.N. can come to the International Court of Justice, and they may agree in advance to accept whatever decision the Court hands down.

308

The Secretariat

THE Secretariat is the organ which takes care of all the paper work of the United Nations. It helps in the economic and social development of nations, assists refugees, arranges for fellowships. The Secretariat is headed by a Secretary-General, whose appointment is recommended by the Security Council and voted on by the General Assembly. All members of the Secretariat are International Civil Servants. This organ works the whole year round.

The first Secretary-General of the U.N. was Trygve Lie of Norway. The second was Dag Hammarskjöld of Sweden. The third Secretary-General was U Thant of Burma.

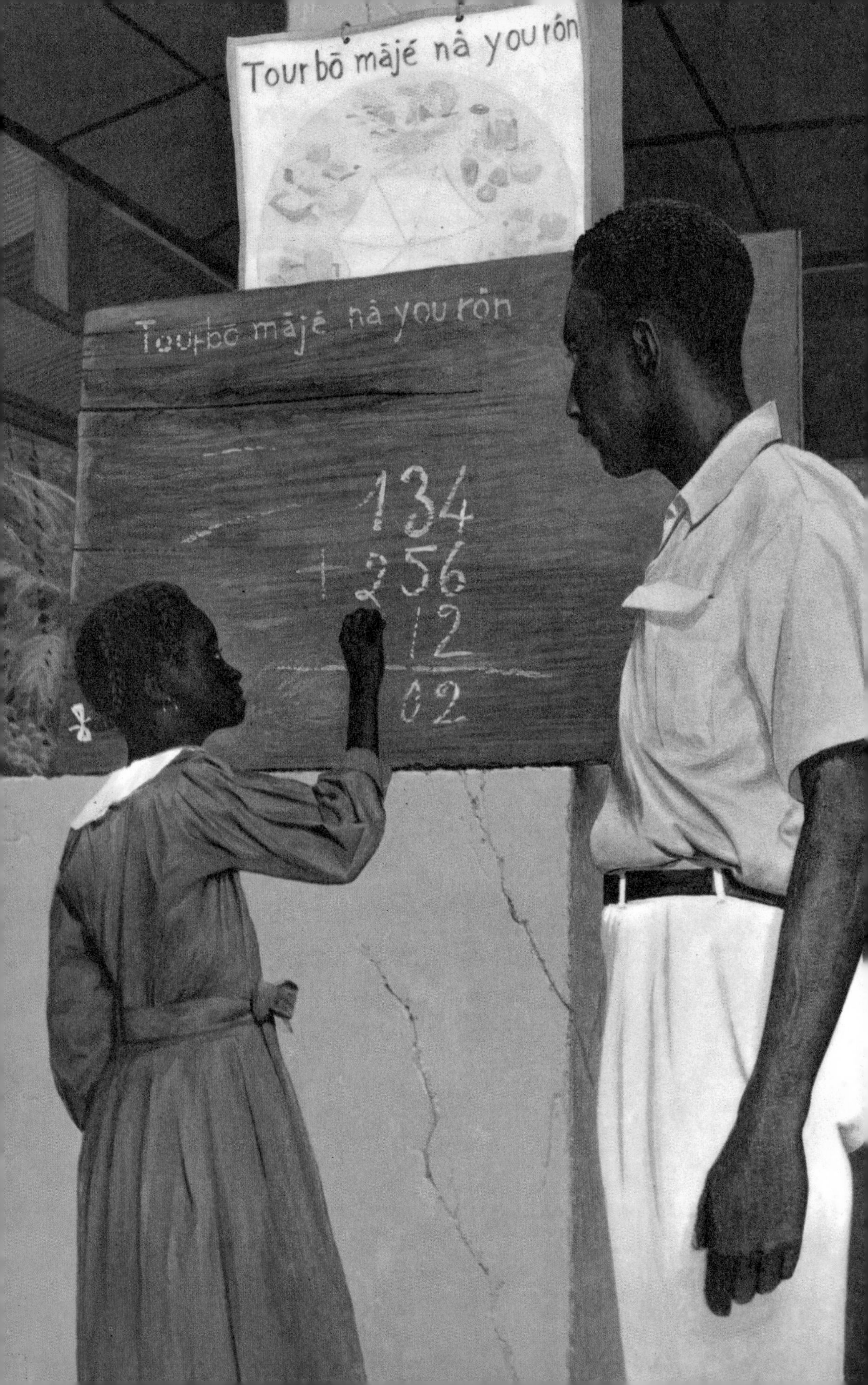

UNESCO

UNESCO—United Nations Educational, Scientific and Cultural Organization—is one of a family of specialized agencies in the United Nations. Its purpose is to promote peace by helping all nations to understand each other through education, science and knowledge of each other's culture.

UNESCO helps to stamp out illiteracy and train teachers by sending educational experts wherever they are needed. It also provides for the exchange of students from many lands; and it teaches about the United Nations, and human rights and freedoms.

UNICEF

UNICEF—United Nations Children's Fund—was established by the U.N. in 1946 to help the children who were victims of World War II. Since then UNICEF has helped care for children and mothers in more than 90 countries, and has worked with the World Health Organization to control such diseases as malaria and tuberculosis. UNICEF gives emergency aid to mothers and children in times of disaster, such as floods and earthquakes. In addition UNICEF has helped to set up maternal and child welfare centers.

UNICEF gets its money mainly from the voluntary contributions of governments and individuals from all over the world.

FAO

FAO—Food and Agriculture Organization—is another specialized agency in the United Nations family of agencies. It tries to teach countries about proper nutrition and to raise the standard of living. It also teaches nations how to develop and conserve their natural resources, such as soil, water and forests. It trains experts in stamping out animal diseases and gives help in stopping soil erosion. FAO teaches farmers of all lands how to irrigate their fields, and trains handlers of food in eliminating spoilage by insects and other pests.

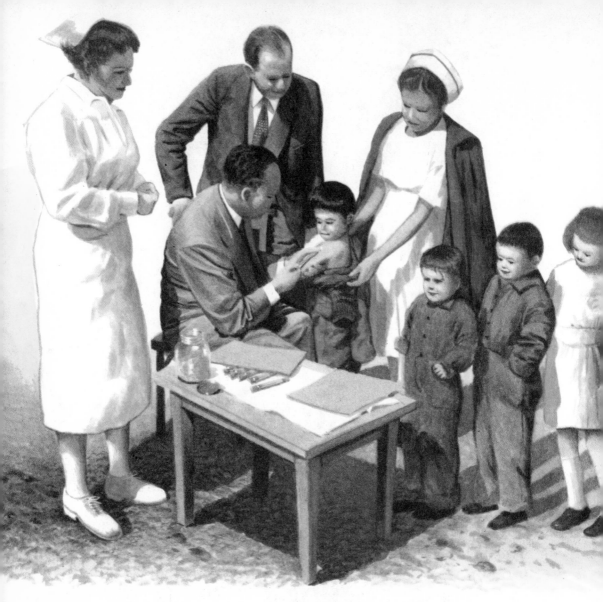

WHO

WHO—World Health Organization—is yet another in the U.N. family of specialized agencies. Its purpose is to make the peoples of the world as healthy as possible. It encourages research in drugs to fight against virus diseases, tries to eliminate malaria by teaching about pest control, and does important work against tuberculosis. WHO puts out books in many languages on scientific subjects. Whenever a new drug is discovered which combats disease, WHO passes on this information to all the nations of the world. WHO also helps to train doctors, public health officers and nurses.

Other Agencies

International Atomic Energy Agency
International Labor Organization
International Bank For Reconstruction And Development
International Development Association
International Finance Corporation
International Monetary Fund
International Civil Aviation Organization
Universal Postal Union
International Telecommunication Union
World Meteorological Organization
Intergovernmental Maritime Consultative Organization
General Agreement On Tariffs And Trade
United National Relief And Works Agency For Palestine Refugees
Office Of The United National High Commissioner For Refugees

Settling Disputes Peacefully

THE United Nations Charter lists many ways for peaceful settlements of disputes between nations, such as:

INQUIRY—a committee finds out the facts.

NEGOTIATION—peaceful talks between the disputing nations.

MEDIATION and CONCILIATION — asking another nation to help settle the dispute.

ARBITRATION—where another nation is the umpire and decides how best to solve the dispute.

The dispute can also be taken to the International Court of Justice.

Unfortunately there have been times when peaceful settlements have not been achieved, such as the case of North Korea's attack on South Korea. When that happened 15 nations banded an army together under the flag of the United Nations and drove the attackers out of South Korea, after which an armistice was signed.

The Meditation Room

ON the main floor of the General Assembly building is the Meditation Room. All religions and all nationalities may use this beautiful room to pray, and think of the tasks which they must perform. At one end of the room is a piece of Agba tree, which is a kind of mahogany from French Equatorial Africa, and is more than 300 years old. Flowers decorate this piece of tree, and a spotlight always shines on it.

There is nothing else in this quiet room except for a rug, some chairs and the flag of the United Nations.

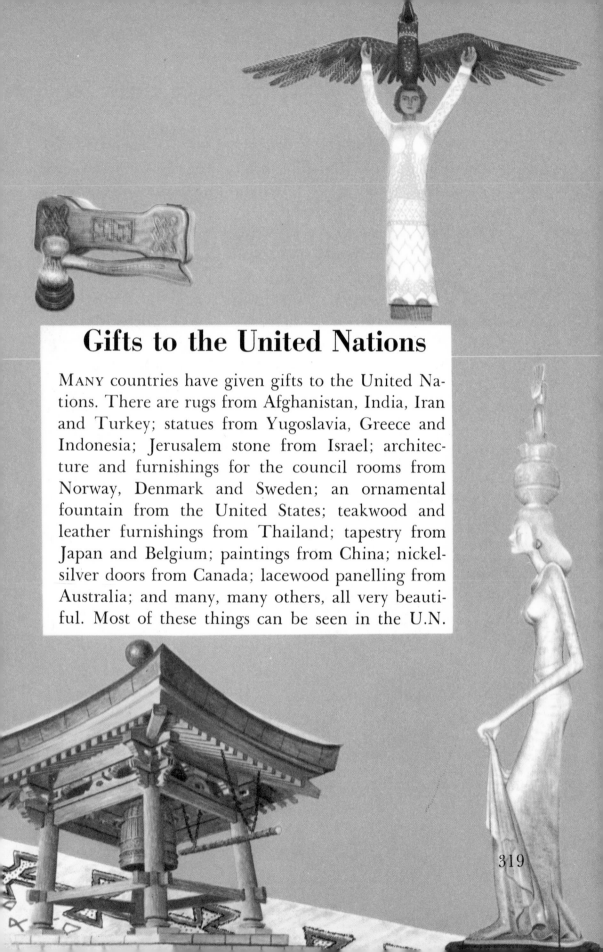

Gifts to the United Nations

MANY countries have given gifts to the United Nations. There are rugs from Afghanistan, India, Iran and Turkey; statues from Yugoslavia, Greece and Indonesia; Jerusalem stone from Israel; architecture and furnishings for the council rooms from Norway, Denmark and Sweden; an ornamental fountain from the United States; teakwood and leather furnishings from Thailand; tapestry from Japan and Belgium; paintings from China; nickel-silver doors from Canada; lacewood panelling from Australia; and many, many others, all very beautiful. Most of these things can be seen in the U.N.

The U. N. International School

THE United Nations International School in New York City was established in 1947 so that children of U.N. diplomats and staff members could be educated and still keep their own particular languages and customs.

The subjects taught there are the same as would be found in any school in the United States. However, during the morning hours, children attend classes held in their own language. In the afternoon, during such subjects as music, art and gymnasium, the students go to classes where the languages are mixed. Children from Sweden sit beside children from China, Israel, Brazil and other lands during those hours.

The U.N. school began as a nursery, and each year one grade has been added to it. At present subjects are taught through the eighth grade, but in time the classes will go right through high school.

The U.N. school is not restricted to children from foreign nations, or from U.N. families. New York City parents may send their children to the school when there is an opening.

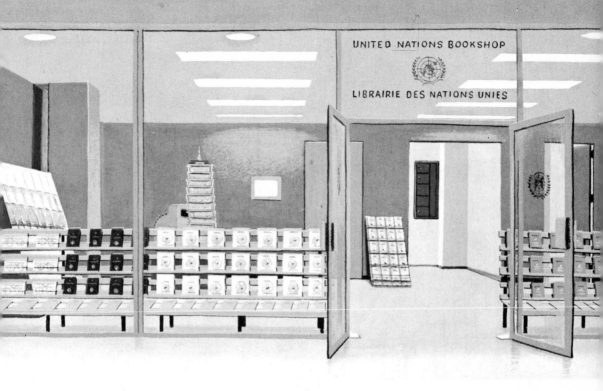

Visiting the U.N.

VISITORS to the United Nations will find that it is almost a small city in itself. There are tours through the buildings, led by charming young guides from every nation, who explain each room, answer all questions and give much information about the United Nations. A gift shop on the lower floor of the visitor's building sells articles from nearly every nation in the world. For example, there are metal plates from Israel, jewelry from Italy, Iran and France, glassware from Sweden, and dolls dressed in the costumes of all nations. There is a special post office which uses only United Nations stamps. The book shop sells books about the U.N. printed in five languages. A souvenir shop sells ash trays and other souvenirs of the U.N. There is a handsome coffee shop for snacks and soft drinks.

In addition there are lectures and lecture series held at frequent intervals throughout the day, on topics related to the United Nations.

THEY SHALL BEAT THEIR SWORDS INTO PLOWSHARES. AND THEIR SPEARS INTO PRUNING HOOKS: NATION SHALL NOT LIFT UP SWORD AGAINST NATION. NEITHER SHALL THEY LEARN WAR ANY MORE

322

ANCIENT
AND
MODERN
WONDERS

The Pyramid
Walls of Babylon
Olympian Zeus
Temple of Artemis
Mausoleum
Roman Forum
Colossus
Pharos of Alexandria
Sphinx
Tower of Pisa
Sistine Chapel
Great Wall of China
Palace of Versailles
Taj Mahal
Grand Coulee Dam
Palace in Lhasa, Tibet
Eiffel Tower
Tower of London and Tower
  Bridge
Suez and Panama Canals
Mount Rushmore
Paintings
George Washington Bridge
Empire State Building
Travel Wonders
Electronic Marvels
Space Satellite and the
  Nautilus
Reactor
Tunnels and Subways

THE world has many wonders made by man. Who can tell which are the greatest? In ancient times Seven Wonders of the World were listed—the Pyramids, the Gardens of Babylon, the Temple of Artemis, the statue of Zeus at Olympia, the Mausoleum, the Colossus of Rhodes, the Pharos of Alexandria. What would the admirers of these structures say if they could see the Empire State Building, the George Washington Bridge, or even the subway that millions in our big cities ride in every day?

And why must only buildings and monuments be listed—are not other works of man also worthy of wonder? Surely a painting by Michelangelo is wonderful! Perhaps the greatest wonders of our time are those which add to the value of living— our automobiles, airplanes, television, and now atomic energy, which promises so much for the earth we know and even space beyond. These are the stories of some Wonders of the World, ancient and modern.

The Pyramid

THE Great Pyramid is the only one of the Seven Wonders of the Ancient World that still stands. It was built at the order of the Pharaoh Cheops, who once ruled Egypt. More than 100,000 slaves labored for twenty years to build it. They had no machines, not even carts—all the work was done by human strength alone. Yet each huge block was so well laid that the Pyramid has stood for 5,000 years.

Walls of Babylon

In Babylon, one of the great cities of the ancient world, was a famous garden which amazed visitors for hundreds of years. It was called the Hanging Gardens, because it was built along arches and towers and looked like a wall of flowers and green shrubs. The garden was kept alive by a hidden pool on the highest terrace, from which the water was drawn to appear in a series of fountains. The gardens were built by King Nebuchadnezzar, who is mentioned in the Bible as the cruel conqueror of Jerusalem.

Olympian Zeus

THE greatest god of the ancient Greeks was Zeus, whom the Romans called Jupiter. The greatest statue of this god was at Olympia, where the famous Olympian Games were played in his honor. The statue was 40 feet high—about seven times as high as a man is tall—and was made of marble, decorated with pure gold and ivory. After 1,000 years, an earthquake tumbled it down.

Temple of Artemis

ONE of the most famous temples of the ancient world stood for 600 years in Ephesus, a great city of Syria. The temple was sacred to Artemis, also called Diana, goddess of the moon. The finest sculptors and painters of Greece decorated this beautiful building, which was destroyed by the barbaric Goths. Only a few pieces of statues and columns remained, to be dug up by modern scientists.

328

Mausoleum

Few remember the tiny kingdom of Caria, which once flourished in what is now southwestern Turkey. But the name of its king, Mausolus, is known because of the word "mausoleum," a massive tomb. The original Mausoleum, built in memory of this king by his widow, Queen Artemisia, was so magnificent that it was one of the Wonders of the Ancient World.

The Roman Forum

EVERY ancient city had a great square where people met to buy and sell goods, hear speeches, see shows, or just talk together. Rome, the greatest ancient city, had the finest square, or Forum. Of all the stately buildings and platforms, only ruins remain, but it is still exciting to walk among the columns where crowds of cheering Romans once stood while Cicero and Caesar made their famous speeches.

Colossus

RHODES, an island near Greece, was one of the richest and busiest towns of the ancient world. Standing across the entrance to its big harbor, was a huge statue of the sun god Helios, famous as the Colossus of Rhodes. Although ships sailed beneath these giant feet, the Colossus was not as large as our Statue of Liberty.

Pharos of Alexandria

THE most famous lighthouse in ancient times was the Pharos, built by Alexander the Great. It guarded the harbor of Alexandria, in Egypt, and its light atop a high tower could be seen for sixty miles. To keep the beacon shining, the lighthouse keepers had to feed a bright fire unceasingly, for the powerful electric lamps behind glass lenses used in our lighthouses were not yet invented.

Sphinx

NEAR the Great Pyramid in Egypt stands a huge sculptured rock called the Sphinx. The face is that of a man, perhaps the Pharaoh Khafre who had it built almost 5,000 years ago. But the body is that of a lion, and between its great stone paws is a small temple. Since no one knows exactly why the Sphinx was built, it remains a symbol of mystery—a riddle.

Tower of Pisa

NEAR the cathedral of Pisa, in Italy, is an eight-story bell tower known as the Leaning Tower. Soon after it was built, it began to shift on its foundation, and it slowly tipped to one side. Despite repairs it will continue to stand at an angle as it did when the scientist Galileo dropped a light and a heavy object from its highest story to prove that both fall with the same speed.

Sistine Chapel

THE Sistine Chapel in the Vatican was named after Pope Sixtus IV, who had it built. It is the private chapel of the Pope, and also a famous treasury of art, for the finest Italian artists painted its walls, and Michelangelo's picture-story of scenes from the Old Testament covers its entire ceiling.

Great Wall of China

FROM the seacoast of China to the mountains of the Far West, for a distance of 1,500 miles, the Great Wall stands as it did 2,000 years ago. Its height is more than twenty feet and its top is wide enough for a roadway. For centuries it was patrolled by soldiers, who also farmed land near their posts. The Great Wall guarded China from the Huns, who once lived in Mongolia, to the north. The Huns have disappeared, but the Great Wall remains.

Palace of Versailles

Louis the Fourteenth was known as the Sun King of France, because of the splendor of his court. At Versailles, near Paris, Louis built the most costly and most magnificent palace in all Europe. It could house 10,000 people, but only the King's friends lived there and strolled in its beautiful gardens, with their fountains, orange trees, strange flowers, and marble statues. Now this royal playground belongs to the people of France, and thousands visit it each year.

Taj Mahal

ONE of the world's most beautiful buildings is the tomb built by Shah Jehan, emperor of India, for his beloved wife—the Taj Mahal. It stands on a high terrace overlooking a long, clear pool, in which its gleaming dome and graceful arches are reflected. The pool has cypress trees on three of its sides,

338

and at the end is the Taj Mahal and four slender towers, one
at each corner of the terrace. The dome and walls are made of
marble and alabaster, in places so delicately thin that daylight
dimly reaches the vault in the interior. On the outside of the
walls, inlaid in precious gems, are writings from the sacred
book of Islam, the Koran.

Grand Coulee Dam

THE Columbia River winds through the state of Washington on its way from the Rocky Mountains to the sea. It is stopped in its course by one of the world's largest structures—the Grand Coulee Dam. Here the water is made to flow where it is needed by farmers and sent through turbines where its force becomes electric power.

340

Palace in Lhasa, Tibet

THE religious leader of the people of Tibet is the Dalai Lama. His palace, the Potala, is in the city of Lhasa, high in the Himalayas. This palace is eleven stories high, looks like a fort, and is painted red and white. Its golden roof can be seen from far off.

Eiffel Tower

The Eiffel Tower was built to attract visitors to Paris for the World's Fair of 1889. It is still popular with tourists, but is also used for broadcasting and weather observation. Elevators reach each of the three platforms, the highest 906 feet above the street, but from there a spiral stairway goes to the top, 984 feet high. For 42 years the Eiffel Tower was the world's tallest structure.

Tower of London and Tower Bridge

THE Tower of London is really a great fortress with many
towers. The oldest is the White Tower, built in the time of
William the Conqueror, 900 years ago. The English crown
jewels are in Wakefield Tower. Bloody Tower was a place of
execution. Part of the area is surrounded by a moat, now dry,
and St. Thomas's Tower borders on the River Thames. The
Tower Bridge across the river is downstream from the older
and better known London Bridge.

343

The Suez Canal

THE 100-mile Suez Canal separating Asia from Africa made possible much shorter trips between Europe and the Far East.

The Panama Canal

BEFORE the Panama Canal opened in 1914, ships bound from New York to San Francisco sailed around the tip of South America, a distance 8,000 miles longer than the present route. The 40-mile canal joined the Atlantic and Pacific oceans.

Mount Rushmore

THE faces of four great Americans—George Washington, Thomas Jefferson, Theodore Roosevelt, and Abraham Lincoln—were carved out of the granite side of Mount Rushmore in South Dakota by the sculptor, Gutzon Borglum. Each face is about 60 feet from forehead to chin, so colossal that they can be seen from a distance of sixty miles.

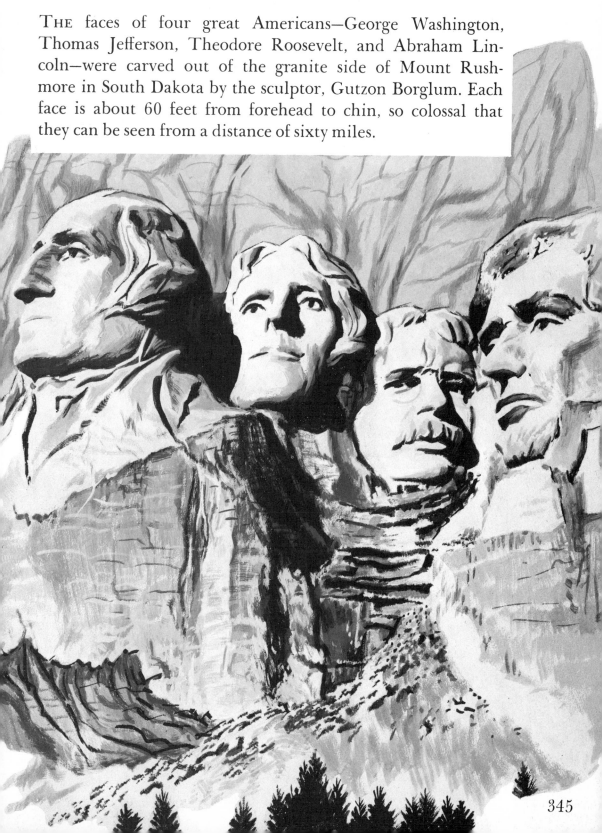

Paintings

GREAT paintings still tell in lovely color and form what men, some of them long dead, saw in the world about them. They tell more than the finest color photographs, for the feeling and imagination of the artists change the real world as if by magic. No one will ever again see through the eyes of Rembrandt or Van Gogh, but their pictures show us what they saw.

The George Washington Bridge

THE George Washington Bridge, crossing the Hudson River to New York City, is 4,760 feet long. It carries an average of 100,000 automobiles a day.

The Empire State Building

THE world famous Empire State Building is 1,250 feet and 102 stories above street level. From the tower you can see for 50 miles.

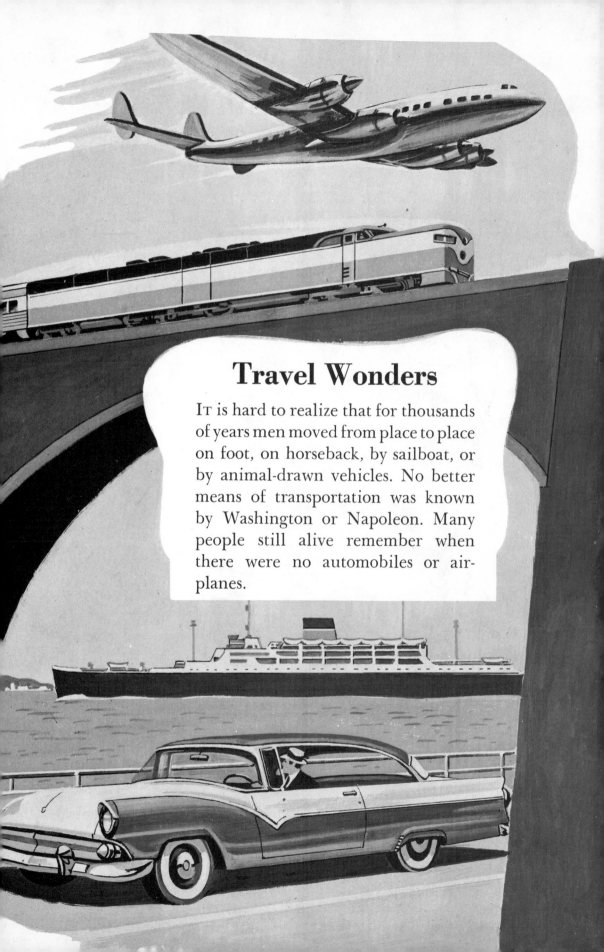

Travel Wonders

It is hard to realize that for thousands of years men moved from place to place on foot, on horseback, by sailboat, or by animal-drawn vehicles. No better means of transportation was known by Washington or Napoleon. Many people still alive remember when there were no automobiles or airplanes.

Electronic Marvels

TRY to imagine what the world would be like without telephones, radio or television broadcasting, phonographs, or even telegraph. It would be a dull world for most of us. Yet less than 100 years ago not one of them existed. It is exciting to imagine what wonders the next 100 years may bring. Whatever they will be, people will find it hard to believe we did not have them.

Space Satellite

SURELY the greatest wonder of modern times has been man's conquest of space. In 1957 Russia's Sputnik satellite escaped the bonds of Earth; a little more than a decade later, in 1969, the United States landed two men on the moon—the first in a series of momentous moon landings and explorations.

Nautilus and Polaris

THE first atom-powered submarine was the U.S.S. *Nautilus*, launched in 1955. It was named after Captain Nemo's submarine in the famous scientific adventure story *Twenty Thousand Leagues Under the Sea,* written in 1870 by Jules Verne.

Atom-powered submarines have many advantages over the older submarines. They not only travel longer distances at higher speeds—they also have much more room for men and equipment because of the space saved by substituting a small reactor for the big diesel engines of the older submarines.

The *Polaris,* the first of the space missiles, was successfully tested in 1960.

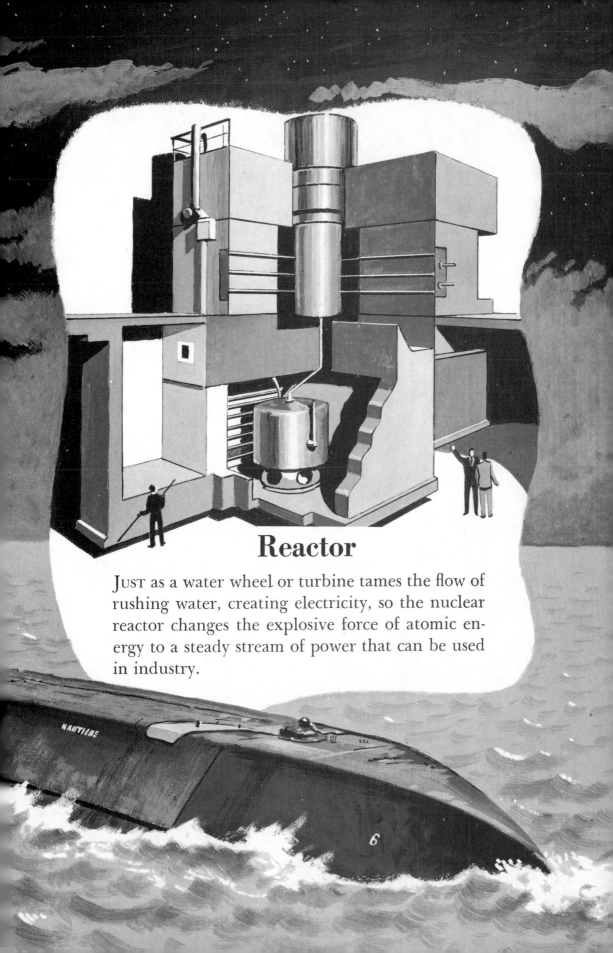

Reactor

JUST as a water wheel or turbine tames the flow of rushing water, creating electricity, so the nuclear reactor changes the explosive force of atomic energy to a steady stream of power that can be used in industry.

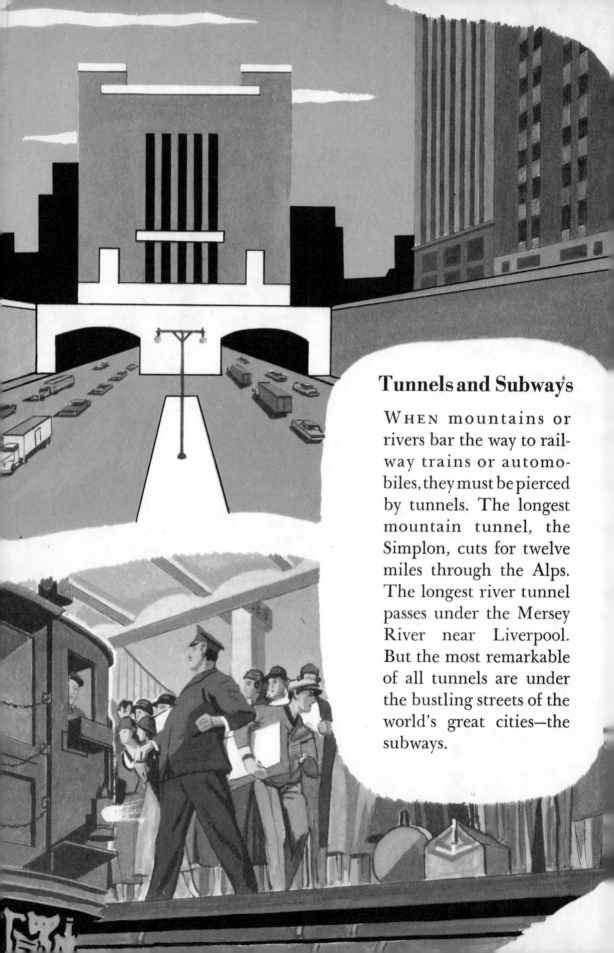

Tunnels and Subways

WHEN mountains or rivers bar the way to railway trains or automobiles, they must be pierced by tunnels. The longest mountain tunnel, the Simplon, cuts for twelve miles through the Alps. The longest river tunnel passes under the Mersey River near Liverpool. But the most remarkable of all tunnels are under the bustling streets of the world's great cities—the subways.

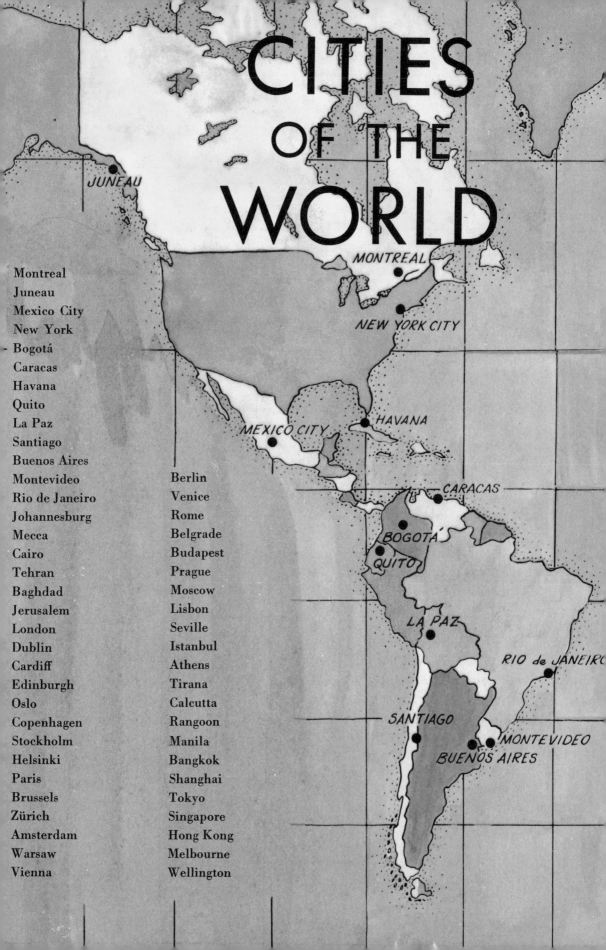

CITIES OF THE WORLD

Montreal
Juneau
Mexico City
New York
Bogotá
Caracas
Havana
Quito
La Paz
Santiago
Buenos Aires
Montevideo
Rio de Janeiro
Johannesburg
Mecca
Cairo
Tehran
Baghdad
Jerusalem
London
Dublin
Cardiff
Edinburgh
Oslo
Copenhagen
Stockholm
Helsinki
Paris
Brussels
Zürich
Amsterdam
Warsaw
Vienna

Berlin
Venice
Rome
Belgrade
Budapest
Prague
Moscow
Lisbon
Seville
Istanbul
Athens
Tirana
Calcutta
Rangoon
Manila
Bangkok
Shanghai
Tokyo
Singapore
Hong Kong
Melbourne
Wellington

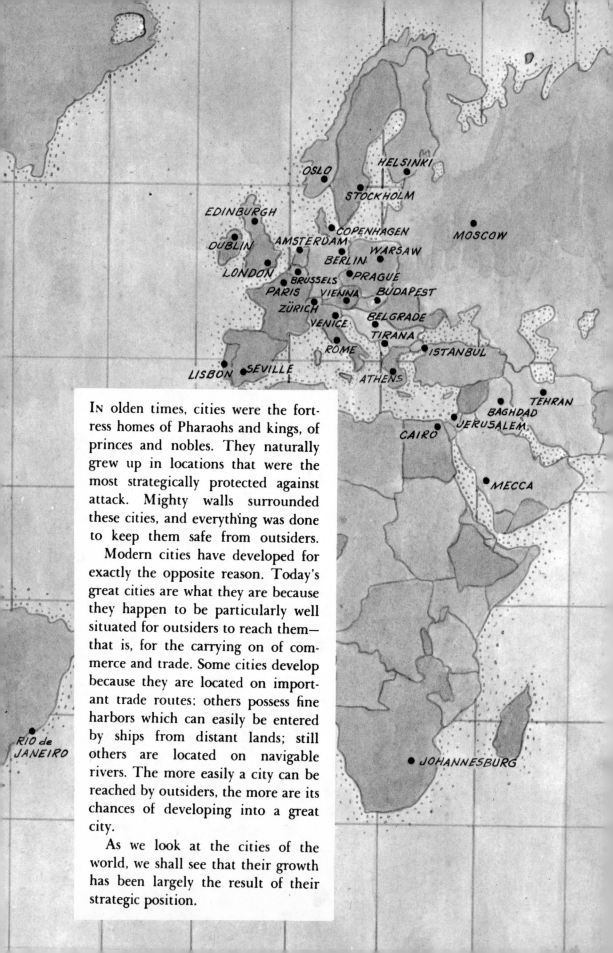

IN olden times, cities were the fortress homes of Pharaohs and kings, of princes and nobles. They naturally grew up in locations that were the most strategically protected against attack. Mighty walls surrounded these cities, and everything was done to keep them safe from outsiders.

Modern cities have developed for exactly the opposite reason. Today's great cities are what they are because they happen to be particularly well situated for outsiders to reach them— that is, for the carrying on of commerce and trade. Some cities develop because they are located on important trade routes; others possess fine harbors which can easily be entered by ships from distant lands; still others are located on navigable rivers. The more easily a city can be reached by outsiders, the more are its chances of developing into a great city.

As we look at the cities of the world, we shall see that their growth has been largely the result of their strategic position.

Montreal

THE largest city in Canada is Montreal. More than two million people live in greater Montreal, and so many of them speak the French language that it is the second largest French-speaking city in the world.

Juneau

JUNEAU, the capital of Alaska, is remarkable for its long, narrow streets. The city is only a few blocks wide, because it is situated along a steep mountain slope. Juneau was founded by gold prospectors in 1880.

Mexico City

MEXICO CITY was originally settled by Aztec Indians about 1325, and for two hundred years was the capital of the great Aztec Empire. Today, it is the capital of Mexico.

357

New York City

NEW YORK has close to 8 million people. What New York lacks in width it more than makes up for in height. Its skyscrapers are the tallest and most numerous of any city anywhere.

Largely because of its splendid geographical location and its immense harbor, New York outranks all other U.S. ports. The Port of New York handles nearly half the na-

tion's yearly imports and exports. The city is rich in industries, especially in the manufacture of textiles. Its Wall Street is the leading financial district of the country. New York is an important cultural and art center.

In the field of amusements, New York is unsurpassed. In fact, Manhattan Island, home of the "Great White Way" along Broadway, takes its name from the Indian expression for "fun-loving island" (*Man-a-hat-ta-nink*).

Bogotá

FEW cities in the world are closer to the equator than Bogotá, the capital of Colombia. Yet this city is situated so high above sea level that its people enjoy a cool climate.

Caracas

CARACAS is the chief city and capital of the United States of Venezuela. Pictured here is the plaza of the *Centro Bolívar*. It is Caracas' Radio City and is three times larger than New York's.

Havana

HAVANA, the most important city of the West Indies, is the capital and major seaport of Cuba. Shown here is the famous fortress, the Morro Castle, which stands at the entrance to the city's marvelous harbor.

Quito

QUITO, one of the oldest cities in the Western world, is the capital of the South American Republic of Ecuador.

La Paz

THE capital of Bolivia, La Paz, lies in a very deep valley, yet it ranks as the world's highest capital city. That is because the valley itself is so far above sea level.

Santiago

SANTIAGO is the capital of the Republic of Chile. Because of the danger of earthquakes, the houses in this city are usually one story high.

361

Buenos Aires

The largest city in South America is Buenos Aires, the capital of Argentina. Next to New York, this modern city exports and imports more goods than any city in the world. Founded by the Spaniards in 1536, Buenos Aires is a Spanish expression for "good airs,". so called because the early settlers believed its atmosphere was particularly healthful.

Montevideo

Montevideo is the capital, largest city, and main port of the small republic of Uruguay. Montevideo has more than a third of the entire population of Uruguay. The name of the city is Portuguese and means "I see a mountain" (*Monte vid'eu*) an expression attributed to one of Magellan's sailors upon sighting a hill along this part of the South American coast in 1514.

Rio de Janeiro

RIO DE JANEIRO, the former capital, is the largest city in Brazil. Portuguese explorers sailed into the magnificent island-dotted bay that fronts the site of this city on New Year's Day, 1502. They mistook it for the mouth of some large river and so named it "River of January" (*Rio de Janeiro*).

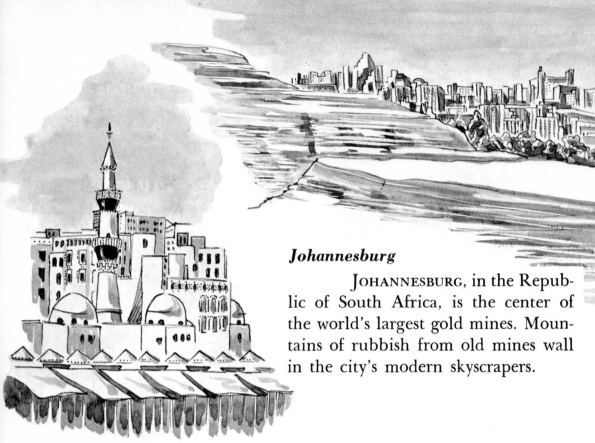

Johannesburg

JOHANNESBURG, in the Republic of South Africa, is the center of the world's largest gold mines. Mountains of rubbish from old mines wall in the city's modern skyscrapers.

Mecca

MECCA, the Holy City of followers of the Islamic religion, is located in Saudi Arabia. Here Mohammed was born and here stands the Great Mosque which shelters the shrine so sacred to Muslims. The faithful believe that angels constructed this shrine long before the creation of man.

Cairo

THE largest city on the continent of Africa is Cairo, the capital of the United Arab Republic (Egypt). Cairo is situated on the eastern bank of the Nile River.

Tehran

TEHRAN is tne capital of one of the world's oldest countries—the ancient kingdom of Persia, now known as Iran.

Baghdad

BAGHDAD, the ancient and fabulous city of the Arabian Nights, is the modern capital of Iraq.

Jerusalem

JERUSALEM is the "Holy City" of three great world religions—Judaism, Christianity and Islam. Jerusalem is also the capital of Israel.

365

London

THE historic city of London is the heart of the British Commonwealth. It is the capital and chief port of Great Britain. Greater London has close to 8 million inhabitants. It includes many, many suburbs and covers the wide expanse of 693 square miles.

Strictly defined, however, London proper or London City, is only 1 square mile, with a population of less than 5,000.

This "city within the city" goes back to the times of the Romans, when it was a walled-in fortress. The walls were rebuilt in medieval

The mighty bell of Big Ben, the clock in the tower of the Houses of Parliament, weighs more than 13 tons. Big Ben is used as the time signal for all British radio stations.

This is Tower Bridge, a massive drawbridge crossing the River Thames. It takes just one and a half minutes to raise and lower the bridge for ships to pass through.

366

times. From here England's great kings ruled and in this small area are located many of London's historic buildings. But over the years, as London developed into the world's leading commercial and governmental center, it needed more and more room. Unlike New York, which has expanded upward in the form of tall skyscrapers, London expanded outward over the surrounding countryside.

Dublin

DUBLIN, the seaport capital of Ireland, is the home of the famous Abbey Theatre where so many of the world's greatest playwrights had their first productions. The city has a little over half a million people.

Cardiff

IN the first century A.D., Cardiff was a Roman stronghold. Today, it is the largest city in Wales, with a population of 248,000.

Edinburgh

EDINBURGH, the capital of Scotland, is one of the most ancient cities in the British Empire. Edinburgh Castle, pictured here, is built on a massive rock and is now used as a barracks.

Oslo

Copenhagen

THE four cities pictured on this page are the capitals and chief centers of the great seafaring nations of northwestern Europe. Oslo is the capital of Norway, Copenhagen of Denmark, Stockholm of Sweden, and Helsinki of Finland. Helsinki is the smallest of the four; Greater Copenhagen is the largest. Copenhagen means "Merchants' Haven."

Stockholm

Helsinki

Paris

MORE people visit Paris than any other city in the world. It is the capital of France. Greater Paris has close to 6,500,000 inhabitants. A thousand years ago, Paris was just a fort on a small island in the Seine River. The modern city has grown up on both sides of this river which is crossed by 30 bridges. The business and wealthy living quarters are on the north or right side of the river. On the Left Bank is the colorful Latin Quarter where students and artists live. Many years ago, when universities taught only in Latin, the students would walk about the streets singing Latin songs, which

is how the Latin Quarter took its name.

On the island where once stood the original Paris is one of the city's great landmarks—the Cathedral of Notre Dame, with its many hideous-faced gargoyles. In medieval times, it was believed that gargoyles frightened away evil spirits.

Brussels

BRUSSELS is more than a thousand years old. It is the capital and largest city of Belgium, with a population of well over one million.

Zürich

ZÜRICH was once a prehistoric village of lake dwellers. It is now an industrial center and the largest city of Switzerland. The city has almost half a million people.

Amsterdam

OFTEN called the "Venice of the North," the Dutch city of Amsterdam is built on about 70 islands which are connected by 500 bridges. Its buildings rest on a foundation of wooden piles.

Warsaw

THE capital city of Poland, Warsaw dates back to the Middle Ages. From the beginning, its people have kept up a heroic struggle against invasion by powerful neighbors.

Vienna

VIENNA is the capital of Austria. The magnificent building on the right was built early in the 18th century as a thanksgiving offering when the city was freed of the "Black Death" plague.

Berlin

BERLIN is not a young city. It was a small river town about the time that Columbus discovered America. Berlin did not become a truly great city until late in the 19th century when it was chosen as the capital of Germany.

Venice

THE celebrated Italian city of Venice is built entirely on piles driven into 118 small islands. There are few streets in this city. The islands are connected by a grand total of 400 bridges. The people of Venice travel in gondolas and in motor boats.

374

Rome

ST. PETER'S Basilica in Rome, Italy, is the world's largest Christian church. In ancient times, this was the site of the famous Circus of Nero where Christians were martyred. The population of modern Rome, the capital of Italy, is 1,750,000.

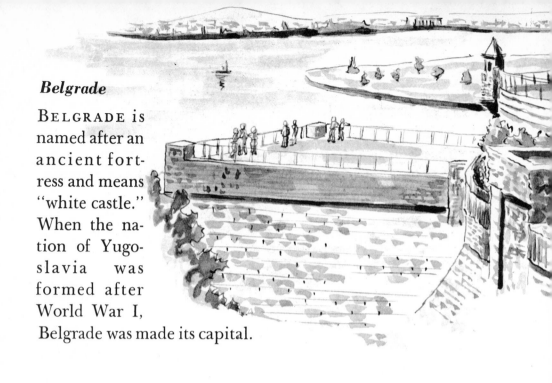

Belgrade

BELGRADE is named after an ancient fortress and means "white castle." When the nation of Yugoslavia was formed after World War I, Belgrade was made its capital.

Budapest

ONCE upon a time two towns faced each other across the Danube River. One town was named Buda, the other Pest. The two towns united in 1872 to form the modern capital of Hungary—Budapest. The bridges that span this dual city are among the most beautiful in Europe.

Prague

THE lofty towers of Prague's ancient palaces and churches make this city look like a great cathedral. The capital of Czechoslovakia, Prague has nearly a million people.

Moscow

Moscow is the capital of the Soviet Union. Greater Moscow has a population of 7,000,000. The heart of the city is the Kremlin, pictured here. *Kremlin* is the Russian word for "fortress." The Kremlin in Moscow houses the main offices of the Russian government.

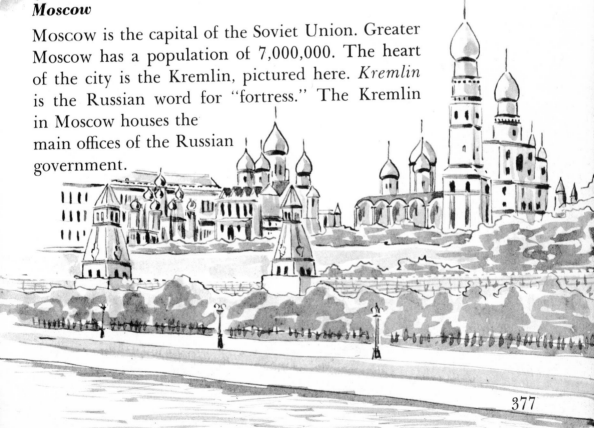

Lisbon

LISBON, the capital of Portugal, is a very hilly city. Towering caged elevators, like the eight-story one pictured here, save tiresome climbing.

Seville

SPANISH Seville is a city of magnificent carnivals, of colorful fairs and exciting bull fights. The people of Seville still dress in vivid costumes and have somehow managed to keep alive the picturesque ways of life followed by their ancestors. Seville is the fourth largest city in Spain. Madrid, the capital, is the largest.

Istanbul

THE port of Istanbul is Turkey's leading city. Throughout the ages it has commanded a strategic position at the crossroads where the continents of Europe and Asia come together. Istanbul used to be known as Constantinople.

Athens

THE majestic ruins high on the Acropolis, overlooking the modern city of Athens, are a magnificent reminder of the city's rich history. More than half a million people live in Athens, which is the capital of Greece.

Tirana

TIRANA is the capital of the small republic of Albania. It is a city of about 60,000 people, of many majestic mosques, of gorgeous gardens and splendid olive groves.

379

Calcutta

CALCUTTA is the most industrialized city of India. However, Bombay (with nearly three million people) is India's largest city. Both are seaport cities. Another seaport on the Indian Peninsula is Karachi. This city, though not as large as either Calcutta or Bombay, is important because it is the capital of the Republic of Pakistan.

Rangoon

RANGOON, the capital of Burma, is another great Oriental port. A war in 1753 destroyed the city of Rangoon. It was rebuilt and given its present name, which stands for "end of the war." To Burmese people, this fanciful lion is the mythical symbol of their country.

Manila

UNTIL 1945, Manila was the capital of the Republic of the Philippines. But the city was so badly damaged during World War II that the capital was moved to one of the suburbs, Quezon. However, Manila is still the largest city of the Philippines. More than 2,000,000 people live in Greater Manila.

Bangkok

BANGKOK is the capital of Thailand (the kingdom of Siam). So many rivers and canals run through Bangkok that the city is usually referred to as the "Venice of the East." It has more than 400 Buddhist temples, like the spiraled one pictured on the right.

Shanghai

SHANGHAI was a small fishing village only a hundred years ago. In 1842, the British forced China to open it to foreign trade. British, French and American businessmen began building settlements which grew up with unbelievable speed. Today, Shanghai is the largest city in China.

Tokyo

TOKYO is the capital of Japan. It is a more modern city than Shanghai. A disastrous earthquake and fire in 1923 ruined a very large part of Tokyo. The city was built up once more, but along modern Western lines. These are second-hand bookstores along the city's "Bookstore Alley." There are over 11 million people in Greater Tokyo. It is the largest city in the world.

Singapore

SINGAPORE, on the Malay Peninsula, is one of the world's leading seaport cities. It is ideally located on the trade routes from Europe and India to the Far East. It is called the "Gateway to the Orient."

Hong Kong

HONG KONG lies on the island of the same name off the coast of southern China. About a hundred years ago the island was the home of only a few scattered fishermen and pirates. Today, Hong Kong, which is also known as the city of Victoria, has more than three-quarters of a million people. The words *Hong Kong* translated mean "beautiful lagoon."

Melbourne

MELBOURNE did not become an important city until 1851, when gold fields were discovered on the city's outskirts. Overnight its population shot upward. Today, Greater Melbourne is the second largest city on the vast continent of Australia, with more than one and a half million people. The largest city in Australia is Sydney.

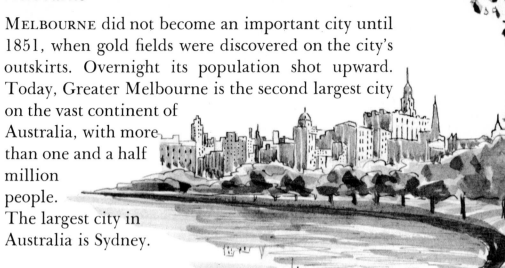

Wellington

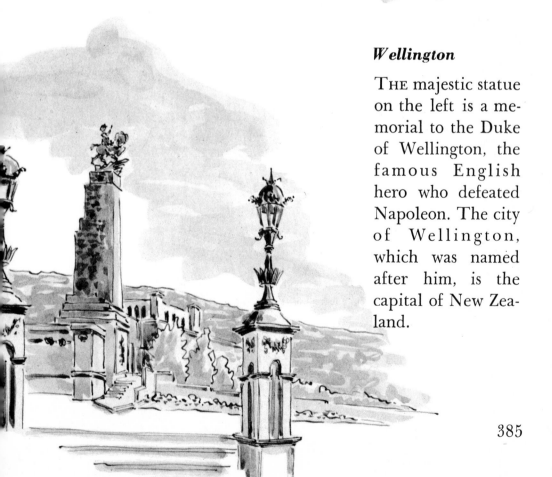

THE majestic statue on the left is a memorial to the Duke of Wellington, the famous English hero who defeated Napoleon. The city of Wellington, which was named after him, is the capital of New Zealand.

385

CALCUTTA

RANGOON

BANGKOK

SINGAPORE

SHANGHAI

HONGKONG

MANILA

TOKYO

MELBOURNE

WELLINGTO

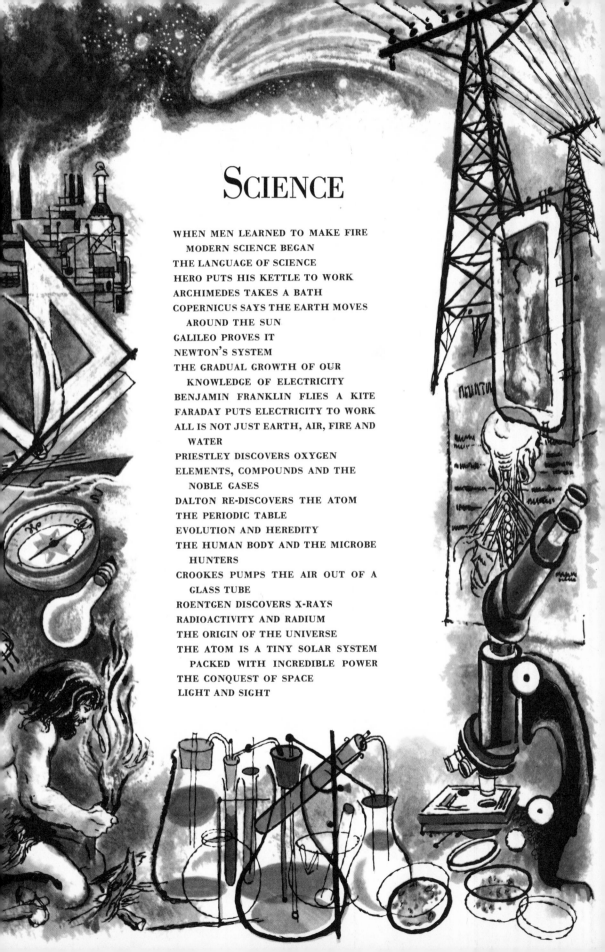

SCIENCE

WE have learned to look with confidence to our scientists in the expectation that they will ultimately solve all our problems. This confidence is not misplaced. They have presented us with numberless wonders in medicine to cure our ills, in devices like radio, television and the airplane to make life more pleasurable, and with explanations for many of nature's miracles.

Daily living with them soon reduces the awe we feel for these inventions. We gradually become accustomed to them. But let us not forget that each discovery came into being because somebody originally was curious about something that puzzled him. He thought long and hard before a brilliant flash of insight came to him. Then he had the courage to try out his bright idea.

Even the discovery of the use of fire, the invention of the wheel and the explanation for lightning came about in this way.

Let us never stop being curious.

When Men Learned to Make Fire
Modern Science Began

PRIMITIVE man must have been frightened by fire at first. He may have seen a tree burst into flame after a loud and fearful thunderclap and flash of lightning. He probably was terrified to observe the fire and smoke coming from a volcano in eruption.

It took a brave man of early times to come close enough to a fire to learn how warm and comfortable it could be. Thousands of years must have elapsed before man learned how to kindle a fire by himself and how to feed it dry leaves and sticks to keep it burning.

Slowly man learned many uses for fire. With it he cooked his food, baked clay to make pottery, burned the insides out of trees to make dugout canoes, and gradually improved his tools and weapons.

The use of fire today is indispensable. It heats our dwellings, purifies our metals, and drives our mightiest engines and our speediest jet planes.

The Language of Science

IT all began because of the great need for learning how to count. Ancient man wanted to know things like how many sheep there were in his flock and how many warriors were in an approaching enemy band. Most primitive tribesmen knew how to count only up to two or three. Beyond that they had to use the word "many."

About five thousand years ago Egyptians began to make a mark on a stone for every day that passed, and they worked out a way to count these marks. Later the Arabs, the Romans, and the Hindus also worked out ways of writing numbers and we still use many of these same systems today.

The ancient Greeks improved upon early arithmetic by adding a reasoning method called "logical proof." Euclid, one of these early Greek thinkers, wrote a book entitled "Elements of Geometry" about lines, circles and angles and their measurement, in which he gave logical proof for all his statements.

Since then men have made great progress in counting and in geometry. We have found new uses and names for numbers like zero which early people did not use or understand. We have found new methods besides addition, subtraction, multiplication and division for working with numbers. We have come to use all these methods which we call "mathematics" to describe and explain the workings of astronomy, business, engineering, military affairs, and of all sciences.

Mathematics, the tool and the language of science, has come to be known as the "Queen of the Sciences."

391

Hero Puts His Kettle to Work

IT was the fire under his kettle that enabled Hero, a Greek scientist of the 2nd century B.C., to get the idea for a steam engine. As he watched the fire make the water boil, he saw the steam lift the lid off the kettle. That gave him an idea. If steam could lift the lid, it could be put to work doing other things. He built the first steam engine. It was only a toy—there was no practical use for it, since all the work could be done by slaves—so it was soon forgotten.

It was not until 1769 that a really practical steam engine was invented by James Watt. In the next 50 years steam engines were put in factories. They were put on wheels and called locomotives. They were put inside ships, which then were called "steamers." Even atomic power generators are "steam engines," since atomic energy converts water to steamy water vapor, which then runs the electric generators.

392

Archimedes Takes a Bath

ARCHIMEDES knew when he stepped into his brimful bathtub that only as much water would run over the edge of the tub as his body would displace.

But would any water overflow from a brimful bathtub if he floated a block of wood in it? He knew that part of the block would be immersed below the surface, but the rest would remain high and dry above the surface of the water. He imagined that the immersed portion of the block of wood must displace some water, which having no other place to go, would spill over the sides of the tub.

But wouldn't a block of light cork float higher than a heavier block of wood of the same size and displace less water?

"Eureka!" he shouted. A flash of insight had come to him. The weight of water displaced must exactly equal the weight of the floating object.

Archimedes' discovery is now used in the design of ships, submarines and even airships.

Copernicus Says the Earth Moves Around the Sun

WHEN Copernicus was born in 1473, most educated people believed that the earth was the center of the universe and that all the heavenly bodies revolved about the earth.

His mathematical and astronomical studies convinced Copernicus, however, that the apparent motions of the sun and the stars could best be explained in another way. In reality, he stated, the earth rotated on its axis at the same time that it revolved around the sun. The stars, he thought, were extremely distant and occupied fixed positions in space.

It took a great deal of courage for Copernicus to oppose the authorities of his day. However, in the year of his death, 1543, his book, "Concerning the Revolutions of the Celestial Spheres," was published. It explained his ideas and eventually convinced most other scholars.

Galileo Proves It

GALILEO (1564-1642) claimed that both light and heavy objects tend to fall to earth at the same rates of speed.

To prove his claim Galileo climbed to the top of the sky-scraper of his day, the Leaning Tower of Pisa, with two cannon-balls of greatly different weight. Before witnesses he dropped both iron balls simultaneously from the top of the tower. They struck the earth together, proving his claim.

The reason why leaves flutter downward so slowly is that they meet the resistance of the air. Behaving somewhat like the outspread wings of a gliding bird, they take many short glides before they alight.

Using a homemade telescope Galileo carefully observed the heavens. His observations and mathematical computations soon convinced him that Copernicus was right in saying that the earth rotates about the sun.

Newton's System

THOUGH men like Copernicus and Galileo explained many things, the mystery remained why the moon continued spinning as it did around the earth and always following a curved path or orbit. It was Isaac Newton who took the knowledge that then existed and made it into a logical system.

He said that any moving object will continue to move in a straight line unless it is stopped or its direction changed by some other force.

If undisturbed, the moon would fly off into space in a straight line away from the earth. A strange force acting between the earth and the moon deflects the moon from its straight-line path and keeps pulling it around the earth. He called this strange force gravitational attraction.

In similar ways our earth and the other planets continue revolving about the sun, each in its own orbit.

To this day, however, there remains very much that scientists would like to know about gravitational attraction.

Newton also discovered that if an object is given a forward motion (say like the shooting of a bullet from a gun), a force of equal strength will be set up in the opposite direction (like the recoil of a gun). The modern jet plane works on this principle—the blast from the rear pushes the plane forward.

The Gradual Growth of Our Knowledge of Electricity

As long ago as 600 B.C., the Greek philosopher Thales knew that amber rubbed with fur or wool would attract small pieces of straw and other light materials. The Greeks also knew that certain rocks of iron ore would attract small pieces of iron. This was also known to the early Chinese, who used this knowledge to make a magnetic compass—a special iron needle that is free to rotate in any horizontal direction. The needle is so attracted by the natural magnetism of the earth that it always turns to point with a fair degree of accuracy toward the north. The compass made navigation of the ocean simpler and safer.

One of the first books showing the connection between magnetism and electricity, based upon actual experiments, was written by Dr. William Gilbert in 1600. It was generally thought that there were two different kinds of electricity: frictional or static electricity—the kind you make when you scuffle your feet over a rug—or when amber is rubbed with wool—and the kind stored in a cell that can be changed into an electric current. Now we know the two kinds are the same.

Benjamin Franklin Flies a Kite

IN addition to all his other accomplishments Benjamin Franklin
was a competent scientist. He marvelled at the newly invented
Leyden Jar and was among the first to realize that it could store
electricity. The natural phenomenon, lightning, also interested
him deeply.

In November 1749, he drew up a list showing twelve ways
in which lightning and electricity were similar. Then he
invented a way "of drawing the electric fire from the clouds
by means of pointed rods of iron erected on high buildings."
He had invented the lightning rod.

In June 1752, he risked his own life and that of his son

398

William, who helped him, to prove that lightning is an electrical discharge. They made a kite of silk on a cedar frame tipped with metal wire. Standing in a doorway, they flew it in a thunder storm. A silk ribbon was attached to the lower end of a silken kitestring. Franklin held a dry portion of that silk ribbon. A metal key was suspended from the kitestring above the ribbon. Below the key was a Leyden Jar. At first nothing happened, but as the kitestring got wet from the rain electricity began to flow. Sparks jumped between the key and the Leyden Jar. The electric current hadn't been able to travel along the kitestring till it got wet. Wet silk, like metal, is a good conductor of electricity. Dry silk is a non-conductor.

Ben Franklin gave the study of electricity a boost. In the hundred years after he flew his kite, Coulomb, Ampere, Ohm, and Volta all made important discoveries. The names of these men will become familiar to you as you grow up. We have honored them by naming the units of electrical measurement after them. Thus, we measure quantity of electricity in coulombs. We measure a current of electricity, that is the quantity that flows past a given spot in a second, in amperes. We measure the push behind the current that makes it flow—we call it electro-motive force—in volts. And we measure the resistance or opposition of the conductor to the flow in ohms.

Faraday Puts Electricity to Work

MICHAEL Faraday, who was born in 1791 and died in 1867, gathered together and set in order all the work of the scientists who had worked on electrical problems before him.

In 1823, he discovered how to make an electrical motor. In 1831, he built the first generator, then called a dynamo. The modern car has both a starting motor and a generator. The starting motor draws electric current from the car battery to start the powerful gasoline engine. The generator is driven by the gasoline engine to recharge the battery and to furnish electric power for all the electrical conveniences in the car.

In 1833, Faraday discovered the effect of passing an electric current through certain solutions. He called these effects the laws of electrolysis. This has made possible the refinement of metals, silver and gold plating, and the manufacture of many chemical products.

As a result of Faraday's work, Morse was able to invent the electro-magnetic telegraph, Bell, the telephone, and Edison, the electric light.

All is Not Just Earth, Air, Fire and Water

THE Greek Aristotle taught that everything in the world was either earth, water, air or fire. This really doesn't tell very much about the composition of the earth. In fact, for centuries, it misled many gifted men, called alchemists, to try to transmute base metals like lead or iron into gold.

In 1662, Robert Boyle urged that things be tested to find out their true nature. He believed that everything was either a simple element that could not be decomposed into other substances or a compound made up of several simple elements. This idea had to wait another hundred years before it was generally accepted.

In the meanwhile it was apparent that matter could exist in three different states: solid, liquid and vapor or gas. Earth was an example of a solid, water of a liquid, and air of a vapor or gas. It was noticed that water, commonly a liquid, did freeze and turn into a solid ice. It also boiled and turned into a vapor. It seemed possible that, like water, everything could be changed, by heating or cooling, from one state to another. But it was found that different amounts of heat or cold are needed to turn the various liquids into gas or solid form.

Priestley Discovers Oxygen

IN 1774 Joseph Priestley, an Englishman, announced that he had discovered a new gas which was like air, only better. A candle could burn brightly in it. Living creatures could breathe it. Mice kept in it lived longer.

He had heated a red substance which we now know as mercuric oxide, and liberated the gas leaving a residue of silvery mercury. This convinced him that the gas and the mercury had been combined.

We now know that the gas, *oxygen,* combines with most metals to form rust and gives off heat slowly. Oxygen from the air we breathe combines slowly inside our bodies with food that we have digested and gives us warmth and energy. Fire is the rapid combination of oxygen with a combustible substance like wood.

Elements, Compounds and the Noble Gases

LAVOISIER, a truly great French scientist, was the first man to take Boyle's idea of elements and compounds seriously. His most important discovery was this: "When elements combine to form compounds they do so in definite proportions by weight."

The best way to explain that is by an example. Carbon is an element very familiar to everyone—it is the "lead" in a pencil, it is coal, and in another and rare form it is diamond. Another element is oxygen, the gas in the air we breathe that keeps us alive. Oxygen and carbon will combine to make carbon dioxide, another gas, the gas that comes out of our mouths and noses as we breathe out. The interesting thing is that it always takes exactly 3 parts by weight of carbon and 8 parts by weight of oxygen to make carbon dioxide. If there is extra carbon or oxygen it won't mix—it is left over. The result will always be 11 (3 plus 8) parts by weight of carbon dioxide. The parts can be ounces, pounds, or tons—but always the proportions are the same.

At first it was thought that the air was made up of only oxygen, and nitrogen, and small amounts of carbon dioxide. But it also contains a small quantity of water vapor which is evaporated from the oceans. It remains in the atmosphere until it "condenses" (forms clouds of tiny droplets) and falls to earth as rain. It then soaks into the ground, comes up in springs, makes little streams that form rivers, and finally reaches the ocean once more. It is the presence of water vapor in the atmosphere which causes humidity.

What gases besides oxygen and nitrogen are found in the air? Cavendish discovered some, and called them the "noble" gases, because they refused to combine with anything else under any conditions. They are snobs! Two of these noble gases, argon and neon, are used to light advertising signs.

Dalton Re-Discovers the Atom

JOHN Dalton was born in 1766 and died in 1844. He became as important to chemistry as Newton was to physics and Faraday to electricity.

Dalton took up an idea of the Greek philosopher Democritus who lived in 400 B. C. He combined it with Lavoisier's law to make a modern science of chemistry.

Democritus believed all matter was made up of tiny, invisible particles he called *atoms*. The atom could not be further divided. It was the final particle of matter, the smallest unit of anything in the universe.

Dalton suggested that all the atoms of the same element were exactly alike in every way. That is, all atoms of hydrogen in the world are exactly alike. All atoms of oxygen are exactly alike.

For instance, the hydrogen atom is the lightest of all. The carbon atom is 12 times as heavy as the hydrogen atom. The atom of oxygen is 16 times as heavy as the hydrogen atom. The atom of aluminum, one of the lightest metals, is nearly 27 times as heavy as the hydrogen atom. The gold atom weighs more than 197 times as much as the hydrogen atom. And uranium, one of the heaviest of all metals, has an atom 238 times as heavy as the hydrogen atom.

PERIODIC TABLE

		Group 0	Group I E₂O EH		Group II EO EH₂		Group III E₂O₃ EH₃		Group IV EO₂ EH₄		Group V E₂O₅ EH₃		Group VI EO₃ EH₂		Group VII E₂O₇ EH		Group VIII EO₄
Period	Series		A	B	A	B	A	B	A	B	A	B	A	B	A	B	
1	1		H 1														
2	2	He 4	Li 7		Be 9		B 11		C 12		N 14		O 16		F 19		
3	3	Ne 20	Na 23		Mg 24		Al 27		Si 28		P 31		S 32		Cl 35.5		
4	4	A 40	K 39		Ca 40		Sc 45		Ti 48		V 51		Cr 52		Mn 55		Fe 55.8 Co 58.9 Ni 58.7
	5			Cu 64		Zn 65		Ga 70		Ge 73		As 75		Se 79		Br 80	
5	6	Kr 84	Rb 85		Sr 88		Y 89		Zr 91		Cb 93		Mo 96		Ma (?)		Ru 102 Rh 103 Pd 107
	7			Ag 108		Cd 112		In 115		Sn 119		Sb 122		Te 127.5		I 127	
6	8	Xe 131	Cs 133		Ba 137		57–71 Rare-earth Metals*		Hf 179		Ta 181		W 184		Re 186		Os 191 Ir 193 Pt 195
	9			Au 197		Hg 201		Tl 204		Pb 207		Bi 209		Po (?)			
7	10	Rn 222	Vi (?)		Ra 226		Ac (?)		Th 232		Pa (?)		U 238				

Np 239	Pu 238	Am 241	Cm 242	Bls 243	Cf 244

*57 L... 9, 58 Ce 140, ... 141, 60 Nd 144. 61 Il (?), 62 Sa 150, 63 Eu 152, 64 Gd 157, 65 Tb 159, 66 Dy 162, 67 Ho 163.5, 68 Er 168, 69 Tm ...9, 70 Yb 173.5, 71 ...5.

The Periodic Table

DALTON's atomic ideas were accepted by scientists all over the world. When he died, 75 elements had been discovered and studied.

The next great discovery was made in 1869 by the Russian chemist, Dmitri Mendeleev. He arranged all the elements in a pattern called the Periodic Table—an orderly pattern of all the chemical facts so far discovered.

The Periodic Table is probably one of the greatest scientific inventions of all time. Without it we could not have entered upon the atomic age. In the table, as Mendeleev wrote it down, he had to leave a few blanks. These were the places that would someday be occupied by elements not yet discovered. Mendeleev predicted exactly what some of these would be like when discovered. His detailed predictions all came true.

Evolution and Heredity

YOUNG Charles Darwin, newly graduated from Cambridge University, asked himself whether all forms of life always existed just as they are now. This was what everyone believed and what he had been taught, but he doubted it very much. Three and a half years traveling around the world on a British ship, *The Beagle,* convinced Darwin that his doubts were justified.

He returned from his travels convinced that man and all the living creatures on earth today are related. All have grown from earlier types, and those from still earlier ones in an unbroken line back to a primitive one-celled creature. The next two paragraphs describe more of Darwin's controversial theory.

More than a billion years ago, a small blob of jelly floated on the shallow seas of the young earth. It and others like it

were the only life on earth. In half a billion years that blob of jelly had become different kinds of sea worms and sea scorpions, seaweeds and other simple sea plants.

During the next half billion years some of this life crawled onto the barren land. The first land animals were "amphibians," equally at home on land and in the water, like present-day frogs. There were also primitive scorpions, the descendants of which became insects or spiders. From the seaweeds that took root on shore came ferns and mosses. The amphibians became reptiles. For one hundred million years they ruled the earth. Out of them came birds and mammals. Gradually the mammals changed into all the different kinds we have today, including man. Each of these changes was very gradual and took thousands of years.

What makes you and your brothers and sisters look somewhat alike? What makes all of you look like your father and mother, and yet also a little different? The answer is to be found in the laws of heredity.

Gregor Mendel, son of an Austrian farmer, wanted to be a scientist but couldn't afford the university. He became an Augustinian monk and, in the years between 1843 and 1865, he became a great scientist. In the garden of the monastery he raised garden peas—pure talls, pure dwarfs, and so on. Then, when he was sure he had pure strains, he began crossing them. He did the same with green and yellow peas. In all he raised and studied more than 10,000 specimens.

From the way these peas transmitted and inherited various traits, such as height or color, Mendel worked out the laws of heredity. They have been found to be true for all types of plants and animals, including man, and have been widely used in the improvement of flowers and agricultural crops and the breeding of dogs and livestock.

The Human Body and the Microbe Hunters

OF course we'd like our doctors to know the internal structure of our bodies. But how do they find out?

Galen, the Greek physician (120-200 A.D.), had some opportunity to see inside the human body when he treated the grievous wounds of the gladiators (professional warriors). He increased his knowledge by dissecting animals, particularly apes. Since he never dissected human beings, however, some of his beliefs were erroneous.

Vesalius, a 16th-century Flemish doctor, performed a wide variety of dissections. As a result of his studies he published the famous book "Structure of the Human Body," which was widely consulted for centuries.

Near the end of the 16th century an English doctor named Harvey, by following the methods of Vesalius, was able to prove that the heart is really a pump. It sends blood to all parts of the body with oxygen from the lungs and food from the digestive system.

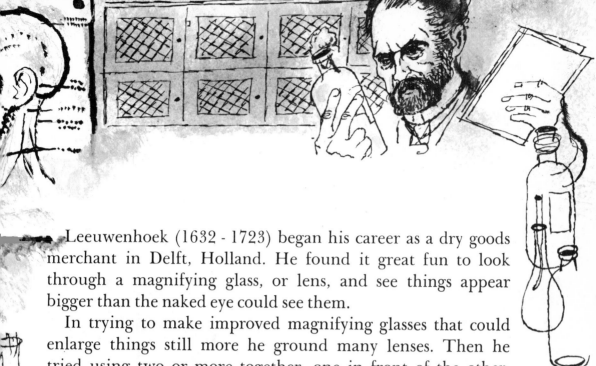

Leeuwenhoek (1632 - 1723) began his career as a dry goods merchant in Delft, Holland. He found it great fun to look through a magnifying glass, or lens, and see things appear bigger than the naked eye could see them.

In trying to make improved magnifying glasses that could enlarge things still more he ground many lenses. Then he tried using two or more together, one in front of the other, and built a microscope. This increased their magnifying power tremendously. What minute things he could now see!

Then he set to work looking at every small thing he could find. He looked at drops of water, particles of dust and even a tiny bit of saliva from his own mouth. In everything he examined he found strange, tiny living things moving about. He had come upon a previously unknown world of living creatures.

Leeuwenhoek had discovered microbes. Not until the 19th century was any use made of this discovery. Then it was found that these microbes, or bacteria as they are now called, are the very things that cause many diseases. When we learned to control bacteria we learned how to prevent and cure many diseases.

In 1885 little Joseph Meister, a young French boy, lay hopelessly ill. His doctors had given up in despair. Louis Pasteur was called in. He had cured the same illness, rabies, in animals by inoculation but he was very reluctant to try his method on a human being.

The boy's parents pleaded with him so Pasteur took a chance. He inoculated the boy. It worked. The boy's life was saved.

409

Crookes Pumps the Air Out of a Glass Tube

IN the 1880's, Sir William Crookes, a British physicist, started something that has led to the atomic bomb and hasn't stopped yet. Carefully he pumped the air out of a glass tube. He did it so well that the air left in the tube was 20 million times thinner than the normal air he had started with.

Then he connected the two ends (electrodes) of a highly charged electric power line to two opposite sides of the evacuated tube and sent an electric current through the tube. To his surprise the glass wall near one electrode gave off a faint green glow.

Crookes tried again. This time he placed a small target midway between the two electrodes before he evacuated the tube. Now he found that the target left a definite shadow within the glowing area. This proved to him that rays of some kind were passing from one electrode to the other.

For 20 years no one knew what these mysterious rays were. More experiments later proved that they were the minute particles, called electrons, which made up the electric current.

410

Roentgen Discovers X-Rays

In 1895, Wilhelm Roentgen, a German physicist, was repeating the experiment of Crookes and of Lenard, who had followed Crookes. Roentgen, however, made a change. He covered the glass walls of the Crookes tube with some black pigment, so that no light could pass through it. Then he turned on the electric current. The mysterious rays went right through the black sides of the tubes and lighted up a specially prepared screen on the outside.

What's more, they went through wood, stone, and even living flesh. They were stopped only by bone and metal. Roentgen had discovered X-rays, which were thought to be a new kind of light.

As you know, X-rays are now used to take pictures inside the body and to locate broken bones, decayed teeth, and diseased internal organs.

Radioactivity and Radium

A PHOSPHORESCENT substance is something that, after being exposed to sunlight and then taken to a dark room, gives off light. An example is phosphorescent paint, used on watch and clock dials so that the time can be read in the dark.

In 1896, a French scientist named Antoine Henri Becquerel wanted to find out if a phosphorescent substance would give off X-rays. He had a piece of uranium ore which he thought was phosphorescent. He wanted to see if, after exposure to sunlight, he could use its light to make a photograph. But nature wouldn't cooperate—it was a cloudy, rainy day. So Becquerel put the uranium ore away in his desk drawer, in which he had already put his photographic plates, all carefully wrapped to prevent any light from falling on them.

When a sunny day came, Becquerel took out his photographic plates to load his camera. He found them all fogged, just as if they had been exposed to sunlight. Becquerel then realized that some kind of radiation was coming out of the uranium ore and that it made no difference whether the ore had been exposed to sunlight or not.

Becquerel had discovered that uranium is a radioactive substance. It was the first such material ever discovered. But what was radioactivity?

What was there in the uranium ore that gave off X-rays? Becquerel had two scientific associates—Pierre Curie, another Frenchman, and his Polish wife Marie Sklodowska Curie. Becquerel turned over the investigation to the Curies.

Ra, 226.05

The problem was to find out what in the uranium ore caused its radioactivity. So they started with several tons of pitchblende, an ore containing uranium that seemed especially radioactive. They worked it over, removing the most radioactive parts and then working those over, throwing away the less radioactive parts. They kept on doing this until they had only a teaspoonful of something that was not uranium, but was a million times more radioactive than uranium.

They called it *radium*. They had discovered a new and very important element.

The discovery of radium in 1898 set the scientific world in an uproar. Suddenly, all the old ideas about the nature of matter were useless. Where was all this energy escaping from the radium coming from? There was only one place it could come from. It must have been coming from empty spaces inside the atoms of the radium. But atoms had been imagined to be solid, like tiny billiard balls. Now we knew that they could not be solid. Then what were they really like?

Four of England's most famous scientists went to work to try to find out. They were Sir J. J. Thomson, Sir Ernest Rutherford, Sir William Ramsay, and Professor Frederick Soddy. The first step was to examine the rays closely. When they were made to pass through a magnetic field, they separated three ways. They were made up of three different rays. Sir Ernest Rutherford named them after the first three letters of the Greek alphabet: *alpha, beta, gamma* rays.

The Origin of the Universe

DID you ever stop to wonder how the earth came into being? Even the scientists don't really know. But they do make some very intelligent guesses.

Some scientists think that our earth and all the other planets were originally huge masses of flaming gas thrown off by our fiery sun. They speculate that these masses of gas gradually cooled off. They then turned to hot, heavy liquids and balled up (as all liquids do when undisturbed) into huge spheres. As they continued to cool off, crusts formed on their surfaces. Their centers still remain hot. We can see this when a volcano erupts and spews forth molten stone.

The British astronomer, Hoyle, has a somewhat different theory. He tells us that our sun was really twins and that one exploded. From the bits of this explosion our solar system and our earth were formed.

But how did the sun come into being? Astronomers concern themselves with problems like this. With their giant telescopes they view the heavens and they see many systems of stars which have reached different stages of development. They surmise that billions of years ago limitless space was filled with clouds of very thin gases. By gravitational attraction these gases slowly contracted and formed the huge fiery balls we now call stars. The sun is one of these stars. Some of these gas clouds have not yet contracted. We call them nebulae.

But how did the clouds of gas get there originally? We don't know. We'll have to leave that problem for future scientists.

The Atom Is a Tiny Solar System
Packed With Incredible Power

EARLY this century scientists discovered that the atom was not solid but like a tiny solar system. At the center there is a heavy core, called a nucleus. In this nucleus there are protons which have a positive electric charge and neutrons which have no electric charge. And then outside the nucleus, like planets around the sun, are tiny particles 1,080 lighter than the nucleus, whirling around it, called electrons.

Each tiny atomic nucleus is packed with incredible power or energy. Albert Einstein, in the Theory of Relativity, told us the extent of this energy in his famous mathematical formula:

$$E = Mc^2$$

This means that energy (E) is equal (=) to mass (M) multiplied by the speed of light multiplied by itself (c^2).

In 1 gram — 1/28 of an ounce — of helium there is enough energy to run 200,000 one-hundred-watt electric light bulbs for ten hours.

The explosion of the first atomic bomb in 1945 verified Einstein's formula.

The Conquest of Space

MAN's first trip to the moon in 1969 was the climax of a series of space conquests that began on October 4, 1957. On that day Russian scientists launched Sputnik I, the first man-made satellite to circle the earth. In 1958, United States scientists orbited Explorer I.

The successful launchings of artificial satellites opened up entirely new possibilities for space travel.

The first men journeyed into space in 1961. The Russian air force officer Yuri Gagarin circled the earth in a spaceship on April 12, 1961. The next month, U. S. astronaut Alan B. Shepard, Jr., made a 15-minute space flight.

These men were followed by an ever-increasing number of astronauts and cosmonauts orbitting the earth for steadily longer periods of time.

Then came *Project Gemini* and *Project Apollo*. In 1965, U. S. astronauts James A. McDevitt and Edward H. White II orbited the earth 62 times in their Gemini 4 capsule. They tested equipment and space maneuvers that would then be used in Project Apollo—the climactic series of missions that landed astronauts on the moon twice in 1969 and twice in 1971.

Light and Sight

SIGHT is a precious gift we take for granted. But our eyes would see not more than those of a blind man if it were not for the light that reaches our eyes from the particular thing we see.

Some things are seen because of the light they give off directly, like the sun, the lighted candle, the electric light. Some things we see because of the light that shines on them from some other source and then is reflected to our eyes. You see this page because light shines on it from some other source and then is reflected to your eyes.

Scientists are still not agreed what light really is. There are different theories about it. One theory, originated by the famous Sir Isaac Newton, stated that light consists of streams of minute particles called corpuscles moving like bullets at great speed. This theory was given up because it could not account for certain behavior of light. Another theory was proposed by the Dutch physicist Christiaan Huygens. He said that light is a form of wave motion. But even this theory, which can account for many of the actions of light that the corpuscular did not, is now being questioned, because it can't explain certain other phenomena of light.

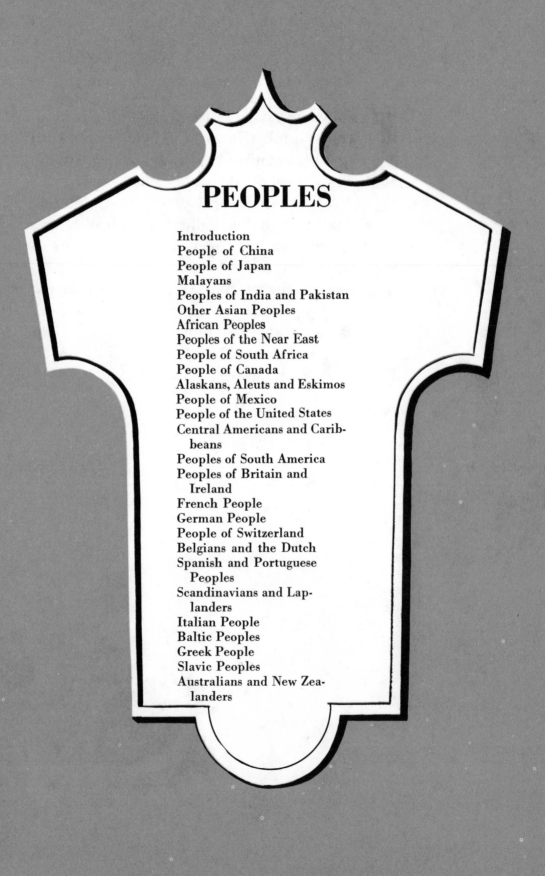

PEOPLES

IF someone gave an American child a piece of whale blubber to eat, the child would turn up his nose and push it away. But the Eskimo children eat whale blubber like candy.

All over the world people have different climates and diets, live in different kinds of houses and speak different languages. These people are as strange to you as you are to them.

But there are many things which are the same the world over. People wake in the morning, go to work or play, eat when they are hungry, and when night comes they go to sleep. They live just as we do.

That is what this section is all about.

Introduction

WHY should anyone want to take the trouble to learn about the peoples of the world? Why should a Norwegian child, who must dress warmly most of the year, want to learn about the African boy who wears little if any clothes?

First of all, it is interesting, that much is easy to see. Second, and most important, by understanding others it is easier to understand ourselves. When the hot afternoon sun makes us drowsy, we can understand why the people of warm Mexico use the noontime to take a nap; we learn not to make the error of judging everyone by ourselves.

The world today is shrinking. Jet planes and fast steamships have cut the time it takes to circle the globe. Radio and telephones allow us to talk to people ten thousand miles away. By learning and understanding the customs of all peoples we come to realize how much each has contributed to the civilization of the world today.

People of China

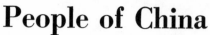

ONE fifth of all the people on earth live in China. It is one of the oldest civilizations known to man.

The Chinese people speak a variety of dialects. Some of them are so different that people from one region cannot understand people from another. It is a musical sing-song tongue, and the whole language depends on the tone of voice used by the speaker.

422

People of Japan

THE Japanese are islanders. Their home, Japan, is off the Asian continent, just as the island where the British people live is off the European continent. Japanese climate is similar to that of Britain and the United States.

The Japanese are both a farming and manufacturing people. Because labor is cheaper in Japan, they can manufacture and sell articles for less money than many other countries.

Animals are scarce on the islands and there are few work horses or oxen for the farms. Because of the meat shortage the Japanese diet is mostly rice, fish and vegetables. But the climate is ideal for farming.

Malayans

MALAYANS live on a long string of islands off the coast of Asia. Types of Malayans who speak a form of the Malay language can be found in Indonesia (the islands of Java, Sumatra, Borneo, Bali, etc. form this republic) and in the Philippines and in Polynesia.

Malayans are largely brown-skinned. Included among them are Muslims, Buddhists and Christians.

The land they live in is rich in rubber, petroleum and tin. Malay farmers grow great quantities of coffee, tea, rice and sugar. Spices such as pepper, nutmeg, cloves and cinnamon come from the fields of these people. They are famous for their teakwood forests, the wood of which is made into prized furniture.

Peoples of India and Pakistan

NOT long ago these two nations of brown-skinned peoples were one. Religion separated them, with the Hindus taking India and the Muslims taking Pakistan.

There are almost 700,000 villages in these two countries. Most of the people are farmers, although a few own their own land. They live in their villages, in huts made of sun-dried bricks of mud; roofs are thatched. There are no sewers, no paved streets and no lights in those poor villages.

The farmers depend greatly on the monsoons (the rainy season) for their crops, as do many other Asian nations. If the rains come too late or too soon, or if there is too little or too much rain, the crops fail. Rice, wheat, barley, cotton, tea and tobacco are grown.

Once in India there was a "caste system." The "untouchables" were the most miserable people on earth and could never rise in life. But new laws are abolishing this system. Still, education is limited in these two countries.

425

Other Asian Peoples

MANY millions of people live in such Asian countries as Korea, Thailand (Siam), Burma, Vietnam and Mongolia. There are great differences among them, and in the way they live.

Koreans are much like the Japanese. Their language is similar, and so are the crops they plant. However they do not manufacture as much as the Japanese do.

Peoples of Thailand, Burma and Vietnam are similar to the great Chinese peoples.

Mongolians are mostly herdsmen in their cold, bleak country. They are nomadic tribes, who raise goats and sheep.

African Peoples

THE African continent is populated by a variety of peoples. Some, like the French in Algeria and the Afrikaans of South Africa, are descendants of European colonizers. Most belong to one or another of the original peoples of Africa. They vary from the fair Berbers of the northern mountains to the black men of Ethiopia in the north-east; from the Muslim Somali people of the Horn to the Bushmen pygmies of the south. Throughout Africa, as their peoples claim the right to control their own lands and lives, new nations are organizing and taking their places among the nations of the world.

Long dismissed by Europe and America as "pagans" of the "dark continent," recent history is forcing a less biased search into African history, civilization and culture.

427

Peoples of The Near East

THE nations that make up this section of the world include
Turkey, Egypt, Israel, and the Arab states of Saudi Arabia,
Jordan, Iran, Iraq, Yemen, Syria and Lebanon.

Turks were formerly invaders of Europe and other lands,
but have since settled down to peaceful pursuits. More than
three fourths of the people are farmers; tobacco is their most
famous crop. Many customs in Turkey have changed.
Harems have been abolished, and the clothing has become
more westernized.

The Arabian states are filled with desert nomads; many
of these wandering tribes are raiders, often attacking small
farms and unprotected outlying villages. There are some
small cities in these lands. The people of the city of Riyadh
live in houses of sun-dried brick, often several stories high.

428

Oil in some of the Arab states has made them wealthy. Camel trains are disappearing, being replaced by trucks, automobiles and planes. Education is getting better.

In Egypt the peasants are still working their farms with ancient tools, and their standard of living is poor. Water is secured from the great Nile River. Meat is scarce.

The State of Israel is composed largely of European refugees who brought their customs with them from other lands. They are a tough, hard working, intelligent and artistic people. They work in farms and factories with equal ability.

Throughout this region are three religions: Muslim, Christian and Hebrew. The Arabs and Israelis have many features in common, since both are Semitic. The people of Iran are more like those of India.

People of South Africa

THE people of South Africa are made up primarily of the descendants of the original European settlers, the Dutch and the British, and of course the African blacks who make up the majority of the population.

Many languages are spoken in South Africa and these are English, Afrikaans (which is a form of Dutch), and the native tribal dialects.

People of Canada

ORIGINALLY the people of Canada consisted of native Indians, English and French settlers, and a small sprinkling of other people from other European countries. Essentially, this is still so; however, many peoples have come into Canada from other lands.

Most Canadians speak either English, French, or both. These are the official languages of Canada. Canada is a member of the British Commonwealth of Nations. Canada belonged to France nearly 200 years ago; in 1873, France ceded the country to England.

Canadian farmers raise crops of apples and wheat, while fisherman take great catches of cod and salmon from the Atlantic and Pacific Oceans. There are vast timber forests in Canada, and the land is rich in nickel, platinum, gold, copper, oil, and uranium.

431

Alaskans, Aleuts and Eskimos

WHEN the United States purchased Alaska from Russia in 1867 little was known about its people. There were Indians and Eskimos on the mainland; the Aleuts peopled the chain of islands off the coast. The Indians were the most advanced, living in log houses and having a tribal form of government.

Many changes have taken place since then. Many U.S. citizens have gone to live in Alaska, and adapted themselves to the climate. The Eskimos are a peaceful people who live mostly on the meats and fish they catch. They are skilled at bone carving, making spearheads and other useful articles. Together with the Indians and Aleuts, they have begun to seek their place within the educational and economic system developing in their land.

People of Mexico

THE people of Mexico are made up partly of descendants of the Spanish settlers and partly of native Indians. The official language is Spanish, but many native Indian dialects are spoken too.

In the Yucatan Peninsula, Maya people speak their own language, plant their corn, and remember the tales of wisdom, which Spanish destruction of their magnificent cities did not destroy.

Mexico's people are proud of the long and brutal revolution they fought for social justice. They often note that their revolt against social and economic oppression came earlier than that of the Russian people.

People of The United States

THE original people of what is now the United States were, of course, Indians. Some experts think they came from northeastern Asia. Between Alaska and Russia is a very narrow strip of water called the Bering Sea, and it is thought that there was once land where the water is now. Perhaps the American Indians crossed this strip of land and migrated south, through Canada and the United States.

There are over 200 million people in the United States, of every race, color and religion in the world, and their customs are a mixture of all. In New York City alone there are hundreds of different churches, and people of African, Puerto Rican, Italian, French, German, Hebrew, Arabic and Scandinavian descent, plus many others.

434

About one fourth of the people throughout the country
work on farms, which produce almost every fruit and vegetable in the world. Many work in factories and produce a variety of things, from automobiles, fine furniture and clothes
through precision parts for atomic reactors. Making movies
is another great industry. American films delight people all
over the world.

The national sport is baseball, but thousands attend football and basketball games. Other popular sports are fishing,
hunting and golf.

Education in the United States is the finest in the world,
and more schools are built every year than in any other country.

Central Americans and Caribbeans

THE nations of Central America are Costa Rica, Guatemala, Honduras, Nicaragua, Panama and El Salvador. All are independent republics, and the people of the countries are predominantly of mixed Indian and Spanish blood. The main occupation in Central America is farming. The export of bananas to the United States helps to make possible a good deal of trade.

Some Caribbeans live on a string of island nations which dot the sea, such as Cuba, Haiti, the Dominican Republic, Trinidad and Tobago. Others live on islands which are still island colonies of European countries, such as the Bahamas, Martinique, etc. Most of these people, too, are farmers. Different languages are spoken on the various islands. Haitians speak French dialects; but in the Dominican Republic Spanish is spoken, while English is the official language of Jamaica.

Peoples of South America

MOST of the South American countries are republics: Chile, Peru, Bolivia, Ecuador, Venezuela, Colombia, Paraguay, Argentina, Uruguay and Brazil.

Spanish is the language of all the rest of South America, except for Brazil, which is Portuguese-speaking. Of course there are a great many native Indian languages and dialects. There is a tremendous mixture of races and peoples in these countries, from Spaniards to the Jivaro Indians of Peru. In Brazil, Colombia and Venezuela are tribes about whom little is known, since explorers have been unable to reach them.

Some Indians have come to live in villages and small cities. Many dress colorfully; for example, the Indian women of Bolivia wear brightly hued clothing, and derby hats!

The people of all South American nations are farmers, miners and cattle ranchers. Minerals, such as oil, gold, silver, tin and copper abound on the continent. To find these precious minerals the people must overcome the dangers of huge snakes, steaming jungles, dry deserts and high mountains.

439

Peoples of Britain and Ireland

LONG ago Great Britain was invaded by Romans, and by Celts, Angles, Jutes, Saxons and Normans. These invaders left their mark on the islands in the form of language and customs. The English language is made up of many words from the Romans, the Saxons and the others.

The British government is a "constitutional monarchy," led by a Prime Minister. The laws are passed by a House of Commons elected by the people, and a House of Lords. The King has little political power.

The Irish are descendants of the Celts who once inhabited the British Isles. Some Celts were driven into the mountains of Wales and Scotland by the invading Angles and other European tribes, and others settled in Ireland.

French People

ONCE France was called Gaul. Caesar's Romans conquered the land and gave it a language; later a Germanic tribe called the Franks invaded it and gave the land its name.

The French people have been friends of the United States since our Revolutionary War. The French Revolution was inspired by ours.

The French are a patriotic and thrifty people, partly farmers and partly factory workers. They are also leaders in the world of fashion. The French are lovers of the arts; their Louvre Museum is world-famous for its fine paintings and sculpture.

French people are fond of fine foods, and their cooking and wines make the country a popular place for tourists.

German People

THE people of Germany are among the most industrious in the world. They have great skill in manufacturing, and German farmers are probably the best in Europe. Germans make beautiful Dresden chinaware; the people of the Black Forest make fine wooden clocks and toys.

A great many of the German young people are educated to be scientists. German schools and teachers are excellent; and Germany has given the world some of the greatest musicians and composers, such as Johann Sebastian Bach, Handel, Beethoven and Brahms.

People of Switzerland

THE Swiss are among the most democratic people in the world. The land they live in is often called "the playground of Europe," and tourists come from all over the world to ski, toboggan, or climb the high and beautiful Alps.

Swiss watchmakers produce almost 20 million clocks and watches each year. These intelligent people put their glaciers to good use; the melting ice and snow is turned into water power for electricity.

Belgians and The Dutch

JUST over a hundred years ago, these two peoples were one nation, but now they are independent countries. However, they still have many things in common. Northern Belgians speak Flemish, which is very close to the Dutch language. Like the Netherlands, Belgium has some dikes to keep back the seas.

Spanish and Portuguese Peoples

LONG ago Spain and Portugal were inhabited by people called Iberians, who fled to northern Spain when invaders came. Today these people are called Basques; their language is different from Spanish or Portuguese.

Romans invaded first; from them came the Spanish and Portuguese languages. Next, from the north came the Vandals and Goths, who mixed with Romans. From these beginnings came the first Spanish peoples.

Portugal's climate is milder than Spain's, therefore Portugal has more farmers. However both peoples grow the same things: cork, wine grapes and olives. Portuguese are fine fishermen.

The national sport of Spain is bullfighting. Spanish music is colorful, the dancing is exciting.

444

Scandinavians and Laplanders

SCANDINAVIANS live in Sweden, Norway and Denmark. These people were the Vikings of a thousand years ago, and traveled to France, England and even to the coast of North America in their small, colorful ships.

The Scandinavian languages are each slightly different but the people have little trouble understanding each other. Each nation is a "constitutional monarchy;" there is a parliament and a king but the king has little political power.

The Laplanders are nomads who wander in the northern parts of Norway, Sweden, Finland and Russia. Their whole lives center around herds of reindeer, and when the animals migrate the people follow. The climate in Lapland is bitter-cold; in winter the people wear two fur coats, one with the fur inside and one with the fur outside.

Italian People

Two thousand years ago the Romans were a great power. They spread their culture and civilization through France, England, Spain and Portugal. Today the Italian people are still lovers of the arts and culture. Great artists have come from Italy, such as Da Vinci and Michelangelo, and great composers, such as Puccini and Verdi.

Italy is a heavily populated country. The people of the south are mainly farmers, while those of the north are factory workers or work in the great seaports.

446

Baltic Peoples

THE Baltic peoples live in the lands of Finland, Estonia, Latvia and Lithuania, along the shores of the Baltic Sea.

Finns are a good deal like the Swedish people, but their language is quite different. They work in the great forests which make up a good part of Finland. They are also expert in cheese-making and other kinds of dairying.

Estonians are much like the Finns in appearance. Lithuanians speak the oldest language in Europe. The Letts, who live in Latvia, are related to the Lithuanians.

Greek People

LIKE the Romans, the Greeks were a great and powerful people in ancient times. They were highly educated and civilized, and their temples and statues were masterpieces of art.

Slavic Peoples

SLAVIC peoples are like a patchwork quilt. In this group can be found Czechs and Slovaks of Czechoslovakia; Serbs and Croatians of Yugoslavia; Bulgarians, Poles, European Russians.

European Russians live mostly on huge collective farms. They are thrifty and hard working. Those who work in factories, especially in the north, are more artistic; their handiwork in embroidery and woodworking is beautiful and practical.

The Czechs, who live in Bohemia and Moravia, are also an artistic people, and show this in their native dress and in manufactured articles. The Slovaks live mostly in small towns in the eastern mountain country. Czechoslovakians are among the best educated people in Europe.

The Poles are Slavic, much like the Russians in appearance. But their culture is more western than that of the Russians.

Yugoslavs love bright colors in their dress. Although most of them are Slavic, many citizens of this country belong to other races. On the same street in a Yugoslav town one is apt to find Armenians, Turks, Hungarians and Greeks, all living together.

449

Australians and
New Zealanders

AUSTRALIA and New Zealand are populated
by two groups of peoples: the white settlers
who come mostly from the British Isles, and
the brown-skinned people who lived in these
countries before the British colonized them.

Australian bushmen are nomadic hunters,
and it is they who invented the famous
boomerang. New Zealand natives are called
Maori.

450

THE UNITED STATES OF AMERICA

TO ALL TO WHOM THESE PRESENTS SHALL COME:

Whereas

Inventions

PRESENTED TO THE Commissioner of Patents A PETITION PRAYING FOR
THE GRANT OF LETTERS PATENT FOR AN ALLEGED NEW AND USEFUL IMPROVEMENT IN

The Wheel
Surveying Instruments
Gunpowder
Printing Press
Steam Engine
Telescope
Spectroscope
Microscope
Gyroscope
Farming Implements
Sewing Machine
Typewriter
Electric Light and Generator
Telegraph
Phonograph
Telephone
Sound and Pictures Through
    Space
Birds, Balloons and Planes
Vulcanizing Process
Cameras
The Automobile
Submarine
Photoelectric Cell
Medical Inventions
Refrigeration
Plastics
Calculating Machines

WE touch a button on the wall—and a dark room is lighted. We speak into a little instrument—and our words are heard almost instantly by people thousands of miles away. We can fly faster than birds, move on land faster than the speediest deer, dart under water swifter than the speediest fish.

It is all the more amazing when we stop to consider that most of the great inventions came around the beginning of the 18th century and later; the things we take for granted today had to be discovered painstakingly, by trial and error method. Great men, like Heinrich Hertz, Eli Whitney, Thomas Edison, Henry Ford, and many, many others, before and after the 18th century, all put their genius to work to make our world a better place in which to live.

452

The Wheel

ONE of mankind's earliest and greatest inventions was the wheel. Without it there could be no industry, little transportation or communication, only crude farming, no water or electric power.

Nobody knows when the wheel was invented. There is no trace of the wheel during the Stone Age, and it was not known to the American Indian until the White Man came. In the Old World it came into use during the Bronze Age, when horses and oxen were used as work animals. At first all wheels were solid discs; later, some time around the year 1800 B.C., spoked wheels were introduced.

The ancient clockmakers, who came to know much about the use of wheels, first devised ways of transmitting and controlling the use of power by means of the wheel.

453

Surveying Instruments

SURVEYING probably began in ancient Egypt. Greeks and Romans used crude instruments, such as plumb lines to make sure an object was straight up-and-down.

The basic instruments of a surveying engineer are: the chain and tape, compass, level, transit, stadia and sextant. Some of these instruments are very complicated.

Chain and tape are used to measure distance. The engineer's chain is 100 feet long, and the surveyor's chain is 100 links, or 66 feet. The compass is used to determine direction. The carpenter's level, which has a "bubble" in it, is used to level off construction work. Imagine living in a house with a tilted floor!

The transit is a complicated instrument; it too has a "bubble level" and is used to align construction work and to measure angles and distances.

A stadia rod is a pole having measured lines marked off on it and is used with a transit to measure distances.

The sextant is an arc used to measure upright angles. It is not so accurate as a transit but it is small and easy to use.

Gunpowder

THE actual date of gunpowder's invention is unknown, but the Chinese and Indians knew about it for many centuries. They used it to blast rocks in the fields. Experience has shown the best gunpowder mixture to be saltpeter, charcoal and sulphur. Since saltpeter was unknown in early China, potassium nitrate was used instead.

Gunpowder first came into use in Europe some time during the second half of the 13th century as a cannon explosive. As demand for gunpowder increased, methods of making it improved. At first it was ground by hand, but this was a very dangerous operation, since black powder exploded easily. Further, care in ramming powder into a cannon was needed, since packing too tightly would cause it to burn slowly or fail to explode, and ramming too loosely produced a short shot. This was remedied by "graining" the powder.

In 1865 Johann Shultze, a Prussian officer, produced a smokeless powder for his field guns, and a few years later Von Lenk used a guncotton powder in his cannon.

Printing Press

BEFORE the invention of the printing press and paper, all books were written by hand on papyrus, on parchment, or on the skin of an animal which was specially treated. In the year 105 A.D. a Chinese named Ts'ai Lun invented paper, and then the Chinese began to print with wood blocks, on which letters were carved out and inked.

The next great printing discovery was movable type made of lead, so that the tiresome job of cutting wood blocks was eliminated. Finally, around the year 1440, Johann Gutenberg invented the first movable-type printing press, which was operated by hand.

Hundreds of improvements have been invented for the printing press. In 1814 Friedrich Koenig invented the first cylinder press, which was later used by the *London Times*, and in 1886 Mergenthaler invented the linotype machine.

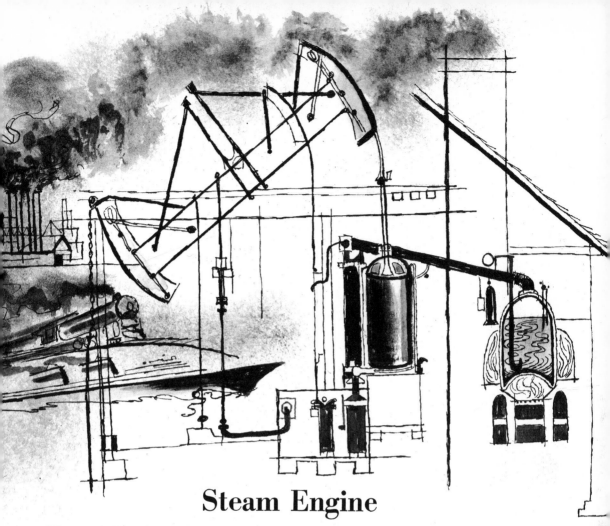

Steam Engine

THE earliest record of anybody trying to put steam to work was the invention of Hero of Alexandria, in 120 B.C. He made a ball with two nozzles through which steam escaped, the jet action causing the ball to rotate. He used this invention to open and close the doors of a temple. Hundreds of years later a man named Giovanni Branca built a steam engine which turned a series of vanes like a windmill.

But these steam engines, and others which followed, were wasteful of fuel. It was James Watt, a Scottish engineer, who perfected the steam engine in 1765.

As water is heated it turns into vapor. This vapor may exert tremendous pressure. It is led into one side of a locomotive cylinder to push a piston forward, then it is led into the other side to push it back. The steam you see escaping is water vapor which has cooled off and condensed.

Telescope

ALTHOUGH several people claim to have invented the telescope, most historians give the credit to Hans Lippershey, an eye-glass maker in Zeeland, Holland, sometime around 1605. It was very small, only a foot long, and could only magnify three or four times.

In 1609 Galileo built a much better one, and kept on experimenting until he had made a telescope which magnified 32 times. With this instrument he laid the foundation for modern astronomy. Others began to build telescopes; one made by Christiaan Huygens was 123 feet long.

The next big step was the Newton telescope. Newton put a mirror into his instrument so that he could use an eyepiece on the side instead of at the end. Later, in 1789, William Herschel built a really fine telescope, and from the Herschel improvement came a good deal of our knowledge of telescopes.

America has several huge telescopes scanning the heavens, including a 100-inch instrument at Mount Wilson and a 200-inch telescope at Mount Palomar, both in California.

458

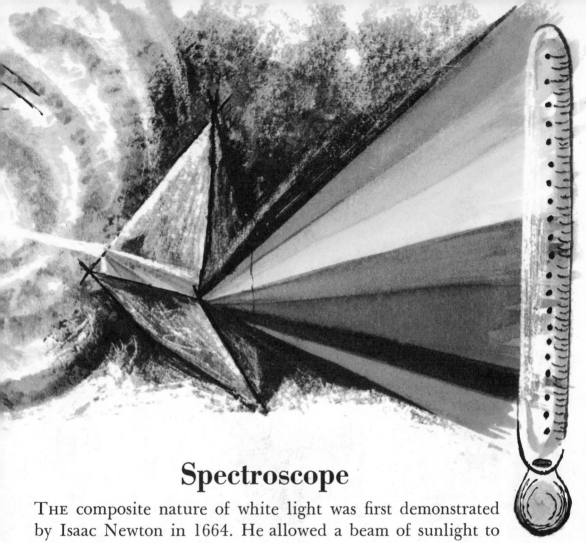

Spectroscope

THE composite nature of white light was first demonstrated by Isaac Newton in 1664. He allowed a beam of sunlight to pass through a round hole in a shutter, through a prism and onto a screen. The result was a spread-out image of the sun, called a spectrum. In 1800 William Herschel studied the distribution of heat in the spectrum with a thermometer and found the hottest temperature was beyond the red color, thus discovering the infra-red spectrum. In 1801 Johann Wilhelm Ritter studied the effect of spectral light on silver salts and found this action went beyond violet, thus discovering the ultra-violet spectrum.

In 1802 Thomas Young worked out the wave lengths of the seven colors recognized by Newton, and in 1814 Joseph von Fraunhofer tried Newton's experiment differently. Instead of a hole he used a slit; he attached a telescope and saw the spectrum interrupted by dark lines, which he later measured to determine the exact wave lengths of the different colors.

459

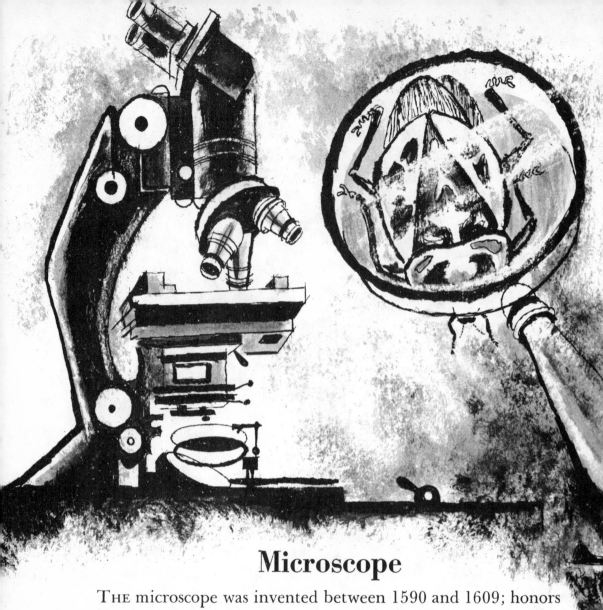

Microscope

THE microscope was invented between 1590 and 1609; honors are divided between Hans and Zacharias Janssen, two Hollanders, and the great Galileo. At first it was little more than a magnifying glass, and most people looked upon it as a toy until late in the 18th century. Up to that time most improvements on it were for ornamental purposes, but with the awakening of scientific interest the microscope was put to great practical use.

There could be no scientific research without the microscope. Germs which the naked eye could not see are very plainly seen under a powerful microscope, and many great medical discoveries have been made because of this wonderful instrument.

460

Gyroscope

THE earliest forms of gyroscopes were toys, such as tops and rolling hoops. It was noted that during the time when a solid body rotated rapidly its axis of rotation did not change direction.

The gyroscope was first used practically in 1774, to create an artificial horizon for seamen. In the mid-19th century some scientists were already using gyroscopes to demonstrate certain laws of mechanics. Jean Léon Foucault, who coined the word gyroscope, used a spinning rotar to demonstrate the earth's rotation. In 1896 it was used by Obry to guide the first true self-propelled torpedo.

Dr. Elmer A. Sperry, an American engineer, made great use of the gyroscope, perfecting a gyrocompass, which is a great aid to seamen. Sperry also perfected an airplane stabilizer and a gyropilot, which allows a plane to be piloted automatically.

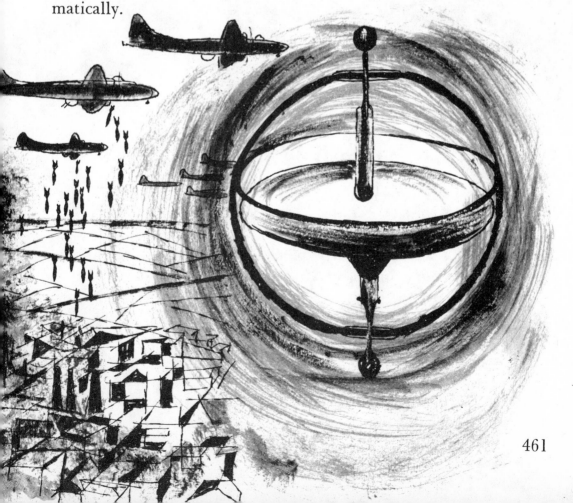

Farming Implements

THE first revolutionary change in farming methods was the invention of the cotton gin in 1790 by Eli Whitney. This machine separated the cotton seed from the fibres, a task which formerly was done slowly by hand. The cotton gin meant that more cotton could be produced, and turned the United States into a great cotton export country; it affected the economic and social conditions of the entire nation, especially in the Southern states.

In 1837 Cyrus McCormick invented his reaper, a machine with rotating blades which cut the grasses and grain quickly and easily. The same year Hiram and John Pitts of Maine in-

vented a thresher, and thereafter invention followed invention
on farms.

In 1870 the harvester appeared—known as the Locke machine. This invention formed grain bundles, compressed and
tied them, all automatically. About 1878 the Appleby Knotter
was added, and became standard equipment on all binders.

In the 1930's the Rust Brothers invented the cotton picker,
a machine which was able to do the work of 50 manual cotton
pickers. The picker stripped the bolls from the cotton plant,
then cleaned the lint from the burrs. However the machines
were very expensive, and are still not in general use for this
reason. More and more cotton farmers, especially in the Southwestern states, are using them because of the speed-up in
production and the saving on farm hands.

Sewing Machine

As far back as 1775 there were attempts to invent a sewing machine, but it was not until 1830 that a practical machine was invented by Barthélemy Thimmonier of France. It was made largely of wood and had a hooked needle which made a "chain stitch." About 1848 the "eye needle" was invented, and the first man to use this needle successfully was the American, Elias Howe. Howe's machine used the "lock stitch," and had a little shuttle which carried the thread through the loop made by the needle. This was the first modern sewing machine.

In 1850 Allen Benjamin Wilson improved the sewing machine by inventing the round bobbin and hook, but, like Howe's machine, it was still operated by hand. It was Isaac Singer who invented the foot treadle and a presser foot device that kept the fabric in place. Today electricity has replaced the foot treadle.

Typewriter

ENGLISH records state that one Henry Mill obtained a patent in the year 1714 for a machine which wrote printed letters one at a time. However this machine was never manufactured. The first American patent was given to William A. Burt of Detroit, who called his invention a "Typographer." This machine was destroyed by fire in the Washington patent office in 1836.

The writing machine we call the typewriter was not perfected until 1867. It was the work of three men: Christopher Latham Sholes, Samuel W. Soulé and Carlos Glidden, of Milwaukee, Wisconsin. In March of 1873 they signed a contract with Remington for the machine; in 1874 the first typewriters were offered for sale by Remington.

Further improvements followed. In 1878 the shift key was designed. Before this typewriters could only print capital letters.

Modern typewriters have progressed in design, so that today there are portables, electric and noiseless models. At present there is some talk about rearranging the keyboard so that the letters which occur most frequently in the English language are nearest our strongest and most agile fingers.

Electric Light and Generator

SCIENTISTS long have known that electricity heated wire, and many tried to use some sort of wire, electrically heated, to create an electric lamp. Thomas Edison tried too. In 1879 he used some cotton thread, heated in an oven so that it turned to carbon; he succeeded in putting this thread inside a glass globe from which the air had been pumped out. It worked! For 40 hours this cotton thread cast a light, then went out. Edison improved the globe by using bamboo instead of thread, and other scientists have used other materials which have improved Edison's lamp still further. William D. Coolidge discovered that tungsten was more suitable as a filament wire, and tungsten is used in many lamps today.

Michael Faraday is credited with inventing the generator to produce an electric current by mechanical power. Although it was crude it did form the basis of many future experiments; Zénobe Théophile Gramme, a Belgian, built a really practical generator forty years after Faraday. Later Robert Van de Graaff, an American, generated electricity by friction, much the same as you would if you rubbed your feet on a rug and touched metal. Static electricity is generated by such action.

The motor is very similar to the generator except that it uses an electric current to produce mechanical power for use in operating machines. The German engineer, Siemens, succeeded in demonstrating his motor on a train engine in 1879.

467

Telegraph

THE earliest practical telegraph was invented by Sir Charles Wheatstone, the famous English scientist, in 1837. The Wheatstone telegraph was used in England for several years, but did not excite as much interest as did the one invented by Samuel Finley Breese Morse, an American.

Morse began work on his model in 1832 and completed it in 1837, the same year as Wheatstone. He proposed that the United States put it to use, and after much debate Congress agreed to build an experimental telegraph line between Washington and Baltimore. On May 24th, 1844, Morse sent his first famous message from Washington. He tapped out in code, "What hath God wrought!" His friend, Alfred Vail, at the other end of the line in Baltimore, received the coded electrical impulses and sent a reply.

Many improvements have been made on the Morse telegraph, including one by Thomas Edison, who invented a method of sending four messages over the same line at the same time.

Phonograph

EDISON's invention of the phonograph was an accident. He was working on a telegraph repeater, and heard a musical note when the needle hit a dent in the paper tape. This gave him the idea for the phonograph; a sheet of tinfoil was wrapped around a cylinder and the speaking mouthpiece vibrated onto the foil. When other parts were put into place the sounds came back.

Telephone

ALEXANDER Graham Bell came from a family that had long been interested in teaching deaf mutes. During his youth he found out about Sir Charles Wheatstone's experiment with the needle telegraph, and he decided to try to invent a musical telegraph.

With the help of an assistant, Thomas A. Watson, he set about building a machine which would reproduce sounds clearly. He was finally able electrically to produce air vibrations, which make up sound, from a thin metal reel.

On March 10, 1876, Bell spoke the first words into his invention: "Mr. Watson, come here. I want you." Watson heard the message in the next room over the telephone line.

469

Sound and Pictures Through Space

TODAY we take radio and television for granted. But they did not come about suddenly. Hundreds of brilliant men from all over the world, many of them internationally famous like Maxwell, Hertz, Marconi, DeForest, Baird and Zworykin, made their contributions to science before these modern wonders were accomplished.

In the present-day transmitting station a microphone is set up to convert speech and music into electrical waves. A television camera picks up a picture and converts it into short electrical pulses and waves. All these pulses and waves are then transmitted out into space from the station antenna.

Your receiving antenna picks up all these electrical pulses and waves and sends them down to your receiving set. There they are assorted. Certain waves are sent to the speaker where they are reconverted into sound. The picture tube reconverts the short pulses and waves into a picture. Even pictures in color can be sent and received this way.

470

Birds, Balloons and Planes

THE idea of flying like a bird has filled man's imagination for thousands of years. More than 300 years ago Leonardo Da Vinci designed a set of flying wings pictured on this page. It took almost another 300 years for man to achieve Da Vinci's dream of flying.

Of course, man had floated in lighter-than-air balloon as early as 1783 but this was not really flying. The balloon, or dirigible, is filled with some gas like helium, which is lighter than air. It rises until it reaches a point where the surrounding air has thinned out so that volume for volume it is just as heavy as the balloon. The balloon can go higher only if some ballast or weight is dropped overboard.

Flying a heavier-than-air plane is something else again. The lower surface of a plane's wings is tilted. As the plane is moved forward by the action of its propeller, or by the thrust developed by its jet blast, its tilted wings press against the resistance of the onrushing air. This lifts the plane just as a kite is lifted by an oncoming gust of air. Birds soar by flapping their wings downward and backward against the resistance of the air.

Since the Wright Brothers made their first successful flight in 1903, vast improvements have been made in aircraft. Jet aircraft now travel faster than sound. They have thus broken the sound barrier. They pass you by before you can hear them coming!

Vulcanizing Process

THREE regions produce all the rubber in the world: South America and the West Indies; Africa and Madagascar; Malaya and Ceylon. Rubber is collected by making a small cut in a rubber tree and hanging a cup under the cut; a tree gives about one fluid ounce of rubber latex per tapping.

Early use of rubber was limited. In 1770 an English chemist rubbed a chunk of crude rubber over pencil marks and found it rubbed out the marks—which is how rubber got its name. Later rubber was used to coat fabrics, and to make rubber shoes and bottles. But these products hardened in cold weather and became sticky in hot weather.

In January of 1839, Charles Goodyear cooked a "stew" on his kitchen stove, containing rubber, white lead and sulphur. This became the vulcanizing process, and from it grew the entire rubber industry.

Today there are several types of "synthetic" or man-made rubber, such as Neoprene, Butyl and others. In many cases these chemically-produced rubber synthetics are better than the natural product.

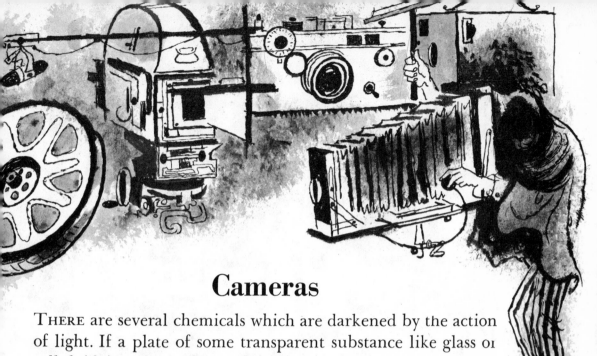

Cameras

THERE are several chemicals which are darkened by the action of light. If a plate of some transparent substance like glass or celluloid is coated with such a chemical substance and then exposed to focused rays of light from a camera lens, an image forms on the plate. This plate is chemically fixed (made permanent) and is called a negative. Light areas in the original scene appear dark here. When coated photographic paper is exposed to light coming through a negative, the original scene reappears. Joseph Niepce and Louis Daguerre were the first to develop a process of permanent photography after many others had worked in the field.

We know that Walt Disney's cartoons are just inanimate sketches. Yet they are so cleverly drawn that when they are flashed upon a screen in rapid succession they give the appearance of being alive. In the movies, 48 still pictures are flashed before our eyes each second. The action is so rapid that the movement of the actors seems continous, and we don't even notice any flicker. It was Charles Francis Jenkins who invented the movie projector in 1894 and gave the first movie show in history.

In 1906, the Englishman Eugene Lauste patented a method of recording sound and pictures at the same time. Although his invention failed, he was on the right track. With the invention of the electron tube and the photoelectric cell it became possible to record sound on film and then to change the recording back into sound.

473

The Automobile

THE idea of a "horseless carriage" came to Europe at about the same time as the first crude steam engines. In the year 1619 two Englishmen, Ramsay and Wildgoose, took out a patent for a vehicle that moved without the aid of horses; years later, in 1680, Sir Isaac Newton devised a machine which moved by steam jets forced from the back of the carriage.

Various inventors experimented with steam automobiles all throughout the 18th and 19th centuries; one of them even had a steam boiler. In 1829 a steam boiler automobile was built which carried fifteen passengers at the rate of 12 miles per hour. Later regular gasoline engines were tried, which were mounted on bicycles and tricycles. The engines were small, and these models were not very successful.

In the 1890's Americans began to give serious attention to the automobile. Henry Ford's first gasoline car, brought out in 1893, was a great improvement on European models, and reached a speed of 20 miles per hour. When gasoline is ignited by an electric spark within an engine cylinder, it expands with explosive force and drives a piston forward. The motion of the piston, through a system of connecting rods, cranks and gears, drives the wheel and moves the car. By the year 1910 improvements in gears, engine cylinders, transmissions and steering devices had been put into automobiles. They grew more and more powerful, until today automobiles with 250 to 300 horsepower are commonplace.

Submarine

MANY inventors, such as Robert Fulton and David Bushnell, tried to invent a practical submarine, and met with some small success, but it remained for Simon Lake and John P. Holland to patent practical undersea boats which, with modifications and improvements, are found in every navy today. The first 14-foot submarine was built by Simon Lake in 1894; Holland's better boat was built in 1898.

All pre-atomic power submarines have Diesel engines for use on the surface and storage batteries and electric motors to drive them while submerged. Breathing undersea is accomplished by using compressed air tanks.

The hull of a submarine is divided into water-tight compartments, and it carries a series of water ballast tanks. To submerge, water is pumped into these tanks to make the sub heavier; to re-surface the water is pumped out again.

476

Photoelectric Cell

IN one form or another the photoelectric cell makes possible television and sound movies, turns on lights and opens doors, acts as a burglar alarm and measures the brightness of stars.

Some preliminary work was done by such scientists as Heinrich Hertz and Wilhelm Hallwachs late in the 19th century, but it was Albert Einstein who explained the details of the photoelectric cell, and for his work in this field he won the Nobel Prize in Physics in 1921. Einstein proved that light and other forms of radiation do not travel in a continuous stream of waves, but in little bunches, or "quanta."

The doors of New York's Pennsylvania Station illustrate how a photoelectric cell works. A beam of light is sent across the passageway where people pass; this light hits a photocell and produces current; the current operates a magnet which holds down a lever keeping the door closed. When the light is interrupted by a person passing, the current stops. The lever is released to make a new contact closing another circuit, which operates motors to open the door.

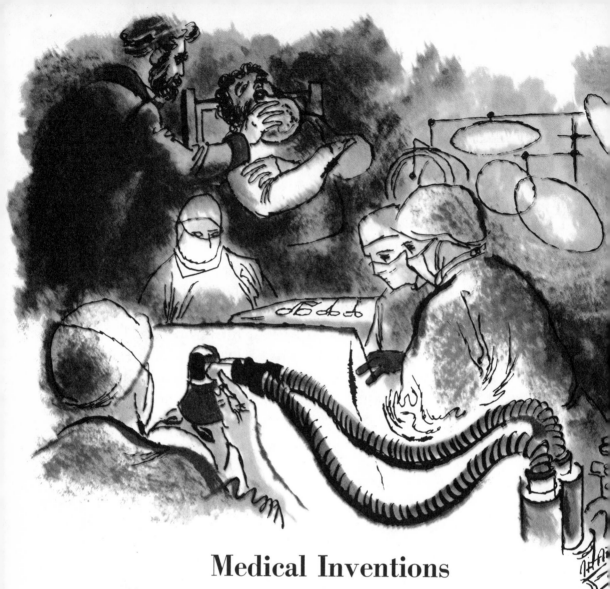

Medical Inventions

THE purpose of all inventions is to make life better and easier for mankind. Freedom from pain and disease is as important as freedom from drudgery, and medical discoveries may therefore be classified as true inventions.

Opium and Indian hemp were pain-killers known to the ancients. Nitrous oxide, discovered by Sir Humphry Davy in 1880, was first used as an anesthetic in 1844 by a dentist named Horace Wells. Ether was introduced in 1842 by a surgeon named Crawford Long; chloroform came in 1847, used by Sir James Simpson. The purpose of any anesthetic, then as now, is to deaden the sensations of touch and pain.

In 1927 Philip Drinker watched a pulmotor save a child overcome by smoke. A pulmotor works like a bellows, forcing air into the lungs and sucking it out again. Drinker wanted to

478

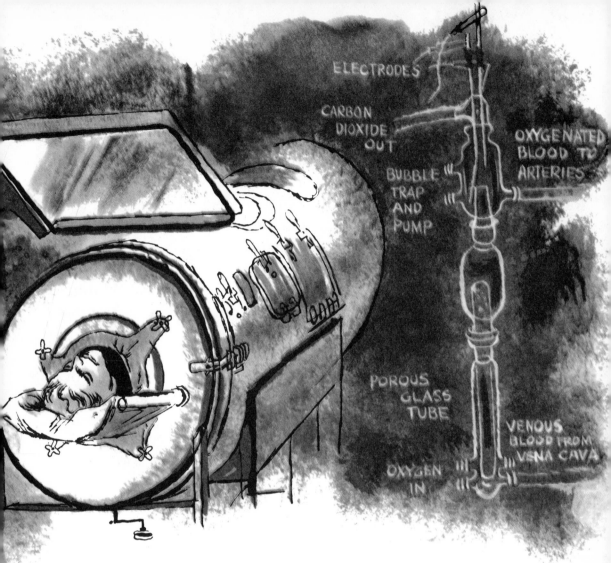

ELECTRODES

CARBON
DIOXIDE
OUT

OXYGENATED
BLOOD TO
ARTERIES

BUBBLE
TRAP
AND
PUMP

POROUS
GLASS
TUBE

VENOUS
BLOOD FROM
VENA CAVA

OXYGEN
IN

invent a machine which would force the lungs to breathe normally. Dr. Thunberg of Sweden had devised a closed room into which he put patients whose breathing muscles were paralyzed. As air was pumped out of, then into the room, breathing was artificially stimulated. Drinker modified this room into a small box-like apparatus, and in 1931 it was put to work successfully to save the lives of polio victims.

The Mechanical (Artificial) Heart was invented in 1933 by Alexis Carrell and Charles A. Lindbergh. It was used in connection with transplanted organs, to observe their functions outside the body. It was also valuable for operations on patients with heart disease; the invention enabled the blood supply to by-pass the heart and lungs while the doctors worked on the injured heart without worrying about shutting off the blood supply of the patient.

Refrigeration

ICE, of course, was the first refrigerator. "Frozen water" was successfully made in quantity in 1834 by Jacob Perkins and used to keep food fresh.

The first mechanical refrigerator was invented (1910-1913) by J. M. Larsen. It was a manually operated machine, and was not put into general use. It remained for the Kelvinator Company to put the first refrigerators on the market in 1918. From their refrigerator it was only a step to the first "sealed" unit in 1926, where the motor was put into an enclosed section atop the refrigerator.

The motor compresses air or some other gas into a small cylinder, thus concentrating its heat. A fan then blows air over the cylinder, cooling it off. When the compressed air is released it expands, cooler than before. Thus cooled, it passes through pipes in the refrigerator. Modern refrigerators even have freezing compartments, where food can be frozen and stored for use far in the future.

In 1897 Joseph McCreary of Toledo patented an air washer, which not only purified the air but also cooled it and made it more humid.

Plastics

THE oldest of the synthetic plastics is cellulose nitrate. Alexander Parkes, an Englishman, prepared various articles from a solution of cellulose nitrate and camphor during a period of time from 1855 to 1865. However it was John Wesley Hyatt, an American, who improved cellulose to a point where it was workable. Hyatt had entered a contest to find a substitute for ivory in the making of billiard balls. He didn't win, but after a series of experiments and improvements celluloid was produced for the making of collars, substitute window panes for carriages, etc.

The next plastic was a shellac molding composition. Emile Berliner used this compound to make phonograph records.

Hundreds of plastics are on the market today, used mainly as substitutes for the more costly stainless steel and aluminum. Polyethylene is used for wire covering and insulation, and vinyls are used in place of leathers. Most plastics are waterproof and do a good job substituting for metals.

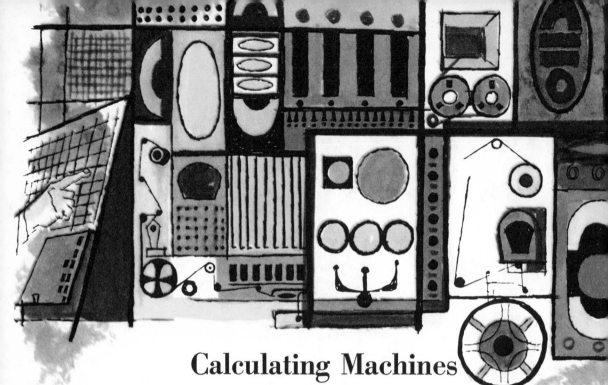

Calculating Machines

THE first instrument which can be called an adding machine was invented by Blaise Pascal in 1642. It consisted of a set of cylinders with numbers marked on the surfaces. For each unit to be added the cylinders changed one space only. It was crude, but it worked with simple arithmetic problems. Many others tried to improve the adding machine; Charles Babbage, in 1843 perfected a device which was the basis of many other calculating machines. It was not until 1888 that William S. Burroughs patented the machine which, with a few improvements, is most similar to the one which is used today. Modern calculating machines can add, subtract, multiply and divide accurately and extremely rapidly.

The greatest advance in calculators has been through electronics. In 1944 an experimental machine was built at Harvard, using 760,000 parts, including cathode-ray tubes. This first model took four days to figure out a problem which would have taken a mathematician 100 years to solve!

The latest "electronic brain" can solve the most complicated problems in minutes; it has a "memory" which enables it to remember numbers and instructions. When properly worked it can even "think for itself." This and other machines have been considerably streamlined in recent years by the development of the tiny transistor.

482

SPACE EXPLORATION

PROJECT MERCURY

This is the United States satellite program carried out by National Aeronautics and Space Administration that pioneered the way for manned space flight. Major goal: to launch an astronaut into a controlled orbit around the Earth and recover him safely. This goal was realized February 20, 1962, when the now famous spacecraft, "Freedom 7," orbited Astronaut John H. Glenn three times around the Earth.

The launch vehicle or booster has a sole purpose: to develop velocity.

Five minutes after blastoff, spacecraft separates from launch vehicle. Altitude is now 100 miles, velocity is 17,500 miles per hour (mph.).

BLASTOFF...

Mercury spacecraft is launched by an Atlas-D rocket. At blastoff, Atlas raises Mercury slowly, then Mercury gains velocity with altitude.

SOME OF THE FIRST SPACE EXPLORERS

Sputnik I and subsequent scientific satellites, planetary probes and manned ships have turned one of man's greatest aspirations — the conquest of space — into a reality. Here are the vital statistics about some of the first of these exploration programs.

SPUTNIK I First man-made satellite to be sent into orbit around the Earth. Launched by U.S.S.R., October 4, 1957. Perigee: 138 mi. Apogee: 598 mi. Weight: 184 lbs. Length: 6'4". Diameter: 22.8".

EXPLORER First United States satellite to be orbited around the Earth. Launched January 31, 1958. Perigee: 2 mi. Apogee: 1,573 mi. Weight: 30.8 lbs. Length: 6'8". Diameter: 6".

WALK IN SPACE Russia took its first walk in space on March 18, 1965, and the United States its first on June 3, 1965.

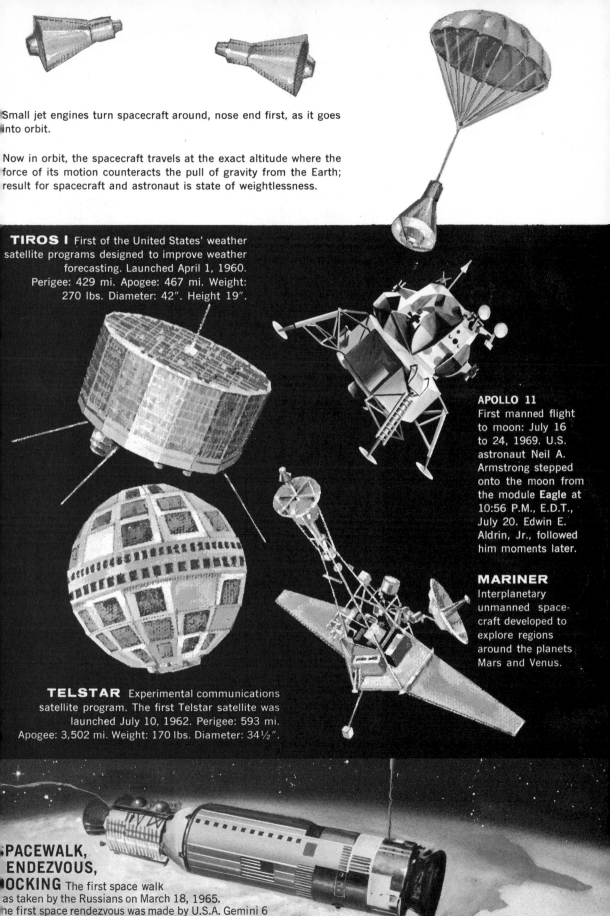

Small jet engines turn spacecraft around, nose end first, as it goes into orbit.

Now in orbit, the spacecraft travels at the exact altitude where the force of its motion counteracts the pull of gravity from the Earth; result for spacecraft and astronaut is state of weightlessness.

TIROS I First of the United States' weather satellite programs designed to improve weather forecasting. Launched April 1, 1960. Perigee: 429 mi. Apogee: 467 mi. Weight: 270 lbs. Diameter: 42". Height 19".

APOLLO 11 First manned flight to moon: July 16 to 24, 1969. U.S. astronaut Neil A. Armstrong stepped onto the moon from the module **Eagle** at 10:56 P.M., E.D.T., July 20. Edwin E. Aldrin, Jr., followed him moments later.

MARINER Interplanetary unmanned spacecraft developed to explore regions around the planets Mars and Venus.

TELSTAR Experimental communications satellite program. The first Telstar satellite was launched July 10, 1962. Perigee: 593 mi. Apogee: 3,502 mi. Weight: 170 lbs. Diameter: 34½".

SPACEWALK, RENDEZVOUS, DOCKING The first space walk was taken by the Russians on March 18, 1965. The first space rendezvous was made by U.S.A. Gemini 6 and Gemini 7 on Dec. 15, 1965. The first docking feat was achieved March 16, 1966 by the U.S.A. Gemini 8.

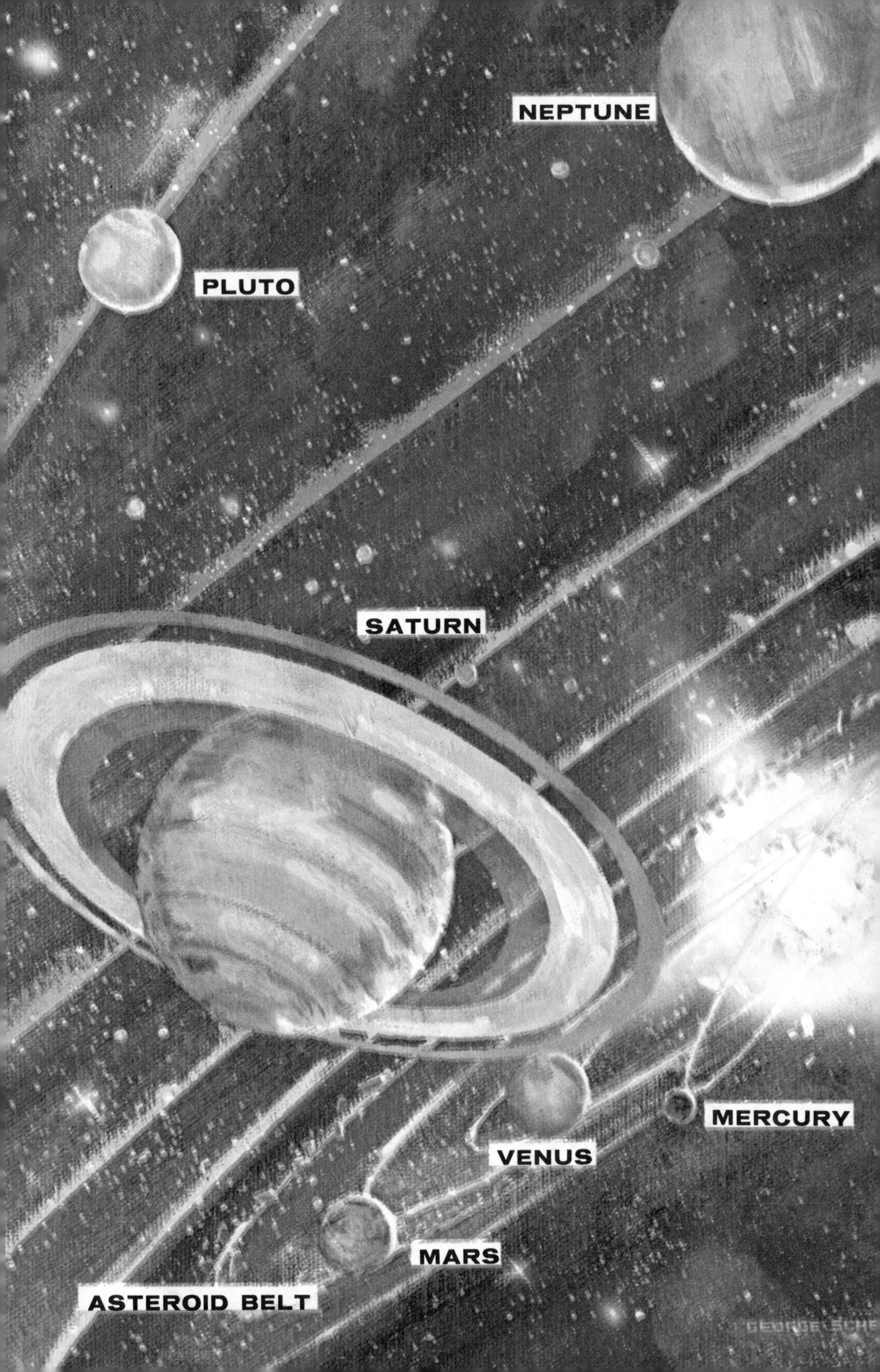
NEPTUNE
PLUTO
SATURN
MERCURY
VENUS
MARS
ASTEROID BELT

ANUS

JUPITER

EARTH

THE SOLAR SYSTEM

Our solar system, with the Sun at its center, and nine planets revolving around it in elliptical (near-circular) orbits, is but one of an esti-mated 100,000 planetary systems similar to it, in the giant disk-shaped Milky Way Galaxy. With-in the Milky Way Galaxy, however, there are at least 100 billion stars; beyond, are millions upon millions of other Galaxies. Many are similar to our Milky Way Galaxy; some smaller, others incredibly larger.

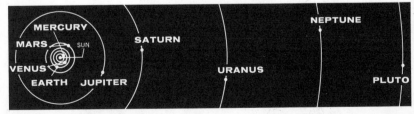

MERCURY
MARS   SUN
VENUS
EARTH   JUPITER
SATURN
URANUS
NEPTUNE
PLUTO

MARS This planet is one of the prime targets for space exploration because of its relative proximity to the Earth. At its closest point, Mars is 35 million miles away. Possessing some atmosphere, the equatorial temperature of Mars ranges from 50° F. above to 90° F. below zero.

PLUTO This is the second smallest of the planets (diameter: 3,600 miles). Pluto takes 284 years to orbit around the Sun.

NEPTUNE This is the fourth largest planet in our solar system. Its diameter is 26,800 miles. The temperature on Neptune is 330° F. below zero. With a deep atmosphere, it receives only a tenth of 1 per cent of the Earth's light and heat.

COMPARATIVE CHART

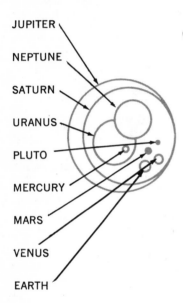

JUPITER

NEPTUNE

SATURN

URANUS

PLUTO

MERCURY

MARS

VENUS

EARTH

THE PLANETS

A spacecraft traveling in a direct line at the velocity of 100,000 miles per hour (mph.) could reach Mars in about 15 hours. Pluto, our outermost planet, would then be reached in four years of continuous flight. But if we tried for the nearest star, beyond our solar system — Proxima Centauri (25 million million miles distant) — it would take 30,000 years to get there.

SATURN Next to Jupiter, this is our solar system's second largest planet. Saturn's orbit around the Sun takes nearly 30 years to complete; its temperature is 250° F. below zero. Saturn has nine satellites revolving around it.

VENUS This planet is other prime exploration targ Often called the Earth's "twin s ter" because of its close rese blance to the Earth in size a density, Venus is within our orbit (26 million miles away at closest point), which makes it closest to us of any of the plan

JUPITER This is our solar system's largest planet, with a diameter of 86,900 miles. It possesses twelve moons. Jupiter spins on its axis faster than any of the other planets — revolving completely every 9 hours and 50 minutes.

MERCURY With no atmosphere, this planet always has one side facing the sun; the temperature on that side is 750° F. above zero; on the other side, it is 400° F. below zero. It is the closest of the planets to the Sun, and is the smallest planet.

URANUS. Distance from the Sun: 1,783 million miles; orbital period: 84 years; diameter: 29,-500 miles. Uranus does not, as do the other planets, spin in an almost upright position on its axis; instead it spins on its side.

EARTH

Our Earth is fifth in size among its sister planets in the solar system. Distance from the Sun: 93 million mi. Diameter: 7,918 mi. It orbits around the Sun at an average speed of 18.52 miles per second. It possesses a very deep atmosphere, four-fifths of its surface is covered with ice caps and seas, and it harbors life.

VAN ALLEN RADIATION BELT

This is the intense radiation zone in space around the Earth detected by Explorer I.

THE MOON
A natural satellite of Earth, the Moon turns with the Earth in its annual revolution around the Sun. Distance from Earth Perigee 221,463 mi.; Apogee, 252,710 mi. The far side of the Moon, hidden from Earth's direct view, was first photographed by Lunik III, U.S.S.R. lunar probe.

BEYOND THE MOON

Now that we have reached the moon a number of times the most challenging space adventure in the years ahead will be to land men on Mars. But remember that the distance between the earth and the moon is roughly 240,000 miles, while Mars—at its closest point—is 35 million miles away! When we do reach the Red Planet, explorations there will bring the richest scientific prize of all—the possibility of finding some form of life on planets other than our own.

GLOSSARY OF SPACE TERMS*

Abort: A space mission aborts when it fails to accomplish its purpose for any reason other than enemy action. An abort may occur at any point from start of countdown to final destination.

Absolute zero: The temperature at which all thermo motion or heat action ceases, approximately minus 273.16 degrees C., minus 459.69 degrees F. or zero degrees Kelvin.

Acceleration: The rate of increase of velocity.

Aerodynamics: That field of dynamics which treats of the motion of bodies relative to the air and the forces which act upon the body, especially as they relate to flight through the air.

Aeronomy: The science that treats of the Earth's atmosphere, or the atmosphere of other celestial bodies, especially in respect to its properties, motions, and reactions.

Air-breathing: The term air-breathing refers to the engine which requires the intake of air for combustion of the fuel, as in a ramjet or turbojet. This is contrasted with the rocket engine which carries its own oxidizer and can operate beyond the atmosphere.

Anoxia: An absence of oxygen in the blood, cells or tissues of the body.

Antigravity: The hypothetical effect upon any mass by which some still-to-be-discovered energy field would cancel or reduce the gravitational attraction of Earth (or any other body).

Aphelion: The point at which a planet or other celestial object is farthest from the Sun in its orbit about the Sun.

Apogee: That point in an elliptical orbit of a satellite at which the distance is greatest between the orbiting body and its primary.

Artificial satellite: A man-made object placed in orbit.

Astrionics: Electronics as applied especially to astronautics.

Astronaut: One concerned with flying through space, or one who actually flies through space.

Astronautics: The science and technology of space flight.

Astronomical unit: The mean distance of Earth from the Sun, 92,907,000 miles.

Astrophysics: The study of the physical and chemical nature of celestial bodies and their environs.

Atmosphere: The body of air surrounding the Earth; also, the body of gases surrounding or comprising any planet or celestial body.

Ballistics: The science or art that deals with the motion, behavior, appearance or modification of missiles acted upon by propellants, rifling, wind, gravity, temperature or any other modifying substance, condition or force.

Biopropellant: A rocket propellant consisting of two unmixed or uncombined chemicals (fuel and oxidant) fed to the combustion chamber separately.

Booster: A propulsion unit used in initial stage of flight.

Boost-glide vehicle: A rocket-boosted winged vehicle under aerodynamic control capable of leaving the atmosphere, entering space and re-entering the atmosphere by gliding.

Burnout: The point in time or trajectory when the propellant of the spacecraft is exhausted or cut off, resulting in the end of combustion.

Celestial mechanics: The study of motion in space, natural or man-made.

Centrifugal force: The apparent force tending to carry an object away from a center of rotation.

Circular velocity: The speed required to maintain a body in circular orbit.

Cislunar: Space between the Earth and Moon.

*From SPACE-THE NEW FRONTIER; published by the National Aeronautics and Space Administration

Closed ecological system: A system which provides for the body's metabolism in a spacecraft by means of cycling carbon dioxide, urine and other waste matters chemically or by photosynthesis, to convert them back into oxygen and food.

Countdown: The step-by-step process leading to space vehicle launching. It is performed in accordance with the predesigned time schedule and marked by a count in inverse numerical order. The countdown ends with T-time, that is "T minus 60 minutes" indicates 60 minutes from launching, except for holds. At the climax the countdown narrows down to seconds, "4-3-2-1-blastoff."

Deceleration: Negative acceleration (slowing down).

Doghouse: A protuberance or blister that houses an instrument on an otherwise smooth skin of a rocket.

Doppler principle: A principle of physics that states, "as the distance between a source of constant vibrations and an observer diminishes or increases, the frequencies appear to be greater or less."

Early warning satellite: A reconnaisance satellite used to detect enemy ballistic missile firings early enough to give warning.

Eccentricity: The degree of deviation from a circular orbit.

Ecliptic: The plane of Earth's orbit around Sun.

Egads button: A button used by the range safety officer to destruct a missile in flight. The word "egads" is an acronym for Electronic Ground Automatic Destruct Sequencer.

Environmental space chamber: A chamber (sometimes a simulated spacecraft) in which humidity, temperature, pressure, fluid contents, noise and movement may be controlled so as to simulate different space conditions. It is normally used for astronaut training.

Escape velocity: The velocity which if attained by an object will permit it to overcome the gravitational pull of the Earth or other astronomical body and to move into space. The escape velocity from Earth's gravity field is approximately seven miles per second.

Fission: The release of nuclear energy through splitting of atoms.

Flight profile: It is the graphic portrayal of the spacecraft's line of flight as seen from the side, indicating the various altitudes along the route.

Free fall: The motion of any unpowered body traveling in a gravitational field.

Fusion: The release of nuclear energy through uniting of atoms.

"G" or "G force": This is the force exerted upon object by gravity or by reaction to acceleration or deceleration, usually from a change of direction. One "G" is the measure of the gravitational pull required to move a body at the rate of approximately 32.17 feet per second.

Gimbal: A gimbal is a mechanical frame with two mutually perpendicular intersecting axes of rotation. A gimballed rocket motor is mounted so as to have two manually perpendicular axes of rotation to provide corrective movements in the pitching and yawing of the vehicle.

Gravity: Gravity is that force that tends to pull bodies toward the center of mass. It is the resultant effect, at the Earth's surface, of the Earth's gravitation and of the centrifugal force of the Earth's rotation upon a free-falling body. It is measured by the acceleration produced in the free-falling body toward the center of the Earth. The acceleration due to gravity (at latitude 45 degrees) is 32.1740 feet per second per second. A body starting at rest falls 16.085 feet in the first second, 48.255 feet in the next second, 80.425 feet in the next and so on.

Ground Support Equipment: GSE is all ground equipment (part of the complete space exploration system) that must be furnished to insure complete support of the space system. It includes all implements, tools and devices either mobile or fixed, required to inspect, test, adjust, calibrate, appraise, gauge, measure, repair, overhaul, assemble, disassemble, transport, safeguard, record, store or otherwise function in support of a space vehicle. This takes in the research and development phase and the operational phase. (GSE is not considered to include land or buildings.)

Gyroscope: A device consisting of a wheel so mounted that its spinning axis is free to rotate about either of two other axes perpendicular to itself and to each other. Once set in rotation the gyro axle will maintain a constant direction regardless of the fact Earth is turning under it.

Hard landing: A hard landing is the deliberate, destructive impact of a space vehicle on a predetermined celestial target. The vehicle is destroyed upon impact, hence "hard landing". The object of such a space shot is to test propulsion and guidance and to prepare the way, normally for a "soft landing".

Interplanetary: Between planets.

Interstellar: Between stars.

Ion: An atom that has lost or acquired one or more electrons.

Ionosphere: A layer or region of the atmosphere characterized by ionized gases.

Light-year: The distance light travels in one year at 186,284 miles per second.

Liquid propellant: A rocket propellant in liquid form.

Lunar: Of or pertaining to the Moon.

Mach: A unit of speed measurement for a moving object equal to the speed of sound in the medium in which the object travels. Mach I, under standard conditions at sea level is about 759 miles per hour. It decreases with altitude.

Mass: The quantity of matter in an object.

Mass ratio: The ratio of a rocket's mass at launch to its mass at burnout.

Monopropellant: A rocket propellant consisting of a single substance, especially a liquid containing both fuel and oxidant, either combined or mixed together.

Nose cone: The cone-shaped leading end of a rocket, missile or rocket vehicle.

Orbit: Path of a body relative to its primary.

Orbital curve: Is one of the tracks over the surface of the primary body being orbited which has been traced by a satellite orbiting about it several times a day in a direction other than due East or due West. Each successive track is displaced to the West by an amount equal to the degrees of rotation of the primary body between each orbit.

Orbital velocity: The speed of body following a closed or open orbit, most commonly applied to elliptical or near-circular orbits

Payload: Useful cargo.

Perigee: The point at which a moon or an artificial satellite in its orbit is closest to its primary.

Perihelion: The point in an elliptical orbit around the Sun which is nearest the Sun.

Perturbation: The effect of the gravitational attraction of one body on the orbit of another.

Primary: The body around which a satellite orbits.

Probe: An unmanned projectile sent into space to gather information.

Propellant: A liquid or solid substance burned in a rocket for the purpose of developing thrust.

Radiation: The emission and propagation of energy through space or a material medium in the form of waves. It is energy traveling as a wave motion. The term when unqualified usually refers to electromagnetic radiation—gamma rays, X-rays, ultraviolet rays, visible light, infrared rays and radio waves.

Retro-rocket: A rocket fitted on or in a vehicle that discharges counter to the direction of flight, used to retard forward motion.

493

Revolution: Orbital motion around a primary.

Rotation: Rotary motion on an axis.

Satellite: A body moving around a primary, especially a celestial body.

Satelloid: An artificial body or vehicle like an artificial satellite except that it is under engine thrust (intermittent or continuous) in its orbit.

Soft landing: The process of landing on the Moon or other spacial body "softly" enough to prevent damage or destruction to the vehicle.

Space: That part of universe between celestial bodies.

Space platform: A large orbiting satellite conceived as a habitable base in space with scientific, exploratory or military applications. Also known as a space station.

Spatiography: The science of space. Spatiography is especially concerned with the charting of magnetic fields, radiation belts, and meteoroid belts.

Specific impulse: The thrust produced by a jet-reaction engine per unit weight of propellant burned per unit time, or per mass of working fluid passing through the engine in unit time.

Speed of light: The speed at which light travels, approximately 186,284 miles per second. This is considered to be the ultimate speed for space travel. Distances in space are measured in light-years. One light-year is equal to 5,880,000,000,000 miles.

Stationary orbit: A circular orbit in which the satellite moves from west to east at such velocity as to remain fixed above a particular point on the equator; sometimes referred to as a 24-hour orbit.

Sustainer engine: An engine that sustains or increases the velocity of a spacecraft once it has achieved its programmed velocity from the booster engine.

Telemetering: A system for taking measurements within a space vehicle during flight and transmitting them by radio to a ground station. The spacecraft telemeter collects and transmits data on such things as speed, temperature, pressure and radiation.

Terrestrial: Of or pertaining to the Earth.

Thrust: The amount of "push" developed by a rocket; measured in pounds.

Tracking station: A station set up to track an object moving through space, usually by means of radio or radar.

Trajectory: The path described by a space vehicle.

Translunar: Beyond the Moon.

Weightlessness: The absence of any apparent gravitational pull on an object. Absolute weightlessness is obtained only by a body falling freely in a vacuum. An orbiting satellite is a special case of free fall. The condition of weightlessness is also induced when a body moves at a speed sufficient to counteract the gravitational attraction of any other body upon it.

FACT QUESTIONS TO CHECK COMPREHENSION
FOR PRESCHOOL AND EARLY GRADES

(Write all the answers on a separate sheet of paper. Do not write in this book. Someone else in your family may want to use these questions.)

PETS (Pages 3-34)

1. What animals were man's first pets?

2. What dogs were called "earth dogs"?

3. What is the Beagle's idea of a good time?

4. For what sport are Greyhounds used?

5. What were Spaniels originally trained to retrieve?

6. Describe the color known as "brindle."

7. What unusual sense does the St. Bernard have?

8. What dog is most often used for farm work?

9. What is the breed name for Police Dogs?

10. What is the usual color of the Irish Setter?

11. What dog has been described as not being high enough to look like one dog, and too long to look like one dog?

12. How much does a Chihuahua weigh?

13. What two kinds of dogs came over on the Mayflower with the Pilgrims?

14. What dog is named after the capital of China?

15. What is the name of the smartest dog?

16. What breed of dog is so old that the Egyptians drew his picture?

17. What breed of dog is named after a German?

18. How can you tell that the Eskimos do not make pets of their dogs?

DOMESTIC ANIMALS (Pages 35-66)

1. What fierce wild animal was the ancestor of our modern pig?

2. What does the word "domestic" mean?

3. What was the most famous trail followed by the cowboys?

4. What country do Brahman cattle come from?

5. Name the two best dairy cows.

6. What kind of horse was used by the Pony Express?

7. Although there are not many left today, what was the name of the most famous type of work horse?

8. How did the Quarter Horse get its name?

9. Explain why Comanche was not killed or captured by the Indians.

10. What horses are only 40 inches high?

11. What name is given to donkeys in Mexico?

12. Is it true that both tame and wild sheep have wool coats?

13. How do the horns of a goat and a sheep differ?

14. How can you tell whether a chicken will lay white or brown eggs?

15. In what way are the feet of ducks and geese alike?

WILD ANIMALS (Pages 67-98)

1. Name a kind of animal that has become extinct.

2. Name two ways that modern man protects wild animals.

3. What is the tallest land animal?

4. How do the stripes of the Zebra help to hide it from its enemies?

5. Is it true that most captured Gorillas grow wild and unfriendly?

6. What member of the monkey family carries on tribal warfare?

7. What animal wears armor like the knights of old?

8. To what family of animals does the Cougar belong?

9. Is the Hippopotamus a closer relation to the horse or the pig?

10. What is another name for the American Buffalo?

11. Is it true that a mother deer is called a buck?

12. Name a shy animal that has more toes on its front feet than on its back feet.

13. What animal sees more of the world upside-down than it does right-side up?

14. When a Bear sleeps all winter long it is called _____ing.

15. What is one food that all Bears like?

16. What is a strange fact about the Elephant's big ears?

17. What member of the antelope family hides in the water?

18. Is it true that the Camel stores water in its humps?

19. Is it true that when you see a Lion with a majestic flowing mane you know it is a female?

20. Which of the wild cats is most dangerous for man?

21. What two animals does the Gnu most resemble?

22. Name a trick used by the sly Fox to escape its enemies.

23. Name an animal that keeps its babies in a stomach pouch.

BIRDS (*Pages 99-130*)

1. In what way is a baby bird like a baby human?

2. Name a bird that can fly backwards.

3. Name a bird that can be heard three miles away.

4. What trick do Blue Jays play on squirrels?

5. What is the first bird to arrive north in the spring?

6. What bird can bark like a dog and meow like a cat?

7. What bird can open up its tail feathers into a huge colored fan?

8. What bird was once trained to hunt for sport?

9. How are Carrier Pigeons used in war time?

10. Is it true that the "wise old Owl" is really not a very smart bird?

11. What bird was named for the man who founded Maryland?

12. Why was the Starling first brought to America?

13. What little bird builds an extra nest to fool attackers?

14. What bird has a bag under its bill like a balloon?

15. What four foot tall bird is a bright pink color?

16. Is it true that the Eagle is bald?

17. How many people could you feed from one Ostrich egg?

18. Is it true that Swans can dive down into deep lakes to get their food?

19. What is the name of a Society that uses its influence to protect birds?

BUTTERFLIES, BEES, BUGS, AND OTHER INSECTS (*Pages 131-162*)

1. Is an insect an animal?

2. Is it true that butterflies never eat; they just drink?

3. What caterpillar protects itself by acting like a snake?

4. What butterfly likes to fight so much it will even battle a grasshopper?

5. What butterfly is protected because it happens to look like another butterfly that birds don't like to eat?

6. If the silkworm is not a worm, what is it?

7. How do moths and butterflies differ in the time they like to fly about?

8. What do scientists think is the reason for those big spots on moths which look like eyes?

9. Name the four stages in the marvelous process through which a butterfly goes.

10. Is it true that the cricket's ears are on its legs?

11. In what way does the "singing" of an insect remind you of playing the violin?

12. What ferocious insect washes its face with its front legs the way a cat does?

13. Is it true that the hard shell of a beetle keeps it from flying?

14. In what way do some beetles help the farmer?

15. In what way are some beetles the farmer's enemies?

16. What insect carries its own battery flashlight?

17. What insect is known as the "darning needle"?

18. Is it true that the queen bee is the only one of the whole colony which is still alive when winter comes?

19. What is the name of the insect which knew how to make paper long before man did?

FISH, SHELLFISH, AND REPTILES (*Pages 163-194*)

1. Name two ways that undersea explorers can describe what they find in the silent world of the ocean.

2. How big are Plankton?

3. Is it true that some Jellyfish have a poisonous *bite?*

4. Pick one shellfish in this list that does not grow its own shell:

   Snail, Hermit Crab, Scallop, Oyster.

5. What kind of an island is made up of the old skeletons of sea animals?

6. Is it true that fish begin to migrate from the sea when winter time comes?

7. Fish are good for us to eat because their flesh contains lots of _____ and _____.

8. Is it true that Mackerel will only drop their eggs in one special place along the coast?

9. What is the name of a little fish that is said to "feed the world"?

10. Salmon start their lives in _____ water, grow up in _____ water, and return to _____ water.

11. It is hard to believe that the Tuna we get from a little can may once have weighed as much as _____ pounds.

12. What is the name of an important foodfish that can lay as many as _____ _____ eggs?

13. What is the name of a fish that swims upright when it is young, and on its side when it grows older?

14. How did the Catfish get its name?

15. Is it true that sportsmen look for Trout in warm, muddy lakes?

16. What fish swims by flapping its gigantic wings?

17. What fish has a big weapon that sticks out in front?

18. What do you know about the Whale that shows it is not a fish?

19. How does an Octopus capture its dinner?

20. Eels start their lives in _____ water, grow up in _____ water, and return to _____ water.

FLOWERS AND PLANTS (*Pages 195-226*)

1. What is the name of the chemical in a plant's leaves which is used to manufacture food for the plant?

2. How do birds and insects help plants to reproduce?

3. To cultivate flowers means to take _____ of them.

4. What flower is named after the Greek word for rainbow?

5. Is it true that the American Beauty Rose was an accident of nature?

6. Name a flower that blooms so early it may have to push its way up through the snow.

7. It is hard to believe, but the_____ belongs to the Lily family.

8. What flower is said to be worn by an unmarried man?

9. How can you tell a Jonquil from a Daffodil?

10. What country do we think of when we see Tulips?

11. How do the Flytrap and the Pitcher Plant get their nitrogen?

12. Why is it that desert plants bloom for only a day or two?

TREES AND SHRUBS (*Pages 227-258*)

1. A good way to tell a tree from a shrub is to remember that a shrub generally has _____ _____ .

2. From what tree do we get wintergreen oil?

3. What tree gives us a syrup that is good on pancakes?

4. The _____ people believed that the first man was formed from a mighty Ash tree.

5. Which tree is shaped like a bursting sky rocket?

6. The _____ and the _____ are used for Christmas trees.

7. What American tree has such hard wood that it is used to make the heads of golf clubs?

8. What nice-smelling tree is used to make closets and clothes chests?

9. From which tree would you pick acorns?

10. Which tree grows so big around the trunk that if you cut a hole you could drive a car through it?

11. What is the best time of the year to pick apples?

12. What is the name of a tree that has no branches and never gets narrower at the top?

13. On what tree might you see a silk-worm?

14. What tree gives a useful sap that is white as milk?

LANGUAGES (*Pages 259-290*)

1. Why does a language die out? When does a language grow stronger?

2. Although English is composed of many other languages, it is basically in the_____ _____ family.

3. How do you say *hello* in German?

4. What ancient language is the ancestor of modern Italian?

5. Other than in Portugal, where do most Portuguese-speaking people live?

6. French is very close to _____ .

7. How did "Romance" languages get that name?

8. The Russian alphabet looks strange to us because it is closely related to the language of ancient _____ .

9. Name a language in which the tone of voice changes the meaning of the word.

10. When a language is written in "pictographs" it means every letter is a kind of _____ .

11. What language is spoken by most of the natives of the many islands spread through the South Pacific Ocean?

12. The Ural-Altaic languages are really named after two _____ s.

UNITED NATIONS (*Pages 291-322*)

1. The main idea of the United Nations is that world problems can be settled by _____ *not* _____ .

2. Who first thought up the name "United Nations"?

3. Where is the permanent home of the U.N.?

4. Is it true that any nation in the world is automatically a member of the U.N.?

5. Is it true that any nation in the world can apply for membership in the U.N.?

6. What is the job of the "interpreters" at the U.N. meetings?

7. On a separate piece of paper list the five official languages of the U.N. in alphabetical order.

8. The six groups which do the work of the U.N. are called _____s.

9. In the General Assembly all nations have _____ vote.

10. List the "Big Five" nations in alphabetical order.

11. Pick one: To veto a problem under discussion means

    A. to say *no* to it;

    B. to say *yes* to it.

12. What are the initials of the special agency in the U.N. which deals with problems of children all over the world?

13. What are the initials of the special agency in the U.N. which deals with problems of health all over the world?

ANCIENT AND MODERN WONDERS (*Pages 323-354*)

1. The _____ is the only Wonder of the Ancient World which is still available for us to see.

2. In Babylon an ancient wonder had huge walls and towers covered with flowers and shrubs. It was called the _____ _____.

3. In Rome, the public square where people gathered to buy things, hear speeches, or just talk to each other was called the _____.

4. The ancient Sphinx has the head of a _____ and the body of a _____.

5. A famous tower that tipped to one side but never fell over is located in _____, Italy.

6. What was the name of the great artist who painted scenes from the Bible on the walls of a Chapel in the Vatican?

7. Is it true that the Great Wall of China was once used to protect the people from floods and ocean waves?

8. One of the major jobs of the Grand Coulee Dam is to use the stored water to make _____ power.

9. The busiest tunnels in the world are built under big cities. They are called _____.

CITIES OF THE WORLD
(*Pages 355-386*)

1. Be able to tell the name of the country for which each of these is an important city: Oslo, Helsinki, Stockholm, Moscow, Edinburgh, Dublin, London, Amsterdam, Copenhagen, Warsaw, Berlin, Prague, Brussels, Paris, Vienna, Budapest, Zurich, Venice, Tirana, Rome, Seville, Lisbon, Athens, Istanbul, Cairo, Tehran, Baghdad, Jerusalem, Mecca, and Johannesburg.

2. What city in Alaska was founded by gold prospectors?

3. What African city is walled in by rubbish from gold mines?

4. What Dutch city was built right in the water?

5. In what city was Mohammed born?

6. In what Italian cities would you take a boat to visit a neighbor just down the "street"?

7. In what city will you find the Kremlin?

SCIENCE (Pages 387-418)

1. Primitive men made the first step towards becoming scientific when they learned how to use _____.

2. What number do we have today that the ancient mathematician did not even know about?

3. Boiling water turns to _____, and this is used for power.

4. According to Archimedes, if a 3-pound block of wood is put into a completely full bathtub, the water that spills over the edge will weigh exactly _____ pounds.

5. Before the studies of Copernicus, the people believed that the Sun and Planets moved around the _____.

6. The force that keeps pulling the Moon around the Earth was called _____ by Newton.

7. The sailor can never lose his direction out at sea because the needle of his compass will always tell him which way is _____.

8. Franklin proved that lightning was really _____ when he caused it to run down a wet string into a jar.

9. Faraday made the first electrical _____.

10. Living creatures could not breathe, and candles could not burn unless there was _____ in the air.

11. The weights of the hydrogen atom, the gold atom, the aluminum atom, and all the other atoms are organized in a chart called the _____ Table.

12. It was Mendel who found that children are like their parents in color and size because of laws of _____.

13. When Leeuwenhoek looked through the microscope he invented, he saw a world of tiny living things which we call _____.

14. When Pierre and Marie Curie discovered radium, they also found that the atom was not _____, but hollow.

PEOPLES (Pages 419-450)

1. Studying the lives of other people helps us to understand _____.

2. The language of the people of _____ is a sing-song where the tone of voice changes the meaning of words.

3. Japan is an _____ off the Asian continent.

4. In a warm climate like Mexico's, people take a rest period around noon which they call a _____.

5. The peoples of South America are a mixture of Indian, Negro, and _____.

6. The people of the British Isles are a mixture of Roman, Celts, Angles, Jutes, Saxons, and _____.

7. Some of the best watches and clocks in the world come from _____.

8. Some of the finest _____ for making wine come from Spain and Portugal.

9. Name the people who live in such a cold climate that they have to wear two fur coats at the same time.

10. Name the people who are the modern descendants of the original Romans.

INVENTIONS (Pages 451-482)

1. Is it true that the American Indian did not know about wheels until the White Man arrived?

2. Surveying instruments are used to be sure the walls of buildings are _____.

3. Gutenberg is credited with inventing the first printing _____.

4. Watt is the inventor of the first practical _____ _____.

5. When an astronomer wants to study the stars he looks through a _____.

6. When a scientist wants to study germs he looks through a _____.

7. Eli Whitney invented the _____ _____.

8. Isaac Singer invented the _____ machine.

9. Samuel Morse tapped out a code message on the first _____ line.

10. Alexander Bell invented the _____.

11. Pick one: If a plane is flying so fast that it has broken the sound barrier:
A. you can hear it pass by before you see it;
B. you can see it pass by before you hear it.

12. Henry Ford is credited with starting a new modern industry with his first gasoline _____.

SPACE (*Pages 483-494*)

1. The first space-craft to carry a man around our planet was called _____ 1.

2. The Americans' first space-craft to carry a man in orbit around the Earth was called _____ 7.

3. Give the meaning of these words:
   apogee; perigee.

4. In order for the Earth to make one orbit each year around the Sun, it must travel at the speed of _____ miles per second.

5. In our _____ system, the Sun is at the center and nine _____ revolve around it.

6. The space-craft cannot launch itself, but is boosted up into the air by a big _____.

7. To give some idea of how big our Universe is, traveling at 100,000 miles per hour, it would take a space-craft _____ years to reach the nearest star.

8. What is the name of the planet that is called the "twin sister" to Earth?

9. The largest planet in our system is _____.

10. Match these important space words with their correct definitions.

A. astronaut	1. the pull of gravity
B. atmosphere	2. where space-crafts are followed by radar
C. countdown	3. the powerful push of a rocket
D. "G" force	4. path around a center point
E. orbit	5. pilot of a space-craft
F. thrust	6. time schedule before blastoff
G. tracking station	7. the air and gas around a planet

INDEX